BUDDHISM AND INTERFAI

Buddhism and Interfaith Dialogue

Part one of a two-volume sequel to
Zen and Western Thought

Masao Abe
Professor Emeritus
Nara University of Education, Japan

Edited by Steven Heine
Associate Professor of Religious Studies
Pennsylvania State University

UNIVERSITY OF HAWAI'I PRESS
HONOLULU

Published in North America 1995 by
UNIVERSITY OF HAWAI'I PRESS
2840 Kolowalu Street
Honolulu, Hawai'i 96822

Published in Great Britain 1995 by
MACMILLAN PRESS LTD
Houndmills, Basingstoke, Hampshire RG21 2XS
and London
Companies and representatives
throughout the world

Printed in Hong Kong

Library of Congress Cataloging-in-Publication Data
Abe, Masao, 1915– .
Buddhism and interfaith dialogue : part one of a two-volume sequel
to Zen and western thought / Masao Abe ; edited by Steven Heine.
p. cm.
Includes index.
ISBN 0–8248–1751–6 (cloth). — ISBN 0–8248–1752–4 (paper)
1. Buddhism—Relations. 2. Buddhism—Doctrines. 3. Buddhism and
philosophy. 4. Philosophy, Comparative. I. Heine, Steven, 1950–
. II. Abe, Masao, 1915–   Zen and western thought. III. Title.
BQ4600.A34 1995
294.3'372—dc20   95–6926
                                                                CIP

Contents

Foreword

Steven Heine

In a remarkable career spanning four decades of teaching, lecturing, mentoring, and publishing in the West, including professorships at some of the major American universities, Masao Abe has had several important accomplishments. First, since the death of D.T. Suzuki he has served as the leading exponent and disseminator of Japanese Buddhism for Western audiences, and many of his most significant writings on Zen in comparison with Western philosophy and religion are included in the award-winning *Zen and Western Thought* (1985). Second, Abe has helped introduce and advance studies of Zen master Dōgen, founder of the Sōtō sect in medieval Japan, through a series of translations with Norman Waddell published in *The Eastern Buddhist* journal in the 1970s and a collection of hermeneutic essays, *A Study of Dōgen: His Philosophy and Religion* (1992). Third, he has been a leader in expressing and examining the texts and ideas of his predecessors and mentors in the Kyoto School philosophical movement, including a translation with Christopher Ives of *Kitarō Nishida: An Inquiry into the Good* (1990) and a collection of essays in remembrance of D.T. Suzuki, *A Zen Life: D.T. Suzuki Remembered* (1986). The fourth and most recent, and in many ways the most compelling, accomplishment has been Abe's participation in continuing ideological encounter and dialogue with a number of highly eminent Western theologians representing a wide spectrum of positions, including existential, mystical, process, kenotic, liberation and feminist theologies, some of the records of which are contained in *The Emptying God: A Buddhist-Jewish-Christian Conversation* (1990) edited by John Cobb and Christopher Ives.

Abe's involvement in interfaith dialogue extends and brings to fruition a basic trend pervasive in the works of Kyoto School thinkers Nishida, Nishitani Keiji and Hisamatsu Shin'ichi, who articulate Buddhist and Zen thought in terms of the concepts and categories of Western philosophy, religion and mysticism, while also clearly and critically demonstrating the differences between the respective traditions. Nishida, the first to integrate German idealism, neo-Kantianism, and phenomenology with Japanese thought, was exceptionally well-versed in Western texts but did not have the opportunity to travel to the West. Nishitani in the late 1920s studied in Germany with Heidegger, an influence that echoed throughout his career, and Hisamatsu lectured in America and engaged in a well-known dialogue with Paul Tillich when both were at Harvard University in the 1950s. Abe, like Suzuki, has spent years traveling back and forth between Japan and the West and has published extensively in English. In the past fifteen years Abe has actively sought out leading Western theologians for a direct exchange of ideas in informal conversations and dialogues as well as formal panels and conferences, including Thomas Altizer, John Cobb, John Egan, Langdon Gilkey, Paul Knitter, Hans Küng and Marjorie Suchocki, all of whom are represented in this volume, in addition to Eugene Borowitz, Catherine Keller, Jürgen Moltmann, Schubert Ogden and David Tracy, among others. Inheriting the legacy of Hisamatsu's F.A.S. Society, founded in 1958 and committed to the dynamic involvement of Zen in world affairs, Abe feels that the creative, constructive encounter between traditions is crucial at this juncture of history. As the forces of modernization, secularization and technologization continue to undermine traditional forms of religiosity while fostering new, urgent, often overwhelming contemporary crises, it is essential that Buddhism and Christianity, and East and West, meet and challenge one another in pursuit of a universal and unifying perspective.

According to Abe, the Buddhist worldview based on the notions of selflessness, dependent origination, and the double negation of emptiness or absolute nothingness is inherently non-dogmatic and free from one-sidedness or bias and thus able to provide a dynamic and flexible paradigm for creating a vibrant and viable unity of world religions and the spiritual liberation of humankind. Yet Abe also fully recognizes that Buddhism cannot contribute to the accomplishment of this demanding task if it stays isolated or aloof from other worldviews. Rather, it must wholeheartedly engage and learn from perspectives that criticize and/or complement it, especially the Christian emphasis on a historical understanding of peace and justice which complements the Buddhist emphasis on monastic, meditative experience of the eternal now. Although Abe argues that Buddhist nondualistic ontology supersedes and completes Christian monotheism, he shows that this flexible ontological vantage-point beyond any commitment to a fixed principle necess-arily encompasses and encourages the Christian ethical standpoint. This volume, which contains Abe's essays and papers previously published in journals or presented at lectures and conferences, is the first part of a two-part sequel to *Zen and Western Thought*. The second volume, forthcoming, titled *Zen and Comparative Studies*, is a collection of writings on the fundamentals of Zen religious ex-perience, Zen and Western philosophy, religion and psychology, current methodological and philosophical issues in Zen studies, and the relation between Zen and Japanese culture and spiritual-ity. In addition, a third volume, *A Study of the Philosophy of the Kyoto School* edited by James Fredericks, is currently in preparation and contains Abe's explication and interpretation of Kyoto School thinkers.

The writings in this volume are divided into three parts. Part One focuses on how Buddhism approaches and contributes to interfaith dialogue, that is, on how Buddhism represents a meth-odological paradigm that serves as a basis for the possibility of dialogical exchange. In a pluralistic, ever shrinking world in which geographical and conceptual boundaries between traditions are continually shattered, the Buddhist notion of *śūnyatā*, Abe argues, is a positionless position that overcomes all forms of self-centeredness and thus alleviates human and karmic suffering at its root. At the conclusion of '"There is No Common Denominator for World Re-ligions": The Positive Meaning of this Negative Statement', he sug-gests that 'on the basis of a positionless position, each religion is fully realized in its distinctiveness and yet is critically judged by other religions as well as by itself in light of its encounter with other religions.' Abe maintains that the Buddhist nondualistic per-spective overcomes the more limited horizons in monotheistic or monistic theologies, but he also shows that 'kenotic' or self-empty-ing theology that is evident in some recent interpretations of Chris-tian scripture is a key notion for comparative and dialogical studies with Buddhism.

Part Two contains four essays on the relation between Buddhism and Paul Tillich, the leading modern systematic theologian who drew on mystical sources and was also receptive to Eastern thought in developing his understanding of non-being or negation. While having tremendous respect and admiration for Tillich and feeling that his theology approaches Buddhism in many important re-spects, Abe contends that Buddhist 'double negation' surpasses the one-sided sense of Tillichian negation by fully completing a paradoxical identity of negation and affirmation, negativity and positivity. According to Abe in 'Negation in Mahayana Buddhism and Tillich: A Buddhist View of "The Significance of the History of Religions for the Systematic Theologian"', 'True nondiscrimination can be realized only through the negation of nondiscrimination. Here again we need the double negation, the negation of discrimination and the negation of nondiscrimination. Through this double negation, and the realization of *śūnyatā*, we arrive at absolute affirmation.' The Buddhist view is at once more completely affirmative by virtue of the fact that it is more completely negational.

Part Three continues a discussion of earlier themes and also opens up several new issues, particularly in regard to the role of meditation East and West and the ethical implications of the Buddhist doctrine of *karma* in comparison with Christian moral activity. Abe considers the Christian mystical notion of 'dazzling darkness' as a touchstone for comparisons with the Mahayana paradoxical equalization and identification of *nirvāṇa* and *saṃsāra*. He further clarifies the meaning of kenotic theology, and he examines the significance of meditation and contemplation in Christian spirituality and Jewish mysticism. For Abe, the Zen principle of self-awakening, despite similarities, takes priority over Western conceptions of faith. But he also recognizes that Buddhism needs to learn from Judeo-Christian historicism and emphasis on the ethical implications of theology.

A prime example is Abe's conversation with Paul Knitter, a prominent liberation theologian also well versed in Zen, which is included as the final chapter here. The dialogue opens with Knitter recalling the unique juxtaposition of experiences in the previous summer when he first traveled to Japan to work on translating Heinrich Dumoulin's history of Zen (from German) and then journeyed to war-torn El Salvador in the company of other Christians. In the first case, inspired by Merton's earlier spiritual adventure in Asia, Knitter is an interested outsider observing and studying in a Buddhist country at peace in the hope that Buddhists and Christians can be 'mutually transformed'. In the other case, he participates in a post-Vatican II attempt 'to enter the grime and mess of the world, especially the world of victims', who were suffering, according to some liberation theology interpretations, largely because of years of indifferent status quo-ism on the part of the

Church. Perplexed in trying to understand the relation between these disparate experiences, Knitter considers the question in terms of the traditional Christian categorical distinctions between contemplation and action, prayer and work, Martha and Mary, spirituality and liberation, and, he adds, 'Japan and El Salvador'. Knitter concludes that in Buddhism, 'You cannot change the world unless you sit', whereas in Christianity, 'You cannot sit unless you change the world'. That is, he appreciates the contribution of Buddhism in stressing the epistemological priority of *gnosis* before *agapé*, and *prajñā* before *karuna*. Yet, without overtly making the kind of biased judgment earlier theologians have made, in Knitter's remarks an old critique of Buddhist 'passivity' clearly resurfaces.

Abe responds in two ways. First, he emphasizes that it is misleading to understand Buddhism merely as a preference for contemplation prior to action, for the relation between these inseparable experiential dimensions is not conditioned by chronological sequence in the sense that one literally comes 'before' the other. Rather, the two are intertwined ontologically so that a *bodhisattva* does not stay in *nirvāṇa* or absolute truth but continually returns to *saṃsāra* or conventional truth in order to aid all sentient beings. Furthermore, Abe stresses that Zen realization of selfhood should not be viewed as a contemplative path that is the flip-side of the active life, as these are provisional designations for two aspects of the selfsame reality. Instead, self-realization is the necessary requirement for authentic contemplative action in pursuit of peace:

> Currently, we have various forms of peace movements, and various other social reform movements. If these movements, however, are pursued only from a political and social standpoint without a basis in our deep realization of True Self, such approaches may not yield adequate solutions.

Yet, Abe also concedes the negative aspect of the positive side of Buddhism in the same paragraph by saying, 'Today's Buddhism is apt to be removed from social realities and confined to temples, and engrossed only in the inner problems of the self.' He concludes with a plea for both religions to learn from each other how to coordinate contemplation and action effectively in the post-modern world.

ACKNOWLEDGMENTS

The material in this volume was originally written or presented in a variety of journals or at conferences. While the majority of the chapters were conceived as objective, scholarly articles, there are several prominent examples of essays composed in response to or in dialogue with a particular Western theologian, including Altizer, Cobb, Egan, Gilkey, Knitter, Küng and Suchocki. The following list explains the initial appearance of each chapter:

Chapter 1, 'Buddhist–Christian Dialogue: Its Significance and Future Task', was delivered in the Ecumenical Chair in Theology Lecture Series at Xavier University, October 1992.

Chapter 2, 'A Dynamic Unity in Religious Pluralism: A Proposal from the Buddhist Point of View', appeared in *The Experience of Religious Diversity*, ed. John Hick and Hasan Askari (Brookfield, Vermont: Gower Publishing, 1985), pp. 163–90.

Chapter 3, '"There is No Common Denominator for World Religions": The Positive Meaning of this Negative Statement', appeared in the *Journal of Ecumenical Studies*, 26/1 (1989), pp. 72–81.

Chapter 4, 'The Impact of Dialogue with Christianity on My Self-Understanding as a Buddhist', was delivered at the session on 'Comparative Studies in Religion' at the annual meeting of the American Academy of Religion in Boston, December 1987, and appeared in *Buddhist–Christian Studies*, 9 (1989), pp. 62–70.

Chapter 5, 'The Problem of Self-Centeredness as the Root-Source of Human Suffering', appeared in *Japanese Religions*, 15/4 (1989), pp. 15–25.

Chapter 6, 'Suffering in the Light of Our Time: Our Time in the Light of Suffering: Buddha's First Holy Truth', was included in the Proceedings of the Conference on Buddhism and Christianity, De Tiltenberg, The Netherlands, 3 (1990).

Chapter 7, 'Negation in Mahayana Buddhism and in Tillich: A Buddhist View of "The Significance of the History of Religion for the Systematic Theologian"', appeared in *Negation and Theology*, ed. Robert Scharlemann (Charlottesville: University of Virginia Press, 1990), pp. 86–99.

Chapter 8, 'Double Negation as an Essential for Attaining the Ultimate Reality: Comparing Tillich and Buddhism,' appeared in *Negation and Theology*, ed. Robert Scharlemann (Charlottesville: University of Virginia Press, 1990), pp. 142–8.

Chapter 9, 'A Response to Professor Langdon Gilkey's Paper, "Tillich and the Kyoto School"', was delivered at the North American Paul Tillich Society in Boston, December 1987.

Chapter 10, 'In Memory of Dr. Paul Tillich', appeared in *The Eastern Buddhist*, 1/2 (1968), pp. 128–31.

Chapter 11, 'Beyond Buddhism and Christianity – "Dazzling Darkness"', first appeared in German translation as '"Leuchtende Finsternise", zum Verstandnis von "letzter Wirklichkeit"' in Buddhismus und Christentum' in *Hans Küng, neue Horizonte des Glaubens und Denkens*, ed. Herman Häring and Karl-Josef Kuschel (Hg. Piper, 1993), 623–50.

Chapter 12, 'Thomas J.J. Altizer's Kenotic Christology and Buddhism', was delivered at the panel on 'Kenosis and *Śūnyatā*' in Berkeley, August 1987.

Chapter 13, 'Zen Buddhism and Hasidism – Similarities and Contrasts', was presented for the Los Angeles Hillel Council, June 1969.

Chapter 14, 'The Interfaith Encounter of Zen and Christian Contemplation: A Dialogue between Masao Abe and Keith J. Egan', was presented at the 'Interfaith Dialogue' at the University of Notre Dame, April 1993.

Chapter 15, 'Interfaith Relations and World Peace: A Buddhist Perspective', was presented at the 'Interfaith Dialogue' at Purdue University with Marjorie Suchocki, November 1991.

Chapter 16, 'Faith and Self-Awakening: A Search for the Fundamental Category Covering All Religious Life' (1981, unpublished).

Chapter 17, 'God, Emptiness and Ethics', appeared in *Buddhist–Christian Studies*, 3 (1983), pp. 53–60.

Chapter 18, 'Responses to Langdon Gilkey', is a portion of a dialogue from the first meeting of the Theological Encounter with Buddhism Group as part of the Second International Buddhist–Christian Conference that appeared in *Buddhist–Christian Studies*, 5 (1985), pp. 67–80.

Chapter 19, 'Spirituality and Liberation: A Buddhist–Christian Conversation', appeared in *Horizons*, 15/2 (1988), pp. 347–64.

We thank the following parties for permission to reprint or use this material: Gower Publishing for Chapter 2; the editor of *Journal of Ecumenical Studies* for Chapter 3; the editor of *Buddhist–Christian Studies* for Chapters 4, 17, and 18; the editor of *Japanese Religions* for Chapter 5; the University of Virginia Press for Chapters 7 and 8; the editor of *The Eastern Buddhist* for Chapter 10; Haerman Häring and Karl-Josef Kuschel for Chapter 11; Donald W. Mitchell, Director of the Purdue Interfaith Project funded by the Lilly Endowment, Inc., for Chapters 14 and 15; the editor of *Horizons* for Chapter 19.

Finally, I greatly appreciate the efforts of the editors at Macmillan, and I am especially thankful for the privilege of working once again with Masao Abe on a project that makes his eminently insightful and compelling works more accessible and widely read.

Preface

In this global age the world is ever shrinking. The East and the West, and the North and the South are encountering and intermingling with each other in a scope and depth never experienced before. This does not, however, mean that the world is being united harmoniously. Rather the difference, opposition and conflict among various ideologies, value systems and ways of thinking become more and more conspicuous throughout the world. How can we find a common spiritual basis in this pluralistic world without marring the unique characteristics of each of the cultural and spiritual traditions? This is the urgent task humankind is now facing. In this regard interfaith dialogue among religions is so extremely important.

Buddhism, which has been relatively aloof from the fierce waves of social and cultural trends of the contemporary world and has not been so active in interfaith dialogue, can no longer avoid the challenge of contemporary pluralism, globalism and secularism. In order to be a genuine world religion Buddhism must confront the cultural and religious pluralistic situation and engage in dialogue among faiths. This is the reason why, being a Buddhist, I have been involved in interfaith dialogue for over three decades.[1]

This book is a collection of essays which I have written on the theme of interfaith dialogue from my own Buddhist perspective. It also includes my dialogical responses to leading Christian and Jewish theologians such as Paul Tillich, Langdon Gilkey, Hans Küng, Thomas Altizer, Keith Egan, Paul F. Knitter, Martin Buber and others.

I also believe that Buddhism can contribute a unique principle which dynamically unites various world religions without marring their particularities and distinctiveness.

Part I 'Buddhist Approach to Interfaith Dialogue' includes discussions on how the Buddhist notion of śūnyatā (emptiness), if properly reinterpreted, can provide an adequate principle of unity of various world religions without marring their distinctiveness. In this regard I offer the notion of 'nondualistic oneness' as distinguished from monotheistic oneness, a 'positionless position' opened

up through the realization of 'no-common-denominator' for all
world religions, a 'boundless openness' without any kind of centrism, and a 'great zero' which, being the source from which one,
two, the many and the whole can emerge, is positive and creative.
On the basis of nondualistic oneness or the positionless position,
or boundless openness, throughout this volume I point out the
problematics involved in monotheism and emphasize the necessity
of going beyond monism and monotheism in the realization of non-
dualistic unity. Thus I state:

> Monistic oneness is realized by distinguishing itself and setting
> itself apart from dualistic twoness and pluralistic manyness.
> Monism essentially excludes any form of dualism and pluralism
> and, therefore, stands in opposition to them. Precisely because of
> this oppositional relation, monistic oneness is neither a singular
> oneness nor a truly ultimate oneness. In order to realize true
> oneness we must go not only beyond dualism and pluralism, but
> also beyond monistic oneness itself. Then we can realize
> nondualistic oneness, because at that point we are completely
> free from any form of duality, including the duality between the
> monistic and the dualistic or pluralistic view.
>
> Monotheistic oneness, being somewhat 'over there', does not
> immediately include two, many and the whole. Even though it
> can be all-inclusive, it is still more or less separated from the
> particularity and multiplicity of actual entities-in-the world. This
> residual condition of separateness is illustrated by the fact that
> the monotheistic God is a personal god who commands and
> directs people. Nondualistic oneness, however, which is based
> on the realization of 'great zero' includes all individual things
> just as they are, without any modification. This is because in
> nondualistic oneness, conceptualization and objectification are
> completely and radically overcome. There is no separation between
> nondualistic oneness and individual things. At this point the
> one and the many are non-dual.

Part II, 'Buddhism in Dialogue with Tillich's Theology,' includes
essays directly or indirectly dealing with Paul Tillich and my dialogues with him. I have been favoured with close contact and the
opportunity of dialogue with many eminent theologians. Among
them Paul Tillich is one of the most provocative and influential
theologians to me. In early 1950 in Japan I read Tillich's *Systematic*

Theology Vol. I and was moved by his existential-ontological interpretation of Christianity. As a research fellow of the Rockefeller
Foundation I came to the U.S. in 1955 to study under Tillich at
Union Theological Seminary in New York, only to find that Tillich
was going to transfer to Harvard University. But during two years,
1955–57, while I studied with Reinhold Niebuhr, John Knox and
others at Union, I often went to Harvard to attend Tillich's 'university lecture' and never missed the public lectures and sermons he
delivered in New York from time to time. Further, in 1960 when
Tillich visited Japan I served as a member of the Welcome Tillich
Committee and organized discussion meetings for Tillich with
Buddhist scholars and theologians. On those occasions he showed
himself to be an open-minded and provocative dialogue partner.
Through these close contacts with Tillich my understanding of
Christianity has been greatly inspired and deepened. As I wrote in
my obituary of Tillich, 'His death is a great loss for Buddhism in
that Buddhism lost an irreplaceable dialogue partner'.

In the articles included in Part II, while I appreciate Tillich's
understanding of God as Being which includes non-being, I also
criticize his understanding of God as the double negation of an
asymmetrical polarity of being and nothing which is essential to
attain the ultimate reality. Tillich's view falls short of the Buddhist
notion of *śūnyatā* as a symmetrical polarity.

[The] difference between God and *śūnyatā* is not a difference in
degree but in quality. The polarity of being and non-being in
Tillich is based on being as we see in his words 'Being embraces
itself and non-being'. [asymmetrical polarity] On the other hand,
the polarity of being and nothing in Buddhism is based neither
on being nor on nothing in their relative sense, but upon absolute nothingness, [symmetrical polarity] that is, nothingness in
the absolute sense.

Although we equally see polarity of being and nothing in both
Tillich and Buddhism, the basis of polarity is radically different.
In Tillich the ultimate reality (God) is conceived as the third in
which being and non-being are united, whereas in Buddhism the
ultimate reality (*śūnyatā*) is not the third nor the first nor the
second. This means that in Buddhism ultimate reality is realized
through the complete turning over of the original horizon of the
polarity of being and non-being. In other words, not only the
complete negation of nothing but also the complete negation of

being, that is the double negation of two poles, is necessary for the realization of ultimate reality as emptiness.

I sincerely hope some theologian will respond to this remark on behalf of Paul Tillich.

Part III, 'Buddhism and Contemporary Theology', includes various forms of interfaith dialogues between some other eminent theologians such as Hans Küng, Thomas Altizer, Keith J. Egan, Wolfhart Pannenberg, Marjorie H. Suchocki, Paul F. Knitter and myself. Some of them discuss religion and World Peace, the future of theology, contemplation and meditation, faith and ethics, spirituality and liberation and so forth, but the most crucial issue to Buddhist–Christian interfaith dialogue may be the encounter between the Christian notion of kenosis and the Buddhist notion of *śūnyatā*. I have discussed this issue rather intensively. In my understanding of the Christian notion of God who is love the notion of kenosis must be applicable not only to the Son of God but also to God the Father. Without the kenosis of God Himself, the kenosis of Christ in inconceivable. If God is understood not to empty Himself even in the self-emptying of the Son of God, then the dynamic identity of kenosis and pleroma, humiliation and exaltation – the essential character of Christ's kenosis – cannot be fully realized.

However, if one breaks through the monotheistic framework and realizes the kenosis of God Himself, the ultimate reality as the dynamic identity of kenosis and pleroma is fully realized. It is right here that the basic tenet of Christianity, "God is love," is completely fulfilled. Once freed from its monotheistic and theocentric character, Christianity not only becomes more open to interfaith dialogue and cooperation without the possibility of falling into exclusivism, but it also becomes compatible with the autonomous reason peculiar to modern humanity and will be able to cope with the challenge by Nietzschean nihilism and atheistic existentialism.

However, Hans Küng insists that the notion of Kenotic God is unbiblical and rejects my interpretation as a 'Buddhist exegesis'.

On the other hand, I argued that the Buddhist notion of *śūnyatā* does not indicate a static state of emptiness but a dynamic activity of emptying – emptying everything including itself, that is self-emptying. In true *śūnyatā* form is ceaselessly emptied, turning into formless emptiness, and formless emptiness is ceaselessly emptied, and therefore forever freely taking form.

Emptiness as the ultimate reality in Buddhism is not monotheistic nor pluralistic nor pantheistic, but the Buddhist notion of ultimate reality is panentheistic in that immanence and transcendence are totally and dynamically identical through mutual negation.

The future task of Christianity is to open up the monotheistic framework through the full realization of the kenosis of God Himself and to realize the ultimate reality as the dynamic unity of kenosis and pleroma.

On the other hand the future task of Buddhism is to break through the static view of *śūnyatā* and is to realize how this self-emptying Emptiness concentrates itself into a single centre in the boundless openness, a centre which is the locus of the real manifestation of a personal deity and the ultimate criterion of ethical judgment and of value judgment in general.

Hans Küng criticizes my interpretation of the kenotic passage in Philippians as 'a Buddhist exegesis of the Christian texts indicating that [Abe] isolates key concepts from Christian texts and transplants them into a Buddhist context'.[2] *Is this really a fair and pertinent understanding of my interpretation of the kenotic passage?* My basic intention in this regard is not to impose Buddhist categories upon the Christian context, and then to give a 'Buddhist' exegesis of the Christian texts. Instead, I have tried to understand the Christian notion of kenosis from within the Christian framework, as much as this is possible. Thus my sincere request to the reader is as follows:

Although I am a Buddhist, I hope my readers will dispel the presupposition that my discussion and interpretation of Christianity is a Buddhist exegesis. I sincerely hope that my discussion of Christianity will be judged not in terms of whether it is Buddhistic or not, but in terms of whether or not it is in accord with Christian spirituality. The interreligious dialogue may adequately and effectively take place if both sides of the dialogue try to grasp the other side's spirituality from within, without imposing its own ontological and axiological categories.

This is my most sincere desire, underlying everything in this volume.

Notes

1. My earliest essay in this category, 'Buddhism and Christianity as a problem of Today' part I, *Japanese Religions* Vol. 3, No. 2 (1963) and part II *Ibid*. Vol. 3, No. 2 (1963), will be published together with responses by a number of theologians and philosophers and my rejoinder under the title *Searching for Common Ground: Buddhism and Christianity Challenged by Irreligion*. Edited by Hakan Eilert and Ronald Kristiansen. Forthcoming, SUNY Press.
2. 'God's Self-Renunciation and Buddhist Emptiness: A Christian Response to Masao Abe' in *Buddhist Emptiness and Christian Trinity*, ed. by Roger Corless and Paul F. Knitter (New York: Orbis, 1990), p. 34.

Part One
Buddhist Approach to Interfaith Dialogue

1

Buddhist–Christian Dialogue: Its Significance and Future Task[1]

I

The contemporary world is rapidly shrinking due to the remarkable advancement of science and technology. East and West are now meeting and exchanging values at all levels of life – in politics, economics and culture. While mutual understanding is going on in some places, the integration of the world makes the multiplicity of human societies and ideologies more conspicuous, causing unprecedented tensions and antagonisms in all areas of life. The coming global age is producing dissension as well as the quest for a greater, more harmonious unity.

Human societies which once maintained their own cultural and intellectual patterns are now being pulled together into one great rushing stream of world history, creating waves which slap and dash one against the other. The synchronization of global space by information and transportation technology requires that all people play their parts on the common stage of world history, and hopefully, come to some awareness of their roles in the drama. Nevertheless, only after divisions and oppositions have been overcome and a new spiritual horizon for humanity has been opened up shall we have a truly united destiny.

A clear, self-conscious realization of *one world history* will not be produced simply by forces working from without, such as the advancement of scientific technology, but will be the work of an innermost human spirituality. Today, however, we know very little about the inner meaning of spiritual and religious traditions not our own. The discovery of new spiritual foundations upon which 'world culture' and 'world history' may be built is contingent

3

upon a dialogue between world religions. Without deep mutual understanding among world religions a harmonious global society can never be established. The ongoing dialogue between Buddhism and Christianity is taking place with this need as its background.

Strictly speaking, however, mutual understanding between religions, although always necessary, is not sufficient. 'Mutual understanding' through dialogue implies that a religion on one side tries to understand the religion on the other side in their currently established forms. Both sides presuppose the legitimacy of their own religion while asking the other party to understand their own legitimacy respectively. However, we now exist in a world in which many people question the legitimacy of not only a particular religion such as Christianity, Buddhism or Islam, but also of religion as such. Many persons in our present secularized world ask 'Why is religion necessary?' and 'What meaning does religion have for us today?' They think that they can live well enough without religion and thus are quite skeptical about, or indifferent to, religion. Moreover, ideologies that negate religion prevail in our society. Scientism, Marxism, traditional Freudian psychoanalytical thought and nihilism in the Nietzschean sense all deny the *raison d'être* of religion not merely on emotional grounds but on various rational or theoretical grounds. Not stopping with criticism of particular religions, these ideologies negate the very being of religion itself. The most crucial task of any religion in our time is, beyond mutual understanding, to respond to these anti-religious forces by elucidating the authentic meaning of religious faith.

Furthermore, 'fundamentalism' has recently arisen within various religions, creating serious religious conflicts. Fundamentalists emphasize the inerrancy of scripture and reject modern theology and the critical study of scripture with assurance that those who do not share their religious viewpoint are not really authentic believers of that religion at all. Accordingly, fundamentalism not only causes frustrating disagreement within the given religion, but also creates an obstacle to interfaith dialogue.

In short, in our current religious situation we are now facing the challenge by anti-religious ideologies on the one hand, and on the other are involved in conflicts between fundamentalists and non-conservatives. If we take 'mutual understanding' as a goal in interfaith dialogue but think that it can be realized apart from the problems raised by anti-religious ideologies and fundamentalism, then the ideals of interfaith dialogue will remain futile hopes. In order properly and adequately to cope with the challenge by anti-religious forces and fundamentalism, we must go beyond 'mutual understanding' and engage in 'mutual transformation'. Only then can the religion-negating ideologies be overcome, for every religion engaged in transformative dialogue should demonstrate its own deepest authentic spirituality by surpassing the traditional verbal formulations of teaching and practice. The life-sustaining value involved in breaking through reified structures applies equally well to the problem of fundamentalism, for the problem of fundamentalism cannot be properly solved within the framework of any of the existing forms of the world's religions. For the sake of overcoming fundamentalism and religion-negating ideologies, a radical reinterpretation of each religion's own spirituality is absolutely necessary. Spirituality is deeper from an existential perspective than mere doctrinal formulations. This is why I insist that in religious dialogue today, mutual understanding, though always necessary, is insufficient; going beyond mutual understanding, interfaith dialogue must be concerned with the mutual transformation of the religions involved. Then and only then will a deep and expansive human spirituality be opened up before each of the world's religions.

With this understanding in mind, I would in the following like to consider how the mutual and ongoing learning between Buddhism and the Western religions should be developed today by discussing three fundamental issues: first, the idea of a monotheistic God in relation to the realization of *Nichts* or Absolute Nothingness; second, two kinds of oneness; and third, the relation of justice to wisdom.

II

First, let us consider the relationship between a monotheistic God and the realization of *Nichts*. Western scholars often discuss religion in terms of a contrast between ethical and natural religion (C.P. Tile), prophetic and mystical religion (F. Heiler), and monotheistic and pantheistic religion (W.F. Albright, A. Lang). The first term in each pair generally refers to Judeo-Christian-

Muslim religions while the second refers to most of the Oriental religions. This kind of bifurcation has been set forth by Western scholars for the purpose of making a comparative judgment with the first of each set (ethical, prophetic and monotheistic) as the standard for evaluation. Consequently, non-Semitic Oriental religions are often not only lumped together under a single category, despite their rich variety, but are also grasped from the outside without any penetration into their inner religious core. Unlike the Semitic religions, which most Western scholars recognize as clearly having a common character, such Oriental religions as Hinduism, Buddhism, Confucianism, Taoism and Shinto exhibit significant differences in their religious essences, and hence cannot be legitimately classified into a single category. Partly in order to bring this point into sharper focus, and partly because I represent Buddhism, I will take up Buddhism alone from among the Oriental religions and contrast it with Judaism, Christianity and Islam.

Most Western scholars correctly characterize Judaism, Christianity and Islam *not* as natural, mystical and pantheistic religions, but as ethical, prophetic and monotheistic religions. All three religions are based on the idea of One Absolute God: Yahweh in Judaism, God the Father in Christianity and Allah in Islam. In each of these religions, the One God is believed to be a personal God who is essentially transcendent to human beings, but whose will is revealed to human beings through prophets and who commands people to observe certain ethico-religious principles. Although we should not overlook some conspicuous differences in emphasis among these three religions, we can say with some justification that each is ethical, prophetic and monotheistic.

In contrast, Buddhism does not talk about One Absolute God who is essentially transcendent to human beings. Instead, Buddhism teaches *pratītya-samutpāda*, or the law of 'dependent co-origination' or 'conditional co-production' as the *Dharma*, or the Truth. This teaching emphasizes that everything in and beyond the universe is interdependent, co-arising and co-ceasing (not only temporally, but also ontologically) with everything else. Nothing exists independently, or can be said to be self-existing. Accordingly, in Buddhism everything without exception is relative, relational, non-substantial and changeable. Even the divine (Buddha) does not exist by itself, but is entirely interrelated to humans and nature. This is why Gautama Buddha, the founder of Buddhism, did not accept the age-old Vedantic notion of Brahman, which is believed to be the only enduring reality underlying the universe. For a similar reason, Buddhism cannot accept the monotheistic notion of One Absolute God as the ultimate reality, but instead advocates *śūnyatā* (emptiness) and *tathatā* (suchness or as-it-is-ness) as the ultimate reality.

Śūnyatā as the ultimate reality in Buddhism literally means 'emptiness' or 'voidness' and can imply 'absolute nothingness'. This is because *śūnyatā* is entirely unobjectifiable, unconceptualizable, and unattainable by reason and will. It also indicates the absence of enduring self-being and the non-substantiality of everything in the universe. It is beyond all dualities and yet includes them.

In the realization of *śūnyatā*, not only sentient beings but also the Buddha, not only *saṃsāra* but also *nirvāṇa*, are without substance and are empty. Accordingly, neither Buddha nor *nirvāṇa* but the realization of the non-substantiality of everything – that is, the realization of *śūnyatā* – is ultimate.

This realization of the non-substantial emptiness of everything is inseparably related with the law of dependent co-origination. Dependent co-origination as the *Dharma* (or Truth) is possible only when everything in the universe is without fixed, enduring substance (although possessing changeable temporal substance) and is open in its relationship with everything else. We human beings have a strong disposition to reify or substantialize objects as well as our own self as if we and they were permanent and unchangeable substances. This substantialization of, and the accompanying attachment to, all kinds of objects causes human suffering. With respect to the goal of intersubjective understanding, the most serious cases of this problem lie in the substantialization of self (which results in self-centeredness) and the substantialization of one's own religion (which entails a religious imperialism). Buddhism emphasizes awakening to *śūnyatā*, to the non-substantiality of everything, including self and Buddha, in order to be emancipated from suffering. Thus it teaches no-self (*anātman*) and awakening to *Dharma* rather than faith in the Buddha.

However, Buddhist emphasis on no-self and Emptiness, as Buddhist history has shown, often causes indifference to the problem of good and evil and especially to social ethics. Buddhists must learn from monotheistic religions how human personality can be comprehended on the basis of the impersonal notion of 'Emptiness', and how to incorporate I–Thou relationships within the Buddhist context of 'Emptiness'.

In Christianity, God is not simply transcendent. Rather, God is deeply immanent in humankind as the incarnation of the Logos in human form, namely in the form of Jesus Christ. And yet the divine and the human are not completely interdependent. For while the human definitely is dependent upon God, God is not dependent upon the human. The world cannot exist without God, but God can exist without the world. Because God is the self-existing deity, ontologically sufficient unto himself, God can and does exist by Himself without depending on anything else. In this regard, Buddhists may ask: 'What is the ground of the one God who alone exemplifies self-sufficient existence?' A Christian might answer this question by stressing the importance of faith in God, this faith being nothing but the 'assurance of things hoped for, the conviction of things not seen' (Heb. 11: 1). Further, God in Semitic religion is not merely the One Absolute God in the ontological sense, but a living and personal God who calls humans through his Word and requires that humans respond to his Word. In his book *Does God Exist?*, Hans Küng says: 'God in the Bible is subject and not predicate: it is not that love is God, but that God is love – God is one who faces me, whom I can address'.[2]

My Buddhistic reaction to this statement is as follows. Can I address God, not merely from outside of God, but also from within God? Is it not the case that God faces me within God *even if* I turn my back on God? The God who faces me and whom I may address and who, in turn, may address me is God as subject. But the God *within* whom I address God and *within* whom God meets me is not God as subject; rather, it is God as universal predicate. Or, more strictly speaking, God as universal predicate is neither God as subject nor God as predicate singly and solely, but is God as *Nichts*. In God as *Nichts*, God as subject meets me *even if* I turn my back on that God and I can therefore always truly address that God as Thou. The very I–Thou relationship between the self and the personal God takes place precisely in God as *Nichts*. Since God as *Nichts* is the *groundless* ground of the I–Thou relationship between the self and the personal God, God as *Nichts* is neither subject nor predicate, but a 'copula' that acts as a connecting, intermediating link between the subject and the predicate always held in dynamic relation. The possibility of dialogic relation between subject and predicate is itself circumscribed by this 'copula' that includes and yet surpasses both subject and predicate. This entails that God as *Nichts* is *Nichts* as God: the personal God is *Nichts* and *Nichts* is the personal God. And on this basis we may say that God is love and love is God because *Nichts* is the unconditional, self-negating love. Even the ground of our freedom to turn our backs on the personal God exists within and through God as unconditional, self-negating love. Without attributing the principle of self-negation to ultimate reality, God will always be conceived from a relative or objectivistic point of view, but not from the point of view of *śūnyatā*. Only from within the fundamental standpoint of *śūnyatā* can one see how God is neither one nor two nor many, but rather beyond and yet inclusive of such relative distinctions. God's self-negation entails God's self-transcendence and creates the possibility of relation between God and the other or human self *within* God as *Nichts*. God as *Nichts* surpasses all relations while yet serving as the transcendental ground for the very possibility of all relations, all revelations and all encounters. This is the absolute interior of God's mystery which is its absolute exterior at one and the same time. We may thus say:

God is love because God is *Nichts*:
Nichts is God because *Nichts* is love.

This interpretation may not accord with traditional orthodoxy. It is here, however, through the principle of self-negation that both human longing for salvation and the deepest mystery of God are thoroughly fulfilled. Furthermore, God as subject who meets one and whom one can address as Thou is incompatible with the ideal of autonomous reason so important to modern humanity, because the autonomous reason, by definition, rejects all forms of heteronomy including theonomy, that is the quality or condition of being subject to God's laws or rule. And the God as subject is also nowadays challenged by Nietzschean nihilism and atheistic existentialism. The notion of God as *Nichts*, however, is not only compatible with but can also embrace autonomous reason because there is no conflict between the notion of

God as *Nichts* (which is neither subject nor predicate) and autonomous reason, and because the autonomy of rational thinking, however much it may be emphasized, is not limited by the notion of God as *Nichts*. In the self-negating or self-emptying God who is *Nichts*, not only are modern human autonomous reason and rationalistic subjectivity overcome without being marred, but also the mystery of God is most profoundly perceived. God as love is fully and most radically grasped far beyond contemporary atheism and nihilism.

This is my humble suggestion towards an understanding of God today.

III

The second topic is an analysis of two kinds of oneness. For any religion, the realization of the oneness of ultimate reality is important because religion is expected to offer an integral and total – rather than fragmental or partial – salvation from human suffering. Even a so-called polytheistic religion does not believe in various deities without order, but it often worships a certain supreme deity as a ruler over a hierarchy of innumerable gods. Further, the three major deities often constitute a trinity – as exemplified by the Hindu notion of *Trimurti*, the threefold deity of *Brahma*, *Viṣṇu* and *Śiva*. Such a notion of trinity in polytheism also implies a tendency toward a unity of diversity – a tendency towards oneness.

This means that in any religion, especially in higher religions, the realization of the Oneness of ultimate reality is crucial. Yet, the realization of Oneness necessarily entails exclusiveness, intolerance and religious imperialism, which causes conflict and dissension not only within a given religion but also between the various religions. This is a very serious dilemma which no higher religion can escape. How can we believe in the Oneness of the ultimate reality in our own religion without falling into exclusive intolerance and religious imperialism toward other faiths? What kind of Oneness of ultimate reality can solve that dilemma and open up a dimension in which positive tolerance and peaceful coexistence are possible among all religions, based on the idea that there is One Absolute reality?

In order to answer this question, I would like to introduce a distinction between two kinds of oneness or unity: monistic oneness or unity, on the one hand, and non-dualistic unity or oneness, on the other. It is my contention that only non-dualistic oneness or unity, not monistic oneness or unity, may provide a real common basis for the contemporary pluralistic situation of world relations. How, then, are monistic and non-dualistic oneness different from one another? I would like to clarify their differences by making the following four points.

First, monistic oneness is realized by distinguishing itself and setting itself apart from dualistic twoness and pluralistic manyness. Monism excludes any form of dualism and pluralism and, therefore, stands in opposition to them. Precisely because of this oppositional relation, however, monistic oneness is neither a singular oneness nor a truly ultimate oneness. In order to realize true oneness we must not only go beyond dualism and pluralism, but also beyond monistic oneness itself. Then we can realize non-dualistic oneness, because at that point we are completely free from any form of duality, including the duality between monism and dualism or pluralism. Non-dualistic oneness is even the ground for the possibility of the binary opposition between the monistic view and the dualistic or pluralistic view.

Secondly, if the monism is monotheistic, then the oneness is realized in a God who is the ruler of the universe and the law-giver to humans and whose mode of being is only remotely similar and comparable to beings of the world. Although the monotheistic God is accessible by prayer and comes to be present among humans through love and mercy, his transcendent character is undeniable. The monotheistic God is somewhat 'over there', not completely right here and right now. Contrary to this case, non-dualistic oneness is the ground or root-source realized right here and right now, from which our life and activities can properly begin. When we overcome monotheistic oneness, we come to a point which is neither one nor two, nor many, but which is appropriately referred to as 'zero or non-substantial emptiness'. Since the 'zero' is free from any form of duality and plurality, true absolute oneness can be realized through the realization of 'zero'. My use of the term 'zero' in this regard may be misleading, however, because the term 'zero' often indicates something negative. But here, in this context, I use 'zero' to indicate the principle which is positive and creative as the source from which one, two, many and the systematic whole itself can emerge. Since I use the term 'zero', not in a negative sense but in a positive and creative sense, I may call it 'great zero'. Monotheistic oneness is a kind of oneness which lacks the realization of 'great zero', whereas non-dualistic oneness is a kind of oneness which is based on the realization of 'great zero'.

Thirdly, the true absolute oneness which can be attained through the realization of 'great zero' should not be objectively conceived. If it is objectified or conceptualized in any way, it is not real oneness. Language can only talk about the 'great zero' elliptically, therefore, and so even my use of the pronoun 'it' must be understood to be a misnomer. An objectified oneness is merely something *named* 'oneness'. To reach and fully realize true oneness, it is necessary to completely overcome conceptualization and objectification. True oneness is realized only in a non-objective way by overcoming even the notion of 'great zero' when it is objectified as an end or goal. Accordingly, overcoming 'great zero' as an end or goal is a turning point from the objective, outwardly aim-seeking approach to the non-objective, immediate approach, or from monotheistic oneness to non-dualistic oneness. Then it may be said that God is not sought outside of one's being, but rather at the ground of one's being. Monotheistic oneness is oneness before the realization of 'great zero', whereas non-dualistic oneness is oneness through and beyond the realization of 'great zero'.

Fourthly, monotheistic oneness, being somewhat 'over there', does not immediately include two, many and the whole. Even though monotheistic oneness can be all-inclusive, it is still more or less separated from the particularity and multiplicity of actual entities-in-the-world. This residual condition of separateness is illustrated by the fact that the monotheistic God is a personal God who commands and directs people. Non-dualistic oneness, however, which is based on the realization of 'great zero', includes all individual things just as they are, without any modification. This is because in non-dualistic oneness, conceptualization and objectification are completely and radically overcome. There is no separation between non-dualistic oneness and individual things. At this point the one and the many are non-dual.

The view of monotheistic unity does not *fully* admit the distinctiveness or uniqueness of each religion united therein, due to the lack of the realization of 'great zero' or non-substantial emptiness. By contrast, the view of non-dualistic unity thoroughly allows the distinctiveness or uniqueness of each religion without any limitation – through the realization of 'great zero' or emptiness. This is because the non-dualistic unity is completely free from conceptualization and objectification and is without substance. In this non-dualistic unity, all world religions with their individual uniqueness are dynamically united without being reduced to a single principle. This is, however, not an uncritical acceptance of the given pluralistic situation of religions. Instead, the non-dualistic unity makes a critical acceptance and creative reconstruction of world religions possible because each religion is grasped from within the one non-dualistic unity – not from one or another external perspective, but from deep within the dynamic laws of a positionless position, i.e. a position which is completely free from any particular position that is surreptitiously taken as the absolute or universal standpoint.

Let me give an example of how world religions can be regrasped from the standpoint of non-dualistic unity in a manner that fosters world peace. When the divine, God or Buddha, is believed to be self-affirmative, self-existing, enduring and substantial, then our idea of the divine becomes authoritative, commanding and intolerant. By contrast, when the divine, God or Buddha, is believed to be self-negating, relational and non-substantial, the idea of the divine becomes compassionate, all-loving and tolerant.

If monotheistic religions such as Judaism, Christianity and Islam place more emphasis on the self-negating, non-substantial aspect of their God rather than the self-affirmative, authoritative aspect of God, or, in other words, if these religions understand the oneness of the ultimate reality or absolute God in terms of non-dualistic oneness rather than in terms of monotheistic oneness, then they may overcome serious conflicts with other faiths and may establish a stronger interfaith cooperation to contribute to world peace.

IV

The third topic concerns the relation of justice to wisdom. In the Western religions, God is believed to have the attribute of justice, or righteousness, as the judge, as well as love or mercy as the forgiver. God is the fountain of justice, so everything God does may be relied upon as just. Since God's verdict is absolutely just, human righteousness may be defined in terms of God's judgment.

The notion of justice or righteousness is a double-edged sword. On the one hand, it aids in keeping everything in the right order, but on the other hand, it establishes clear-cut distinctions between the righteous and the unrighteous, promising the former eternal bliss, but condemning the latter to eternal punishment. Accordingly, if justice or righteousness is the sole principle of judgment or is too strongly emphasized, it creates serious disunion among people. This disunion is unrestorable because it is thought to be the result of a divine judgment.

Although religious emphasis on the law and the doctrine of exact retribution is Jewish, Jesus went beyond such a strong emphasis on divine justice and preached the universal equality or divine indifference of God's love. Speaking of God the Father, Jesus said: 'He makes His sun rise on the evil and on the good, and sends rain on the just and the unjust' (Matt. 5: 45). Thus, he emphasized, 'Love your enemies and pray for those who persecute you, so that you may be sons of your Father who is in heaven' (Matt. 5: 44). Nevertheless, in the Judeo-Christian tradition the notion of divine election is persistently evident. The Old Testament preaches God's choice of Israel from among all the nations of the earth to be God's people in the possession of a covenant of privilege and blessing (Deut. 4: 37, 7: 6; I Kgs. 3: 8; Isa. 44: 1–2). In the New Testament, divine election is a gracious and merciful election. Nevertheless, this election is rather restricted, for as the New Testament clearly states, 'Many are called, but few are chosen' (Matt. 22: 14). Thus 'the terms [election or elect] always imply differentiation whether viewed on God's part or as privilege on the part of men.'[3] Paul says that all humans are condemned under the law, and justifiably so. This is why salvation is through spiritual rebirth in love for Christ and not through obedience to the Judaic laws (Rom. 3: 28). Nevertheless, many Christians, rather than giving their lives to the spirit of Christ's sacrificial love, instead interpret Paul to mean that only those humans who have committed themselves to the *name* and *form* of Jesus will be elected by God for eternal bliss. Unfortunately, such an interpretation precludes salvation for non-Christians. In Christianity, the notion of the 'Elect of

God' often overshadows the 'universal equality' of God's love. If I am not mistaken, this is largely related to the over-emphasis on justice or righteousness.

While Christianity speaks much about love, Buddhism stresses compassion. Compassion is a Buddhist equivalent to the Christian notion of love. In Christianity, however, love is accompanied by justice. Love without justice is not regarded as true love and justice without love is not true justice. In Buddhism, compassion always goes with wisdom. Compassion without wisdom is not understood to be true compassion and wisdom without compassion is not true wisdom. Like the Christian notion of justice, the Buddhist notion of wisdom indicates clarification of the distinction or differentiation of things in the universe. Unlike the Christian notion of justice, however, the Buddhist notion of wisdom does not entail judgment or election. Buddhist wisdom implies the affirmation or recognition of everything and everyone in their distinctiveness or in their suchness. Furthermore, as noted above, the notion of justice creates an irreparable split between the just and the unjust, the righteous and the unrighteous, whereas the notion of wisdom evokes the sense of equality and solidarity. Again, justice, when carried to its final conclusion, often results in punishment, conflict, revenge and even war. Wisdom, however, entails rapprochement, conciliation, harmony and peace. Love and justice are like water and fire – although both are necessary, they go together with difficulty. Compassion and wisdom are like heat and light – although different, they work together in complementarity.

The Judeo-Christian tradition, however, does not lack the notion of wisdom. In the Hebrew Bible, wisdom literature such as Job, Proverbs and Ecclesiastes occupy an important position in which *hokma* (wisdom) frequently appears. This term refers to both human knowledge and divine wisdom. As a state of knowing given by God, wisdom enables the human person to lead a good, true and satisfying life through keeping God's commandments. In the New Testament, *sophia* is understood to be an attribute of God (Luke 11: 49), the revelation of the divine will to people (1 Cor. 2: 4–7). But most remarkably, Jesus as the Christ is identified with the wisdom of God because he is believed to be the ultimate source of all Christian wisdom (1 Cor. 1: 30). Nevertheless, in the Judeo-Christian tradition as a whole, the wisdom aspect of God has been rather neglected in favour of the justice aspect of God. Is it not important and terribly necessary now to emphasize the wisdom aspect of God rather than the justice aspect of God in order to solve the conflict within religions as well as among religions?

On the other hand, in Buddhism the notion of justice or righteousness is rather weak and thus Buddhism often becomes indifferent to social evil and injustice. If Buddhism learns from Western religions the importance of justice, and develops its notion of compassion to be linked not only with wisdom, but also with justice, it will then become closer to Judaism, Christianity and Islam in its interfaith relationship and may become more active in establishing world peace.

Notes

1. The author is very grateful to Mr David Cockerham for his revision and valuable suggestions.
2. Küng, H. *Does God Exist? An Answer for Today* (New York: Random House, 1981), pp. 109–10.
3. Harrison, E.F. (ed.) *Baker's Dictionary of Theology* (Grand Rapids, MI: Baker Book House, 1960), p. 179.

2

A Dynamic Unity in Religious Pluralism: A Proposal from the Buddhist Point of View

I

Religious pluralism is a remarkable cultural and religious phenomenon in our time and one of the important issues to be addressed by religious thinkers and writers of all traditions today. The 'challenge of religious pluralism' has thus been discussed extensively in recent years. In this respect I would like to make the following two points.

First, although religious pluralism is an issue commonly challenging all religions in our time, the degree of its seriousness and the manner of its challenge are not necessarily identical for all religions. For instance, there is a considerable difference between Christianity and Buddhism in this connection. Although in its early centuries Christianity confronted the problems of religious pluralism it has, in recent centuries, enjoyed a virtual religious monopoly in Europe and America. Only recently, with the collapse of the Europe-centered view of the world and the rapid development of international interaction in various fields of human life, have Christians come again to experience intensely the reality of religious pluralism. In this connection they have come to recognize the existence of non-Christian religions and the integrity of non-Christian systems of belief and values, not only in foreign lands, but in Europe and America as well. Hence, religious pluralism now appears to many Christians to be a serious challenge to the monotheistic character of Christianity.

On the other hand, Buddhism, throughout its long history, has

existed and spread throughout Asia within a religiously pluralistic situation: in India, it coexisted with Brahmanism, Jainism
and many diverse forms of Hinduism; in China with Confucianism and Taoism; and in Japan with Shinto and Confucianism.
Thus to most Buddhists the experience of 'religious pluralism'
has not been the serious shock it has been to most Christians.
Furthermore, the diversity within Buddhism is greater even than
that within Christianity. Admittedly, a considerable degree of
diversity is found within Christianity, between Catholic, Protestant, Greek and Russian Orthodox, Coptic and other churches.
The diversity within Buddhism, however, is more radical, as is
illustrated by the drastic divergences between Theravada and
Lamaism, Zen and Pure Land Buddhism, Esoteric Buddhism and
Nichiren. The primary explanation for this greater Buddhist
diversity is that the various forms of Christianity, however
culturally diverse they may be, take as their fundamental source
a single volume of Sacred Writings (i.e. the Bible). The various
forms of Buddhism, on the other hand, beyond their cultural
diversity, have *each* a fundamental scriptural source unique to
itself, with the exception of Zen which rejects any reliance upon
scripture. (Zen insists on 'an independent transmission outside
the teaching of the scriptures'). Another reason for the greater
diversity in Buddhism than Christianity may be found in the fact
that, while Christianity is based upon faith in One God who is
believed to be the ruler of the world and of history, Buddhism
takes its foundation in the law of 'dependent co-origination' or
'Emptiness' (*śūnyatā*). When faith in One God is essential to a
religion, diversity in that religion is naturally limited and a
pluralistic relation to other religions is difficult to maintain. In
contrast, when 'dependent co-origination' or 'emptiness' is the
basis of a religion, diversity in that religion will be significant
and a pluralistic relation to other religions is easily maintained.

For these two reasons at least, pluralism is more familiar to
Buddhism both as a problem of the religions and as a problem
of its own forms, than it is to Christianity. Such familiarity,
however, does not mean that pluralism does not confront Buddhism
today with a serious challenge. As the globe rapidly shrinks and
East and West interact with one another on a novel scale and
depth, Buddhists also face a more broad-based and more inten-
sive encounter with religious pluralism. This is the most import-

ant reason why Buddhists themselves need an ongoing series of interfaith dialogues as do Christians. Buddhism is also now exposed to the irreligious challenge posed by technology, industrialism, Marxism and so forth, which are the products of the modern West. In summary, while 'religious pluralism' is now a common challenge to Christians and Buddhists, the seriousness and nature of the challenge is not altogether equal in the two instances. In this regard, one may say that in our time, Christianity has moved from a relatively non-pluralistic situation to one radically pluralistic, whereas Buddhism has moved from the old pluralistic situation to a new pluralistic one.

Second, pluralism in our time includes not only 'religious pluralism', but also a conflict between religion and non-religion. Roughly speaking, until a century or so ago most people took for granted the meaning and necessity of religion for humanity. However, since sometime in the nineteenth century and particularly in our century, many people have become indifferent to or doubtful about the *raison d'être* of religion. Questions such as: 'Is religion truly indispensable to humanity?' 'Cannot people live their life without religion?' and 'Is religion not, perhaps, an obstacle to progress?' have been raised. A characteristic of our time is the existence of many ideologies and philosophical schools which *in principle* deny that religion serves any useful purpose for human beings. These modern secular schools of thought attack not necessarily a particular religion such as Buddhism or Christianity, but religion in general and deny the philosophical and cultural validity of religion itself. Further, they do so not from an emotional standpoint, but from a philosophical-theoretical foundation. As examples of such religion-negating ideologies, I mentioned scientism, psychoanalysis, Marxism and nihilism, particularly Nietzschean nihilism.[1] The followers of all religions are now exposed to attack by these anti-religious ideologies. All religious persons are thus, in our time, forced to defend and reconfirm the religious truth as they believe and live it. To do so properly, it is insufficient merely to tackle pluralism within the realm of religion and to develop mutual understanding among the followers of religions. It is now absolutely necessary for all religions to break through the traditional framework of their doctrine and practice and to re-examine themselves most radically in order to grasp the quintessence of their own faiths.

Only when they can deepen and revitalize the quintessence of their faith and overcome religion-negating ideologies prevailing in our society, can they be said to cope with the challenge of pluralism today. In short, all religious persons are now standing at the intersection of two types of 'challenge from pluralism'. That is, they face the challenge of pluralism in terms of religion and non-religion or anti-religion. To open up a new religious dimension at the depth of that intersection is an urgent task for the adherents of all religions today.

II

The primary reason that the pluralistic situation of religion is such a problem to the adherents of various religions is the fear that it will threaten each religion's claim to absoluteness. People fear that an affirmation of religious pluralism will lead to a vicious relativism and finally to a self-defeating skepticism. They see it as a viewpoint that will undermine their religious commitment. The major reactions to religious pluralism may be classified as the following three attitudes.

First, a person may view religions other than his or her own as rivals or enemies and simply reject them or try to convert their adherents to his or her own faith. This attitude has prevailed in the Semitic religions until recent times and, to a greater or lesser extent, has been present in all religions.

Second, a person may attempt to find parallels between his or her own religion and other religious traditions and to evaluate the religious significance of the beliefs of others without prejudging or rejecting them. In contemporary Christianity, Richard Niebuhr and R.C. Zaehner may be mentioned as examples of this sympathetic approach. Niebuhr emphasizes the need for Christians to be open and responsive to the criticisms by other religious believers of the Christian confession of Jesus as the Christ. He argues that through open-minded dialogue, believers in different traditions can deepen and enrich their own grasp of religious truth. Such a fair recognition and positive esteem of parallel truths among different religions are clearly evident in the writings of Niebuhr. But, at the same time, we must recognize that he is much less concerned with Eastern religions than with non-Christian Western movements such as Marxism,

Freudianism and Existentialism. On the other hand, Zaehner is deeply involved in the study of Hinduism and Buddhism, as well as Islam and Zoroastrianism. In his writings he has emphasized the urgent need to understand these religions from within. However, while finding parallels between Christianity and other religious traditions, he finally asserts Christianity as the fulfilment or consummation of all other religions, thereby rendering doubtful his own intended openness and objectivity toward non-Christian (and non-Catholic) religions.[2]

Third, a person may, with even greater openness, recognize a common Reality underlying the different religious traditions and claim that they are different manifestations of this common Reality. Such an attitude is most evident in Indian religions such as Hinduism, but is not difficult to uncover in contemporary Christian thinkers. William Ernest Hocking and Wilfred Cantwell Smith are two illustrious examples. Emphasizing that religion is universal and inherent in all humankind, Hocking takes the essence of all religions as 'a passion for righteousness, . . . conceived as a cosmic demand'.[3] Although he rightly recognizes particular and separative aspects of religion, especially in terms of the communication of religious truth, he talks much about 'the same God' and the 'need for a common symbol'.[4] On the other hand, clearly denying that all religions are the same, Cantwell Smith talks about 'the unity or coherence of humankind's religious history'.[5] By saying that 'the evident variety of their religious life is real, yet is contained within an historical continuum',[6] Smith emphasizes the interrelatedness and continuity of the history of religions as the possible basis for the common term 'faith'.

> The history of man's religious life, which for some centuries was divided into self-conscious parts, is beginning to include also a developing history of diverse instances of self-consciousness of the whole, open to each other.[7]

The attitude that all religions partake of one and the same Reality at their depth has been taken repeatedly, *mutatis mutandis*, in the West as well as in the East, though predominately in the East. In Japan, this attitude has been expressed in a poem as follows:

Though paths for climbing a mountain
From its foot differ,
We look up at the same moon
Above a lofty peak.

In the contemporary context of religious pluralism, such an attitude seems to be getting rather widely accepted.

John Cobb challenges this widespread attitude. He emphasizes that 'the insistence of a given identity among the several religious Ways continues to block the urgently important task of learning from one another.'[8] To make this point clear, he describes the features of his own first-hand experience of dialogue with Japanese Zen Buddhists. In this connection, he remarks that 'they [Buddhists] have experienced Emptiness and what they have experienced is not describable as most Christians want to describe God.'[9] He also examines the writings of Catholic fathers who have been involved practically in Zen disciplines and refers to Father William Johnston's view by saying that 'he has increasingly seen that Zen and Christian mysticism are different throughout, regardless of the parallels that may be found.'[10] Cobb concludes as follows:

> This strongly suggests that to insist as Christians that Emptiness is a Buddhist name for what we call God is dangerous and misleading. It cuts us off from our Biblical heritage, forcing us to take as normative the Neo-Platonic mystical stream in our tradition. Even then it demands of us changes in this tradition which break its last ties to the Bible. The result is to reinterpret 'God' in terms of Emptiness. We can no longer understand God in terms of Yahweh or the Father of Jesus Christ.[11]

This conclusion, which John Cobb has recently reached through his own experience and observation of ongoing Buddhist-Christian dialogue, is important and justifiable. On its basis he proposes as a working hypothesis that 'What is named by "Yahweh" and "the father of Jesus Christ" is not the same as what is named by "Emptiness".'[12] On the basis of this hypothesis, rather than rejecting one of them as unreal, 'We could allow parallels and similarities to appear, but we would have no need to obscure differences at the most fundamental level.'[13] He continues in this vein:

If we do not need to find some common denominator in all religious movements, then we can listen carefully to the important nuances of difference in all of them and learn from each without imposing common categories. Similarly, the distinction between religious and secular loses importance.[14]

In this connection, Cobb further suggests that:

There is a very deep assumption that when two traditions both claim to deal with what is transcendent and ultimate, they must be understood as relating to the same reality. What is ultimate, it is assumed, is truly ultimate, and therefore must be ultimate for all.[15]

Clearly rejecting this deep assumption, Cobb tries to establish his own dialogical standpoint on the understanding that there is no common denominator in all religious traditions.

So far, I have no objection at all to John Cobb's position. Rather I find in him a standpoint which is congenial with the Buddhist one. As is well known, the Buddha answered with silence any metaphysical question concerning 'ultimate Reality', such as whether the world is eternal or not. His silence, however, does not indicate agnosticism but rather a thoroughgoing criticism of all possible metaphysical propositions implied in various philosophical schools of his day, hence his teachings of *anātman* (no-self) and *madhyamā pratipad* (the Middle Way). The Middle Way should not be construed as a position in the sense of a third position lying at a middle point between the two extremes, but as a no-position or no-standpoint which supersedes both of the other opposed views. It is a positionless position or a standpoint which is free from any standpoint. *Pratītya-samutpāda* (dependent co-origination) is no less than another term for this Middle Way. This positionless position unique to the Buddha is more clearly and definitely grasped by Nagarjuna in terms of 'eightfold negation' and *Śūnyatā* (Emptiness). The positionless position together with 'eightfold negation' and 'Emptiness' can be properly realized only *existentially*, not merely logically or conceptually. This Mahayanist position established by Nagarjuna rejects any view or theory of the 'ultimate Reality' as a thought-construction and does not admit any notion of 'common denominator' or 'ultimate unity' in all philosophical or religious traditions. Instead, by taking a positionless position represented by 'dependent co-origination' and 'Emptiness', he freely recognizes the distinctiveness and the relative or contextual ultimacy of other philosophical positions. On the one hand, the Mahayana positionless position does not at all admit one absolute, ultimate Reality because it realizes 'Emptiness' or the non-substantiality of everything; but, on the other, it freely recognizes the relative or contextual ultimacy of various philosophic-religious traditions without eliminating their distinctiveness. Herein, the plurality of various spiritual traditions is given a positive significance without falling into a mere relativism or skepticism. For, in the positionless position made possible by the realization of 'Emptiness' or the non-substantiality of everything, the relative is ultimate and the ultimate is relative. In other words, the relativity of various religions and the ultimacy of each religion are dynamically non-dual and identical. This dynamic position is possible only through the denial of a 'common denominator' or 'ultimate unity' in various spiritual traditions. In the sense that Cobb also rejects a 'common denominator', I find in his writings a standpoint which is congenial with Buddhism.

We must, however, raise a question as to whether Cobb's position can really afford to affirm the dynamism which freely recognizes the relative ultimacy of plural religious traditions without eliminating their distinctiveness, such as is done by Buddhism with its positionless position. Let us examine Cobb's position more closely.

Emphasizing the complementary rather than contradictory character of Buddhism and Christianity, Cobb says:

> Instead of speaking of ultimacy in general, it is better to examine more exactly what Mahayana Buddhists would mean by the ultimacy of Emptiness, should they employ such terminology. Similarly, we should investigate what the Biblical writers would mean by the ultimacy of Yahweh or of the heavenly Father, should they use this language. I am convinced that the respective claims of the Buddhist and Christian scriptures are profoundly different and that finally they are complementary rather than contradictory.[16]

He then elucidates the different nature of the ultimacy of Buddhist 'Emptiness' and Christian 'God' by saying that:

It (Emptiness) is the ultimate answer to the question *what* one is and *what* all things are. It is not the answer to the question *how* and *why* things have the particular character or form they have. The study of forms and why and how they inform our experience and our world was pursued far more intensively in the eastern Mediterranean (in terms of the Biblical God) than in the sphere of Buddhist influence.[17]

Consequently, Cobb argues:

There is no reason in principle to assume that the Buddhist and Christian claims exclude each other. The fact that all things are empty does not directly contradict the claims that I should place my ultimate trust in God.[18]

This, then, is how John Cobb understands the complementary relationship between Buddhist and Christian claims of ultimacy. It seems to me, however, that the *ground* or *reason* for such a complementarity is not as clear as it might be. Even if we admit with Cobb that the Buddhist and Christian claims do not exclude or directly contradict each other, such an admission is only a negative, not a positive, basis for the complementarity. Again, even if we acknowledge that Buddhist 'Emptiness' is the ultimate answer to the question of *what* things are and that the Christian 'God' is the answer to questions of *how* and *why* things are, the very relationship between the questions *what* and *how-why* and between their respective answers is quite unclear. Cobb seems to distinguish Buddhist and Christian ultimacy and just to juxtapose them. As stated before, he clearly denies the existence of a 'common denominator' or 'ultimate unity' underlying the various religious ways, and instead proposes as a working hypothesis for Buddhism and Christianity the complementarity of their two different forms of ultimacy. However, the complementarity between the two religions is asserted without revealing its positive ground. The question should be asked: Whenever Cobb emphasizes the complementary relation between the ultimacy of 'Emptiness' and the ultimacy of 'Yahweh', where is he taking his own stand? Is he taking the ultimacy of 'Emptiness', the ultimacy of 'Yahweh', or some third position as his own stand? Since it is impossible to *properly* talk about *complementarity* between two items by merely taking *one of them* as one's own position, we must assume that Cobb is consciously or unconsciously taking some *third* position as his own. If this is the case, what is that third position? Isn't his position that of a speculative metaphysics? Isn't he emphasizing the complementary nature of the relationship between Buddhist and Christian ultimacy on a conceptually established ground? These questions lead me to suggest that Cobb's working hypothesis lacks a dynamism through which the plurality of religious traditions can be truly given positive significance, and the relativity of various religions and the ultimacy of each religion can be realized as dynamically nondual. The positionless position realized by Mahayana Buddhism, on the other hand, possesses just such a dynamism.

III

In this connection, I would like to make a concrete proposal from the Buddhist point of view. In order to do so the three-body (*trikāya*) doctrine may be introduced herein.

The three-body doctrine concerns the Buddha-body (*buddhakāya*) or the forms in which the Buddha is manifested. After the Buddha's death, his disciples and followers gradually began to idealize his historical existence and various forms of the Buddhabody doctrine have been widely and profoundly developed, particularly in Mahayana tradition. The three-body doctrine, that is the doctrine of the threefold Buddha-body: *nirmāṇa-kāya*, *saṃbhoga-kāya* and *dharma-kāya*, is the most representative form of the Buddha-body doctrine and has been predominant for centuries in Mahayana Buddhism. *Nirmāṇa-kāya*, which means assumed-body, apparitional-body or transformation-body, is no less than the historical Buddha in the person of Gautama. The historical Buddha who was believed in and reverenced by his disciples and followers as the Enlightened One or the One who awakened to *Dharma*, lived, preached and passed away. Through the great shock of confronting the death of Gautama Buddha, his disciples eventually came to believe that, behind the appearance of the historical Buddha, there is a suprahistorical or nonhistorical Buddha. Gautama was a realizer of *Dharma* but, having a physical body, was limited by time and space. According to this doctrine, however, he was the transformation-body of the suprahistorical Buddha who is beyond time and space, and who thus is the formless, colourless, unlimited, eternal Buddha. In other words, the historical existence of Gautama Buddha is understood and believed to be an accommodated body through which the suprahistorical Buddha revealed himself to the earthly disciples because of his great compassion. This suprahistorical Buddha is, in turn, divided into two different bodies, that is *saṃbhoga-kāya* and *dharma-kāya*. *Saṃbhoga-kāya*, which means bliss-body, reward-body or enjoyment-body, is the suprahistorical Buddha who has fulfilled *Dharma* and is enjoying various virtues because of the merit he has attained. While *saṃbhoga-kāya* is suprahistorical or non-historical, freed from time and space, and in this sense is formless and colourless, it may nevertheless be said to have a particular form, though invisible, according to the kinds of virtue which it is enjoying as the merit of its fulfilment. *Dharma-kāya* is the truth-body without any personal character. (Therefore, the term 'body' is here rather misleading.) It is *Dharma* (Truth) itself which is to be fulfilled and enjoyed by *saṃbhoga-kāya*. As *Dharma* itself, *dharma-kāya* is beyond time and space, is universal and eternal, and is completely formless and colourless.

I explained the three-body doctrine above in order of *nirmāṇa-kāya*, *saṃbhoga-kāya* and *dharma-kāya*. Essentially speaking, however, this order should be reversed. Without *dharma-kāya* as their foundation, *saṃbhoga-kāya* and *nirmāṇa-kāya* cannot appear. Again, without *saṃbhoga-kāya* as its basis, *nirmāṇa-kāya*, that is transformation-body, is inconceivable. At the same time, in essence, the threefold body of Buddha is not divided. The Awakened One in his transformation body, of which Gautama was the first instance, is still one with the formless *dharma*-body and invisible reward-body. All three bodies, although different, are in actuality one living, acting Reality.

In Mahayana Buddhism, *dharma-kāya* is identified with *śūnyatā* or Emptiness. As *Dharma* or Truth itself, which is the ultimate ground of both reward-body and transformation-body, *dharma-kāya* is in itself. More strictly speaking, *dharma-kāya* neither *is* in itself, nor *is not* in itself. It is neither *existent* nor *not existent*, neither *fulfilled* nor *unfulfilled*. It is empty and entirely formless. It is, however, not 'emptiness' nor 'formlessness' in the static mode, rather it is always emptying itself. Constant activity of emptying everything including itself is no less than the reality of *Dharma* itself which is termed *dharma-kāya* in the three-body doctrine. Again, *dharma-kāya*, negating any form, constantly negates its own formlessness and takes various forms freely without hindrance. This is the reason that as the ultimate ground *dharma-kāya* takes a form of invisible *saṃbhoga-kāya* (reward-body) and a form of visible *nirmāṇa-kāya* (transformation-body) freely without losing its own formlessness. *Dharma-kāya* is not less than dynamic activity as the ground of everything and is non-objectifiable and inconceivable.

In contrast to this, *saṃbhoga-kāya*, as the reward-body which is attained as the virtue of the fulfilment of *Dharma*, is the suprahistorical embodiment of the formless *dharma-kāya*. Use of the term 'fulfilment' raises a question about the fulfilment of *what* and *for what*. 'Of what', in this case, is 'of *Dharma*'. 'For what' is 'for itself and all other creatures'. Therefore, *saṃbhoga-kāya* bears a kind of form and a kind of subject–object dichotomy. Although suprahistorical, *saṃbhoga-kāya* stands for others as well as for itself. Thus, it may well be said to be *personal*. *Saṃbhoga-kāya*, however, is different from *nirmāṇa-kāya*, i.e. the historical Buddha who appeared with visible form and colour among man in this world. By means of its virtue, *saṃbhoga-kāya* never remains in the self-enjoyment of its own fulfilment of *Dharma*. It necessarily takes a historical form of Buddha-body, *nirmāṇa-kāya*, as its own transformation in order to share its fulfilment with all fellow beings.

In short, *saṃbhoga-kāya*, unlike *nirmāṇa-kāya*, is beyond time and space and thus formless, colourless, unlimited and eternal, and yet, unlike *dharma-kāya*, has a kind of form as a Buddha who was fulfilled *Dharma*, and thus in some sense stands facing others. It is the reality of *fulfilled Dharma for itself*, and at the same time, is the reality of *unfulfilled Dharma*, which is to be fulfilled *for all others*.

In Mahayana Buddhism both *saṃbhoga-kāya* and *nirmāṇa-kāya* are plural, not singular. This is because *dharma-kāya* as the ultimate ground for both is not One God or One Substance, but formless Emptiness or boundless Openness which, emptying itself, takes forms freely. Among various forms of *saṃbhoga-kāya* (reward-body) Amida Buddha and Mahāvairocana Buddha are very important. Amida Buddha is a *saṃbhoga-kāya* whose virtues are immeasurable life and immeasurable light and upon whom Pure Land Buddhism is based. On the other hand, Mahāvairocana Buddha is originally a *saṃbhoga-kāya* who is the Sun Buddha, the

Great Luminous One whose virtues are wisdom and compassion.[19] For some forms of Esoteric Buddhism, Mahāvairocana Buddha is the principal image. Amida Buddha and Mahāvairocana Buddha have been worshipped as the central Buddha by Pure Land and Esoteric Buddhists respectively for many centuries, but this difference in worship has led to no serious conflicts between them. This is simply because both Amida and Mahāvairocana are regarded as different manifestations of one and the same *dharma-kāya* which is in reality empty, open and formless. This is quite different from the case of Yahweh in the Judeo-Christian tradition, 'Whose name is jealous and is a jealous God'[20] (Exod. 34: 14). In Mahayana Buddhism, in addition to Amida and Mahāvairocana, there are many *saṃbhoga-kāya* in the form of Buddhas and Bodhisattvas.[21] They are all reward-bodies with a particular name and form who have fulfilled *Dharma* and are enjoying various virtues for themselves and at the same time are encouraging all others to attain the same fulfilment.

As for *nirmāṇa-kāya*, that is, the assumed-body or transformation-body, Gautama Buddha is not the one and only instance. There are innumerable forms of the transformation-body throughout Buddhist history. Gautama Buddha is simply the first instance. For Buddha as *nirmāṇa-kāya* is no less than the one who, if any, awakened to *Dharma*. Accordingly, Indian masters such as Nagarjuna (around AD 150–250) and Vasubandhu (420–500), Chinese masters such as T'ien-t'ai Chih-i (531–597) and Shan-tao (–681), all have been revered alongside Gautama Buddha and, according to the three-body doctrine, may be said to have been regarded as *nirmāṇa-kāya*. In Japanese Buddhism, this is more conspicuous. The founders of powerful Japanese Buddhist sects such as Kūkai (774–835), Hōnen (1133–1212), Shinran (1173–1262), Dōgen (1200–1253) and Nichiren (1222–1282) have been worshipped by their respective followers almost in place of Gautama Buddha. Again, according to the three-body doctrine, these figures can be properly regarded as *nirmāṇa-kāya*. In Christianity, however great and important St. Thomas Aquinas and Martin Luther may be to Catholic and Protestant churches respectively, they are not revered alongside Jesus. Even St. Paul cannot be an exception. This is simply because Jesus is the only incarnation of the Godhead – the transformation-body of God. This great difference stems from the fact that while Jesus Christ is believed to be the only son of Father God Yahweh, Gautama Buddha and other great Buddhist figures are understood to be, in essence, equally representative of the transformation-body of one and the same *Dharma* which is entirely empty, open and formless. Accordingly, however crucial Gautama Buddha may be, and however important the founders of various sects may be to the adherents of these sects, there has been little conflict between Gautama and these founders, or between founders themselves.[22] A notable exception is Nichiren, the founder of the Nichiren Sect in Japan. Taking the *Lotus Sutra* as the most authentic scripture expounded by the eternal Buddha, he severely criticized other Buddhist sects prevailing in his day. Even so there has been scarcely any bloodshed or religious war among various forms of Buddhism throughout its long history. This fact stems almost exclusively from the notion of *Dharma* (or *dharma-kāya*) as the ultimate ground which is dynamically formless. Because Gautama and the founders of various sects are regarded as various forms of the transformation-body of the non-substantial, open and formless *Dharma*, there is little possibility for serious conflict.

BUDDHISM

Principle	Manifestation			
NIRMĀNA-KĀYA (Transformation-body)	Gautama (Original Buddhism)	Kūkai (Estoric Buddhism)	Shinran (Pure Land Buddhism)	Bodhidharma (Zen)
SAMBHOGA-KĀYA (Reward-body)	Vairocana, Amida, etc.			
DHARMA-KĀYA (Truth-body)	Formless and boundless reality of Emptiness (Openness)			

Diagram 1

In this connection, the following two points are worth consideration:

1. Although the formless *Dharma* (or *dharma-kāya*) is the ultimate ground for all forms of Buddhism, some Buddhist schools take a certain form of *sambhoga-kāya* rather than formless *dharma-kāya* as central for the soteriological point of view. The most conspicuous example is Pure Land Buddhism. Through the existential realization of one's sinfulness, living in the age of

degeneration of *Dharma*, Pure Land Buddhism emphasizes that salvation is possible only through the virtue of the unconditional compassion of Amida Buddha who is a reward-body. Pure Land Buddhism is *saṃbhoga-kāya* centered, not *dharmakāya* centered. Although this *saṃbhoga-kāya*-centeredness is soteriologically essential, it somewhat diminishes the dynamic function of formless *Dharma*.

2. In Buddhist countries, especially in Japanese Buddhist circles, there are *saṃbhoga-kāya*-centered forms of Buddhism as well as *dharma-kāya*-centered forms. Since they are now very much institutionalized because of their long history, the dynamic function of formless *Dharma* is more or less lost. The result is a rather indifferent attitude of each form of Buddhism towards others and a lack of ecumenical awareness. Their relatively peaceful coexistence is not a sign of dynamic unity among various forms of Buddhism but rather a lifeless juxtaposition among them. To revitalize the present forms of Buddhism, it is important to break through their established form of teaching and practice and to regrasp the most fundamental idea of the *Dharma* which is dynamically formless.

IV

Is it not possible that the Buddhist doctrine of the threefold body may contribute to the establishment of a dynamic unity in religious pluralism? In this connection as a working hypothesis, the following threefold reality may be offered: 'Lord', 'God', and 'Boundless Openness'. 'Lord' roughly stands for *nirmāṇa-kāya*, a historical religious figure that is the centre of faith; 'God' approximately represents *saṃbhoga-kāya*, a personal God who is suprahistorical but has a particular name and virtue(s); 'Boundless Openness' or 'Formless Emptiness' generally expresses *dharmakāya*, Truth itself, which is also suprahistorical and is the ultimate ground for both a personal 'God' and a central historical religious figure as 'Lord'. 'Lord', 'God' and Boundless Openness' are three different realities which nevertheless have a dynamic identity with 'Boundless Openness' as its ultimate ground.

In the Judeo-Christian tradition, the term 'Lord' is often used to refer to Yahweh. As Paul said (1 Cor. 8: 6), however, for Christians it may be said that there is only 'one God, the Father', and only 'one Lord, Jesus Christ'. In the present proposal, in clear distinction from the term 'God', the term 'Lord' is used to refer to someone like Jesus Christ or Gautama Buddha – a historical transformation or embodiment of the formless Reality which appeared in a particular form of religion. Further, the term 'Lord' here is used in a still wider sense by applying its connotation of 'master'. In this wider sense the term may include such religious figures as Moses and Muhammad. However crucial he may be to Judaism, Moses is not a transformation-body of Yahweh. In the Jewish tradition, however, Moses is regarded as the 'founder' of Hebraic religion and as the unique law-giver of Israel. Further, the Christian tradition has always considered Moses as the forerunner and 'type' of Christ. Moses delivered the Old Israel, Christ the New.[25] Again, however important he may be to Islam, Muhammad is not more than a prophet and is never regarded as a transformation-body of Allah. In this sense he cannot be identified with Jesus Christ. As the central figure of Islamic history, however, the role of Muhammad is so indispensable and crucial to Islamic faith that he may be here included, together with Moses, under the term 'Lord' (or Master). Such a free and flexible usage of the term 'Lord' is not, I hope, arbitrary because in the present proposal the term is understood basically as a historical embodiment of the 'Boundless Openness', not simply as a historical incarnation of One God.

The term 'God' is also here used somewhat flexibly although it always indicates a personal God with a particular name and virtue(s). This refers to Yahweh, Allah, Isvara (Śiva, Viṣṇu, etc.), Amida and so forth. Most of these Gods are believed by their adherents to be the one absolute deity and as the very centre and focus of their faiths. These Gods are also believed to have as virtues love, justice, eternal life, wisdom, compassion and the like. Although in a majority of cases, these Gods are regarded as ultimate Reality, in the present proposal they are to be regarded as reward-bodies (*saṃbhoga-kāya*), i.e. the deity who attained the fulfilment of ultimate Reality – Boundless Openness or Formless Emptiness – in terms of a particular name and form (though invisible) through which they can be distinguished from each other.

In the present proposal, ultimate Reality for all religions is understood as formless, colourless, nameless, unlimited, impersonal 'Openness' or 'Emptiness', which stands for *dharma-kāya*. As stated earlier, this Emptiness is not a static state of emptiness, but rather a dynamic activity constantly emptying everything including itself. It is formless by negating every form, and yet, without remaining in formlessness, takes various forms freely by negating its own formlessness. This is the reason that 'Formless Emptiness' or 'Boundless Openness' is here regarded as the ultimate ground which dynamically reveals itself both in terms of personal 'Gods' and in terms of 'Lords' that are historical religious figures.

In Christianity, Father God Yahweh is believed to have begotten the son of God, Christ, who gave up the form of God and 'emptied himself, taking the form of servant, being made in the likeness of men' (Phil. 2: 7). This kenosis is a great self-negation of Father God to reveal himself in the form of Jesus Christ in this historical world. Even so Yahweh still remains as Father God and his Self-negation is not thoroughgoing. It was Christian mystics such as Meister Eckhart and St. John of the Cross who went beyond Father God and became united with the Godhead. For them, the Godhead is impersonal, formless and nameless 'Nothing'. Herein, God's kenosis is fully realized.

In Hinduism, Isvara is regarded by his devotees as a central manifestation of Brahman, the impersonal, highest principle of the creation of the universe. Accordingly, Brahman should not be identified with a personal God such as Yahweh, Allah or Amida, but rather with the source of personal Gods. In the present proposal, however, Brahman is not taken as 'Boundless Openness'. For although *neti neti* ('not this, not this') is necessary for the acknowledgment of Brahman, Brahman, which is identified with Ātman (eternal Self), is strictly speaking still somewhat substantial and not completely formless or empty. This is the reason Gautama Buddha did not accept Brahman as the ultimate Reality and instead emphasized Anātman (no-self) and dependent co-orignation which is no less than another term for 'Emptiness'.

Space limitation does not allow a detailed discussion of Amida Buddha in Pure Land Buddhism. It may only be mentioned that, though suprahistorical, Amida has a personal form with a particular name and is thus well regarded as 'God' in the above sense, but not as 'Boundless Openness'. In order, however, to find a positive significance in the present situation of religious diversity and to establish a dynamic unit in religious pluralism, it is not appropriate to take 'God' (as understood in the present proposal) as the ultimate Reality. Going beyond 'God', one should return to and take one's stand on the root-source from which various 'Gods' are understood to emerge. For Gods, with particular names and particular virtues, however universal the nature of their virtue may be, are by nature not truly compatible with, but rather exclusive of, each other because each of them is believed by their adherents to be the positive centre and focus for their religious faiths. Only when one goes beyond 'God' and takes 'Boundless Openness' as the ultimate ground can a dynamic unity in religious pluralism be established without eliminating each religion's claim to absoluteness. 'Boundless Openness' or 'Formless Emptiness', here offered as the ultimate ground, is certainly the basic principle which integrates all religions dynamically, but is not a common denominator or an underlying given identity among the various religious traditions. Unlike Brahman, which is regarded in Hinduism as the underlying principle of the identity of everything in the universe, 'Boundless Openness' or 'Formless Emptiness' is entirely non-substantial and self-emptying or self-negating without a claim to a particular form of absoluteness. Accordingly, while it is working as the dynamic, self-negating principle of unity for all religions, 'Boundless Openness' does not eliminate but rather allows or guarantees each religion's claim to absoluteness in terms of 'God' and centeredness in terms of 'Lord'. This is because the various forms of 'God' and the various instances of 'Lord' in the various religious ways are equally and respectively grasped as manifestations of the dynamic 'Boundless Openness' as the ultimate ground.

The key point of the present proposal lies in its emphasis on the necessity for the clear realization of dynamic 'Boundless Openness' or 'Formless Emptiness' as the ultimate ground for all religions and as the basis for a dynamic unity in religious pluralism. In order, however, to open up a dynamic unity in religious pluralism, which is an urgent task for all religions today, each religion, especially religions based on the notion of 'God', must break through their traditional form of personal-God-centeredness, and return to and take their stand on the realization of dynamic 'Boundless Openness' as the ultimate Reality. Likewise, a religion which is not based on a personal 'God' but on the underlying absolute unitary principle, such as Brahman, must go beyond its substantial, self-identical principle and awaken to the dynamic, self-negating 'Boundless Openness' as the ultimate ground.

WORLD RELIGIONS

Principle	Manifestation			
LORD (Nirmāṇa-kāya)	Jesus	Muhammad	Kṛṣṇa (?)	Gautama[26]
GOD (Saṃbhoga-kāya)	Yahweh	Allah	Isvara (Śiva, Viṣṇu Brahmā)	Amida
BOUNDLESS OPENNESS (Dharma-kāya)	Formless and boundless reality of Emptiness (Openness)			

Diagram 2

This means that although 'Boundless Openness' embraces various forms of 'God' and 'Lord' as their ultimate ground, this is not a blind acceptance but a critical acknowledgment of them. While 'Boundless Openness' is all-embracing and thus able to accept various religions without eliminating the distinctiveness of their Gods and Lords, it is at the same time constantly emptying them – even asking them to abnegate themselves and return to itself ('Boundless Openness') as their ultimate ground. The *dynamic* nature of 'Boundless Openness' in regard to various religions indicates no less than this dynamic identity of the all-embracing acceptance and the critical approach of constant emptying.

Every religion must be involved in a cultural and social milieu in order to actualize its spirit and life. However, when this historical-cultural involvement creates an institutionalization and fixation of doctrine, ritual, religious order and so forth, it stereotypes that religion and leads to unnecessary conflicts with other religions. This possibility is especially serious in our time in which religious pluralism is so evident.

It is thus extremely important and necessary for each religion today to break through its traditional forms of doctrine and practice and to realize the dynamic ground, 'Boundless Openness', as its own basis. This is necessary not only in order to develop real mutual understanding among religions, but also to encourage learning from each other in the interfaith dialogue. Such a breakthrough is also urgently necessary if each religion is to grapple with the challenge posed by contemporary anti-religious ideologies. As stated earlier, all religions are now exposed to the attack of various religion-negating forces prevailing in our time. The *raison d'être* of religion is now questioned on numerous fronts. To cope with this situation, all religions must re-examine themselves radically and grasp the quintessence of their own faiths. It is here suggested, standing at the intersection of the two forms of challenge, the challenge of pluralism within religion and the challenge by anti-religious ideologies, that the realization of 'Boundless Openness' may serve as the ultimate ground to meet the double challenge.

John Cobb is right when he says, 'What is named by "Yahweh" and "the Father of Jesus Christ" is not the same as what is named by "Emptiness" (in Buddhism).'[27] For in my understanding, 'God Yahweh' and 'Emptiness' are standing on two different levels of religious realization and thus are not comparable. Cobb is, however, unclear in what sense or on what basis 'Yahweh' and 'Emptiness' must be said to be not the same. Accordingly, Cobb is not justified in insisting on the complementarity of the ultimacy of Yahweh and the ultimacy of Emptiness. This is the reason I earlier raised the questions: 'From what standpoint is he talking about the complementarity of these two ultimacies?' 'Is he not, consciously or unconsciously, taking a third position in regard to the two ultimacies, a position which is constructed conceptually?' 'What is, after all, the ground of that complementarity?' To use the term complementarity, an answer to the last question should be this – the ground of 'complementarity' between the ultimacy of God, Yahweh, and the ultimacy of Emptiness lies in Emptiness itself. This is because the positionless position, which is constantly self-emptying and self-negating, Emptiness, can negate its own ultimacy and give the foundation to the ultimacy of God Yahweh. They are 'complementary', not *immediately* but in the sense that God Yahweh is a manifestation of 'Formless Emptiness' or 'Boundless Openness' through its dynamic activity of self-emptying or self-negation. Through complete kenosis, God Yahweh abnegates his name and himself and returns to the Godhead which is now realized as 'Boundless Openness' or 'Formless Emptiness'. The ultimacy of Yahweh is an affirmative and positive ultimacy whereas the ultimacy of Emptiness is a negative and self-negating ultimacy. Since the ultimacy of Emptiness is a self-negating one, it can give the foundation to, and is complementary with, the ultimacy of God Yahweh.

One may say that such a proposal of threefold reality, that is 'Lord,' 'God' and 'Boundless Openness', as the basis for a dynamic unity in religious pluralism is nothing but a form of Buddhist imperialism because it is based on the Buddhist notion of Emptiness. It is true that the proposal is suggested by the Buddhist *trikāya* doctrine and that 'Boundless Openness', as the ultimate ground in the present proposal, stands for the Buddhist notion of *dharma-kāya*. However, only if 'Boundless Openness' or 'Formless Emptiness' is substantial, not self-negating, and represents *a position affirmatively insisting on its own ultimacy* must the present proposal which is based on it be said to be a form of Buddhist imperialism. Since, to the contrary, as repeatedly emphasized, 'Boundless Openness' or 'Formless Emptiness' is a dynamic activity of ever-self-emptying and thus is a positionless position which makes other positions possible and alive in a dynamic harmony, it cannot be imperialistic. Rather, it is this 'Boundless Openness' that opens up a dynamic unity in religious pluralism in our time.

(The author is grateful to Professor Bruce Long and Mr Garry Bollinger for their thoughtful revision of and suggestions for the paper in its final stage.)

Notes

1. Masao Abe, 'Religion Challenged by Modern Thoughts', *Japanese Religions*, Vol. 8, No. 2, (1974), pp. 2–14.
2. R.C. Zaehner, *Christianity and Other Religions* (New York: Hawthorn Books, 1964), p. 8. See also Donald K. Swearer, *Dialogue: The Key to Understanding Other Religions* (Philadelphia: Westminster, 1977), p. 32.
3. William Ernest Hocking, *Living Religions and A World Faith* (New York: Macmillan, 1940), p. 26.
4. Ibid., pp. 265–6.
5. Wilfred Cantwell Smith's *Towards A World Theology* (Philadelphia: Westminster, 1981), Chapter 1.
6. Ibid.
7. Ibid., Chapter 8.
8. Ibid., p. 154.
9. Ibid., p. 156.
10. Ibid.
11. Ibid., pp. 156–7.
12. Ibid., p. 157.
13. Ibid.
14. Ibid., p. 158.
15. Ibid.

16. Ibid.
17. Ibid., p. 159.
18. Ibid., p. 160.
19. Originally regarded as a *saṃbhoga-kāya*, Mahāvairocana Buddha has come to be identified with *dharma-kāya* through the development of the Esoteric tradition. Kūkai himself, the founder of Japanese Shingon Esoteric Buddhism, only in his later years defined Mahāvairocana Buddha as the *dharma-kāya*. See Yoshito S. Hakeda, *Kūkai: Major Works* (New York: Columbia University Press, 1972), p. 82.
20. A comparison of Amida and Mahavairocana with Yahweh may be questionable. However, at least in so far as all of them are not the completely formless Reality but a personal deity with a particular name and virtues, they are comparable.
21. To mention only a few, *Avalokiteśvara* (Kannon) Bodhisattva represents the virtue of compassion, *Samantabhadra* (Fugen) Bodhisattva, discipline, and *Mañjuśrī* (Monju) Bodhisattva, wisdom.
22. In this context, Zen takes a quite unique position. Rejecting the theory of a threefold Buddha-body, Zen stresses 'an independent transmission outside doctrinal teaching or the teaching of the scriptures,' and 'directly pointing to man's Mind, awakening of one's Original Nature, thereby actualizing one's own Buddhahood.' Thus Zen emphasizes that everyone in his Original Nature (Mind) is a Buddha (an awakened one) and that a Buddha can be realized only as man's Original Nature. Hence, Ma-tsu (707–786) says: 'Outside of the Mind, no other Buddha; Outside of the Buddha, no other Mind.' Rejecting particularly the notion of *saṃbhoga-kāya*, Zen insists upon the complete identity of the realization of Dharma and the realization of the True Self. Bodhidharma, the founder of Zen, Rinzai, Dōgen *et al.* are regarded as realizers in this sense. In this connection, even Gautama Buddha as *nirmāṇa-kāya* is not needed for Zen realization.
23. In his later thought, Kūkai regarded Vairocana Buddha as *dharma-kāya* rather than *saṃbhoga-kāya*. (See note 19.) So Diagram 1 indicates only his earlier understanding. Kūkai has been regarded by the majority of his followers as the transformation-body of Vairocana Buddha.
24. It is clear that in his self-understanding Shinran never regarded himself as a transformation-body of Amida Buddha. On the contrary, he strongly understood himself as a severe sinner who could not be saved without the unconditional compassion given through Amida's Original Vow. However, Eshinni, his wife, regarded Shinran as a transformation-body of *Avalokiteśvara* (Kannon) Bodhisattva and the majority of Shinran's followers, in later centuries, have worshipped him almost in place of Gautama Buddha. *Mieido* or *Goeido*, the hall in which an image of Shinran is enshrined, is larger than Amida Hall in both East and West Honganji Temples, the head temples of Pure Land Shin Buddhism. It is also notable that Shinran himself regarded both Shan-tao, a Chinese Pure Land master of the T'ang dynasty, and Hōnen, Shinran's own master, as the transformation body of Amida Buddha.

25. Richardson, A. (ed.) *A Theological Word Book of The Bible* (New York: Macmillan, 1953), p. 156.
26. This indicates the Pure Land Buddhist position in which Gautama Buddha is regarded as the transformation body of Amida Buddha which is, in turn, regarded as the reward-body of formless *dharma-kāya*.
27. Ibid., p. 13.

3

'There is No Common Denominator for World Religions': The Positive Meaning of this Negative Statement

PRECIS

The most serious and crucial question in the current situation of religious pluralism is whether there is a basic unity or common denominator for world religions. After examining the positive and negative views concerning this question as presented by various theologians and religious scholars, the author points out that both the positive and the negative views start from the dualistic question: either the religions have a common essence, or they do not. He suggests overcoming this dualistic question itself and realizing that there is a common denominator *neither* in the affirmative *nor* in the negative sense. If we accept the no-common-denominator stance in all religious traditions, then a positionless position, a standpoint that is free from any position, is opened up. The clear realization that there is no common denominator for all world religions would serve as the common basis for the pluralistic situation of world religions.

I

Religious pluralism on a worldwide scale is a reality newly experienced by human beings and a serious challenge to the followers of all religions. In this pluralistic situation of world religions, questions such as the following are seriously asked: How should one confront religious pluralism while maintaining the claim of the ultimacy of one's own faith? Are other religions false, insufficient, or equally true in comparison with one's own faith? How are interfaith dialogue and mutual understanding between religions truly possible without marring one's own faith? Perhaps the most serious and crucial question is whether there is something common to, something universally true for, all religions. That is to say, 'Is there a basic unity or common denominator for world religions?' From this follows another question, namely: 'If there is such a basic unity or common denominator, what is it?' This is the question of whether there is an absolute One as the common essence of all religions.

In recent years theologians and religious thinkers of various traditions have engaged in many discussions and theological attempts to answer these questions. Quite a few of them insist on the existence of some sort of common denominator for world religions, often offering at the same time an elaborate interpretation of the characteristics of their own religious truth. Such theologians and religious thinkers constitute what may be called an affirmative group. A number of other theologians and religious thinkers reject the notion of the existence of a common denominator of world religions and insist on the absence of common unity. They form what may be called a negative group.

In this presentation I will first discuss these two opposing stands by referring to a few representative thinkers of the groups. I will then present my own proposal that there is no common denominator for world religions. Although this appears to indicate the idea of the negative group, it differs essentially from the negative position. For, when the negative group states that there is no common denominator, the *non-existence* or *absence* of a common denominator underlying the various world religions is indicated, as opposed to the affirmative group which maintains the necessity and possibility of the *existence* or *presence* of some kind of common denominator. By sharp contrast, my statement does not indicate the mere non-existence or absence of a common denominator underlying the world religions but, rather, a *complete negation of both the affirmative and the negative views*. It implies that in both views there are hidden presuppositions of the existence or non-existence of a common denominator, that is, the common essence for world religions, and that these presuppositions are made somewhat conceptually. In order to return to Reality one must break through all presuppositions, positive and negative, together with all conceptualizations. Reality at the basis of the pluralistic religious situation can be realized as it is only by negating and overcoming both positive and negative views of a common denominator. My formulation, 'There is no common denominator for world religions,' does not indicate the mere negative view of a common denominator but the necessity of negating both affirmative and negative views and of destroying all presuppositions. It thereby shows a *positionless position*, in which both the diversity and the unity of world religions are fully and dynamically realized, hence my subtitle.

II

I will begin by discussing the affirmative group, which insists that it is necessary and possible to recognize some common denominator or common essence for world religions.

In his book, *God Has Many Names*, John Hick proposed his 'Copernican revolution' in theology by emphasizing the necessity of 'a paradigm shift from a Christianity-centered or Jesus-centered to a God-centered model of the universe of faiths'.[1] He wrote: 'One then sees the great world religions as different human responses to the one divine reality, embodying different perceptions which have been formed in different historical and cultural circumstances.'[2] His view is not simplistic, and in his more recent publications Hick has used 'the Real' or 'Reality' rather than 'God' to include non-theistic religious experiences such as Hinduism and Buddhism, and he writes much about 'Reality-centeredness'.[3]

Wilfred Cantwell Smith, while also very critical of simplistic views of the common essence of all religions, has advanced the notion that a new, cooperative unity of religions is both possible and necessary. As the starting point in working toward this unity, Smith proposed the notion of 'faith' as the common essence of all religions. To him faith stands for 'an inner religious experience or involvement of a particular person; the impingement on him of the transcendent, putative or real'.[4]

Raimundo Panikkar may be regarded as another extremely important proponent of the common-essence theory in a unique way. He also rejects the simplistic theory of a neutral symbol such as the one God who exists over and above the names of the various religions. For Panikkar, the divine 'reality is many names and each name is a new aspect, a new manifestation and revelation of it. Yet each name teaches or expresses, as it were, the undivided Mystery.'⁵ He calls this shared mystery 'the *ultimate* religious *fact* [that] does not lie in the realm of doctrine or even of individual self-consciousness,' but it may well 'be present everywhere and in every religion.'⁶ The fundamental religious fact is the mystery known in every authentic religious experience, but always more than that experience can feel and say. Panikkar, however, rejects the notion that the meeting of religions can or should take place on some neutral ground such as that proposed by Hick or Smith. For him the meeting of religions can take place only in the very heart of the various religious traditions themselves. For the Christian this means the experience of the Trinity,⁷ especially the universal Christ as distinguished from the particular Jesus.

Still another exponent of the common-essence view of religion who should not be overlooked is Frithjof Schuon. Unlike other religious thinkers, Schuon makes a particular distinction between exoteric and esoteric, which runs horizontally across all religions.⁸ To him the real divisions in the religious world are not the many religions but two different types of religious persons: exoteric believers and esoteric believers. Moreover, among the esoteric believers there is a common essence or unity, regardless of the religion to which they belong. Schuon calls this common essence of religions the 'transcendent unity,' which indicates the nonduality between the absolute and the finite. In the preface of his book by that title, Schuon wrote:

[I]t must be emphasized that the unity of the different religions is not only unrealizable on the external level, that of the forms themselves, but ought not to be realized at that level . . . If the expression 'transcendent unity' is used, it means that the unity of the religious forms must be realized in a purely inward and spiritual way and without prejudice to any particular form. The antagonisms between these forms no more affect the one universal Truth than the antagonisms between opposing colors affect the transmission of the one uncolored light.⁹

Although John Hick, Wilfred Cantwell Smith, Raimundo Panikkar and Frithjof Schuon are significantly different from one another in their understanding and interpretations of the common essence of religion, they all state that the recognition of the common denominator for world religion is possible and necessary.

III

In contrast, we have the negative group, a number of theologians and religious thinkers who reject the existence of the common-denominator or the common-essence view of world religions as something abstract. Some of them reject it by emphasizing historical relativism, others by insisting on the irreducible uniqueness of their own faiths. The former position is that of Ernst Troeltsch, while the latter is represented by Karl Barth.

For Troeltsch, each religion is a different cultural manifestation of the human struggle from the divine source to the divine goal.[10] Emphasizing this historical relativism, Troeltsch originally maintained that Christianity was not an exception and 'is in every moment of its history a purely historical phenomenon, subject to all the limitations to which any individual historical phenomenon is exposed, just like the other great religions'.[11] Though he wanted to argue for a superiority or normativity of Christianity over the other religions and attributed to Christianity a kind of 'provisional' or 'qualified' absoluteness,[12] in his later years he acknowledged the failure of his attempt. Although his insight must be appreciated, his acceptance of pluralism was inconsistent and did not set forth the positive basis common to all historical religions.

Barth stood almost in diametrical opposition to Troeltsch. Construing religion as a human phenomenon, which may be studied as any human phenomenon is studied, Barth strongly emphasized the uniqueness of Christianity by saying that it was not a human phenomenon but a witness to what God has done in Jesus Christ. Yet, he recognized that Christians also produced a religion. To him, however, Christianity as a religion was not an expression of faith but, rather, a sinful effort. Faith in Christ frees people from religion and from the world. Thus, Barth strongly rejected the existence of a common denominator in world religions.

Wrestling with the theological legacy of Troeltsch, John Cobb has asked, 'How is one to understand the Christian faith in light of the challenge to its claim to absoluteness constituted by Troeltsch's life work?'[13] Cobb has clearly recognized that Christianity is one historical movement alongside others and is in the process of being transformed by other religious traditions. However, his dynamic and open interpretation of Christianity does not lead to relativism. On the contrary, for Cobb, 'The fullness of Christianity lies in the ever-receding future.'[14] He emphasizes that 'to give complete devotion to the living Christ – as Christ calls us in each moment to be transformed by the new possibilities given by God for that moment – that is not idolatrous or faithless. That is what Christianity is all about.'[15] Indeed, Cobb is quite open to religious pluralism. He has even gone so far as to say: 'While Christianity is Buddhized, Buddhism can be Christianized.'[16] To him, Christianity and Buddhism are complementary, not contradictory and incompatible.

Cobb's openness to religious pluralism, however, does not entail the recognition of a common essence of all religions. On the contrary, he has been quite skeptical about the common-essence view and critical of the approaches taken by Smith and Hick, rejecting the very assumption that we can identify what is common to all. Referring to Smith's usage of the term 'faith' as the common basis for all religions and the key term for a world theology, Cobb wrote:

I am not asking merely for a more careful account of what is common to all religious people. My point is that we should give up the use of any language that first separates religion from other phenomena and then tries to identify what is normatively characteristic of all religion. Let us allow Buddhists to be Buddhists, whether that makes them religious or not. Let us allow Confucianists to be Confucianists, whether that makes them religious or not. Let us allow Marxists to be Marxists, whether that makes them religious or not. And let us allow Christians to be Christians, whether that makes us religious or not. Quite apart from any such categories as religion or faith, there is plenty of reason to see that these proper names point to diverse ways of living and experiencing that are important for both the past and the future of the world. Hence, we should take them all seriously, as far as possible in their own terms, and allow each to challenge our beliefs and assumptions. That is a better way to a world theology than the effort to determine what is common to all.[17]

Cobb applied much the same objection to Hick's effort to find a common focus in God:

> The choice of the term *God*, despite all disclaimers, has the same effect as Smith's choice of *faith*. It suggests lack of attentiveness to what Buddhists are trying to tell us. But shifting terminology to the transcendent or the absolute does not help. The problem is the quest for what is common. Truly to accept pluralism is to abandon that quest.[18]

IV

In what follows I would like to present my own view and proposal. I agree with Cobb when he criticized Smith by saying that the choice of the terms 'faith' and 'God' as the common essence of all religions was quite problematic (that is, too narrow and provincial). Further, I also concur with his complaint that in their approach they begin 'with the assumption that we can identify what is common to all'.[19] However, I do not agree with Cobb's statement above: 'The problem is the quest for what is common. Truly to accept pluralism is to abandon the quest.'[20] For, if the very quest for what is common is the problem, and we should abandon that quest in order to truly accept pluralism, we must be led to a mere diversity without unity. This implies a relativism in the negative sense, because a diversity without unity entails skepticism or anarchy in value judgment. It is, however, human nature or innate character to seek an integral and comprehensive understanding of human life and the universe. The problem is not the quest itself for what is common among world religions but to start the quest with a presupposition that we can identify what is common to all. Cobb is right in rejecting the affirmative group of theologians and religious thinkers – especially Smith and Hick, who start with the assumption of some sort of common denominator for all religion. However, it is too much for him to ask that we abandon the quest as such.

In order truly to accept pluralism, Cobb emphasizes as cited above:

Let us allow Buddhists to be Buddhists, whether that makes

them religious or not. Let us allow Confucianists to be Confucianists, whether that makes them religious or not. Let us allow Marxists to be Marxists, whether that makes them religious or not. And let us allow Christians to be Christians, whether that makes us religious or not.[21]

In this emphasis on the full recognition of the pluralistic situation, it is unclear on what basis Buddhists, Confucianists, Marxists, and Christians can be respectively just as they are. The nonexistence or absence of a common denominator may yield full acceptance of pluralism, but that acceptance is without basis and thereby uncertain. If we are firmly to accept pluralism without falling into a vicious relativism, we need a basis common to all religions and traditions. In so saying, however, I am not suggesting a return to the affirmative view that advocates a particular common denominator of world religions. On the contrary, I am suggesting the importance and necessity of the clear realization of the 'no-common-denominator' in both the affirmative and negative sense. If we realize 'no-common-denominator' in all religious traditions thoroughly, by overcoming both the affirmative view of the presence of a common denominator and the negative view of its absence, then a complete emptiness is opened up. This is a *positionless position*, a standpoint that is free from any standpoint. This horizon of emptiness or positionless position is reached for us at the end of the double negation of the affirmative and the negative views of a common denominator for all religions; however, being free from all human presuppositions and conceptualizations, it manifests itself as the reality in terms of the standpoint at the basis of all religions. The clear and complete realization of 'no-common-denominator' for all world religions will serve as the *common basis* for the pluralistic situation of world religions.

V

In this connection I shall distinguish two kinds of unity or oneness: first, monistic unity or oneness; second, nondualistic unity or oneness. It is my contention that not the former but the latter kind of unity or oneness may provide a real common basis for the contemporary pluralistic situation of world religions.

Now, how are monistic unity and nondualistic unity different from one another? I would like to clarify their differences by making four points.

First, the view of monistic unity affirms the existence of a common denominator of world religions, such as the notion of 'God' or 'faith', by rejecting the nonexistence view of such a common denominator. It is based on the question of whether or not there is a common denominator. In other words, it poses the question in a dualistic 'either . . . or' way (either the religions have a common essence, or they do not) and concludes in the affirmative: such an essence exists. By contrast, the view of nondualistic unity rejects the dualistic 'either . . . or' question as the starting point of the affirmative conclusion and adopts a 'neither . . . nor' position. By this double negation it rejects both the existence view and the nonexistence view of a common denominator. It insists on the necessity of overcoming the dualism implicit in both the affirmative and the negative positions on the common-denominator issue and replaces that dualism with a positionless position that is free of dualism altogether. Since monistic unity stands against a nonexistence view of the common denominator of world religions, it does not escape dualism because its opposition to its alternative keeps it in a dualistic framework. In order to reach a true unity of world religions, we must go not only beyond the negative nonexistence view but also beyond the affirmative monistic view to a truly nondualistic view of unity.

Second, a monistic unity is usually viewed from the side of the pluralistic situation as an end or goal of unity. It is viewed as existing somewhat 'over there', not right here. It is conceived and objectified from the outside. Contrary to this, nondualistic unity is realized right here, right now – that is, in the very midst of the pluralistic situation. It is the ground or root-source from which our life and actions can properly begin. When we overcome monistic unity or oneness, we come to a point where there is neither one, nor two, nor many; instead, it is a point that is appropriately referred to as 'zero'. Since the 'zero' is free from any form of duality and plurality, true oneness or true unity can be realized through the realization of 'zero'. This true unity indicates 'no-common-denominator' in the absolute sense and is a positionless position. Monistic unity is a kind of unity that lacks the realization of 'zero', whereas non-dualistic unity is a kind of unity that is based on the realization of 'zero'.

Third, the true unity that can be realized through the realization of 'zero' should not be objectively conceived. If it is objectified or conceptualized in any way, it is no longer the real unity. An objectified unity is merely something called 'unity'. To reach and fully realize that true unity it is necessary to completely overcome conceptualization and objectification. True unity is realized only in a non-objectified way by overcoming even 'zero' objectified as the end. Accordingly, overcoming 'zero' as the end is a turning point from the objective, aim-seeking approach to the non-objective, immediate approach, from monistic unity to non-dualistic unity. Monistic unity is a unity before the realization of 'zero', whereas non-dualistic unity is a unity through and beyond the realization of 'zero'.

Fourth, such monistic unity as Hick's notion of 'God' or 'Reality' and Smith's notion of 'faith' is realized by reducing the uniqueness of one's religious experience and life. In the case of Hick, he proposes the notion of God or one ultimate reality behind all religions by emphasizing the necessity of a paradigm shift from a Jesus-centered to a God-centered model and to the reality-centered model of the universe of faith.

Of course, for Hick this paradigm shift does not entail the denial of the uniqueness of Jesus Christ but a reinterpretation of the traditional Christology. Against the traditional Christology, which has ontologized the incarnation and the image of the Son of God into absolute and exclusive categories such as God the Son co-substantial within the triune Godhead, Hick understands the incarnation as a myth and insists that God is to be encountered not only in Jesus but is *truly* to be encountered in Jesus. Thus, while maintaining the uniqueness of Jesus Christ, Hick allows room for interfaith dialogue. To him, however, interfaith dialogue presupposes the one Divine Reality or the one Logos behind all religions.

In the case of Smith's emphasis on a universalist faith and the need for a new unity among all religions, he requires of Christians a certain 'theological surrender'. That is, Christians 'will have to be willing to let go of their traditional beliefs that their religion or even their Christ is superior to and normative for all others.'[22] Smith thus rejects the normativity of Jesus Christ for other religions but insists that God has 'really', not necessarily 'fully', been revealed in Christ, and this revelation is 'potentially fuller than it is actually'.[23] Christology lays the foundation for interreligious dialogue. His approach is certainly not Christocentric but theocentric, based on a universalist faith as the common essence of all religions.

The view of monistic unity necessarily arouses a theological attempt to maintain the distinctiveness of one's own faith completely and still to allow a sort of openness to religiously pluralistic situations. Cobb is one of the unique theologians who, openly accepting the pluralistic situation, is trying to maintain the fullness of Christianity. As I said above, however, I do not see a firm basis for accepting pluralism in his theology.

The view of monistic unity does not *fully* admit the distinctiveness or uniqueness of each religion united therein, due to the lack of the realization of 'zero' or non-substantial emptiness. By contrast, the view of non-dualistic unity thoroughly allows the distinctiveness or uniqueness of each religion without any limitation – through the realization of 'zero' or emptiness. This is because the non-dualistic unity is completely free from conceptualization and objectification and is without substance. In this non-dualistic unity, all world religions with their uniqueness are dynamically united without being reduced to a single principle. This is, however, not an uncritical acceptance of the given pluralistic situation of religions. Instead, the non-dualistic unity makes a critical acceptance and creative reconstruction of world religions possible because each religion is grasped in the non-dualistic unity – not from the outside but deeply from within on the dynamic basis of a positionless position.

This is the positive meaning of the negative statement, 'There is no common denominator for world religions.' In other words, on the basis of a positionless position, each religion is fully realized in its distinctiveness and yet is critically judged by other religions as well as by itself in light of its encounter with other religions. This non-dualistic stance indicates an affirmative and positive common-denominator stance, but it is essentially different from a mere affirmative stance of the common denominator of all religions – precisely because it is beyond the polarity of the affirmative and the negative stances and is realized through the realization that 'there is no common denominator for world religions.'

Notes

1. John Hick, *God Has Many Names* (Philadelphia: Westminster Press, 1982; orig. London: Macmillan, 1980), p. 18.
2. Ibid.
3. John Hick, 'On Grading Religions', *Religious Studies*, Vol. 17, No. 4 (1981), p. 453.
4. Wilfred Cantwell Smith, *The Meaning and End of Religion: A New Approach to the Religious Traditions of Mankind* (New York: Macmillan, 1962, 1963), p. 156.
5. Raimundo Panikkar, *The Unknown Christ of Hinduism*, rev. ed. (Maryknoll, NY: Orbis Books, 1981), p. 24.
6. Raimundo Panikkar, *The Intrareligious Dialogue* (New York: Paulist Press, 1978), p. 57.
7. Raimundo Panikkar, *The Trinity and the Religious Experience of Man* (Maryknoll, NY: Orbis Books, 1973), p. 42.
8. Frithjof Schuon, *The Transcendent Unity of Religions*, tr. Peter Townsend (New York: Harper & Row, 1975), Chapter 3.
9. Ibid., p. xxxi.
10. Harold Coward, *Pluralism: Challenge to World Religions* (New York: Orbis Books, 1985), p. 24.
11. Ernst Troeltsch, *The Absoluteness of Christianity and the History of Religions*, tr. David Reid (Richmond, VA: John Knox Press, 1971), p. 85; also see p. 71.
12. Paul F. Knitter, *No Other Name? A Critical Survey of Christian Attitudes toward the World Religions* (Maryknoll, NY: Orbis Books, 1985), p. 27.
13. John B. Cobb, Jr., 'The Meaning of Pluralism for Christian Self-Understanding', in Leroy S. Rouner (ed.), *Religious Pluralism* (Notre Dame, IN: University of Notre Dame Press, 1984), p. 161.
14. Ibid., p. 174.
15. Ibid.
16. Ibid., p. 176.
17. Ibid., p. 172.
18. Ibid.
19. Ibid., p. 171.
20. Ibid., p. 172.
21. Ibid.
22. Knitter, *No Other Name?* p. 47
23. Wilfred Cantwell Smith, *Towards a World Theology: Faith and the Comparative History of Religion* (London: Macmillan Press; Philadelphia: Westminster Press, 1981), p. 175.

4

The Impact
of Dialogue with Christianity
on My Self-Understanding
as a Buddhist

I

I have been asked to talk about the theme, 'The Impact of Dialogue with Christianity on my self-understanding as a Buddhist'. Although I am a Buddhist I have been interested in Christianity and Western philosophy from my student days. However, I began a dialogue with Christianity publicly in 1963, when I published an article, 'Buddhism and Christianity as a Problem of Today' in the journal *Japanese Religions*.[1] To my pleasant surprise, there came to me many sincere echoes from the West of this small voice in a corner of the East. These responses are the starting point of the 'Symposium on Buddhism and Christianity' which was published in the subsequent issues of *Japanese Religions*[2] in the following several years.

In that initial article, 'Buddhism and Christianity as a Problem of Today', I made the following four points:

1. In Christianity God is personal and human beings alone were created 'in the image of God' as a free being. Unlike other creatures human beings can respond directly to the Word of God. It is here that the ground for the Christian doctrine of human personality, ethics and history is to be sought.
2. It is, however, precisely the idea of 'a personal God' that is confronted and challenged by the modern age which asks: 'How can the Christian idea of a personal God comprehend the objective rationality of modern science on the one hand, which attempts to treat everything mechanistically, in its

lifeless phase (i.e. a phase of death), and on the other hand, the existential negativity of radical nihilism in the Nietzschean sense which is determined to endure nihility without God?

3. In marked contrast, Buddhism, which is based on the principle of Absolute Nothingness or non-discriminating Wisdom, is not alienated from, but embraces and comprehends, the impersonal rationality of modern science and the radical negativity of nihilism. For Buddhism provides a basis on which both human self and nature may attain emancipation. On this basis, often called *jinen*, that is, 'primordial naturalness', all things, including humans, nature and even the supernatural, are themselves, just as they are.

4. Due to its idea of non-discriminating Wisdom and primordial naturalness, however, Buddhism must face the following problems: How can it account for the human being as a 'person' with freedom and hence the possibility of doing evil? Where can Buddhism find a basis for ethical responsibility and for social and historic action?

These four points have been more or less the basic issues for my subsequent Buddhist–Christian dialogue. After the above 'Symposium on Christianity and Buddhism' I have been participating in 'the Zen–Christian Colloquium' which has been meeting annually in Japan since 1967, 'East–West Religions in Encounter' sponsored by Professor David Chappell and held every four years beginning in 1980, and the 'Buddhist–Christian Theological Encounter Meeting' which Professor John Cobb and myself organized in 1983 and which has met annually since 1984. Through these frequent meetings and personal discussions with leading theologians including John Cobb, Langdon Gilkey, Schubert Ogden, Gordon Kaufman, Thomas Altizer, Paul Knitter and Hans Küng, I have been stimulated and inspired in my self-understanding of Buddhism. In the following I would like to clarify only three issues which are, I think, most important, that is, my understanding of Śūnyatā, Buddhist ethics and the Buddhist view of history.

II

First, my understanding of Śūnyatā. Whenever I have talked about the Buddhist notion of Śūnyatā, or Emptiness, as the

ultimate reality in Buddhism at Buddhist–Christian dialogues
the questions that are raised repeatedly are: How can such a
negative notion as 'Emptiness' be ultimate reality without falling
into nihilism? How can human personality be comprehended on
the basis of the impersonal notion of 'Emptiness'? How can
ethics and history be grounded in Buddhism by taking 'Emptiness' as the ultimate principle? Whenever I tried to answer these
questions I painfully realized that the English term 'Emptiness',
although it is the usual translation for the Sanskrit original
'*Śūnyatā*', is quite misleading. For, fundamentally, the term '*Śūnyatā*'
is not a metaphysical, but a religious and soteriological notion.
As Nagarjuna pointed out, *Śūnyatā* is synonymous with *pratītya-
samutpāda*, that is, dependent co-origination. It also implies
asvabhāva, that is, no-self-nature, no-own-being, or non-substantiality. Accordingly, when one awakens to *Śūnyatā* in everything
one is emancipated from the substantialization of and attachment to everything and realizes the interdependent relationality
of everything including oneself. Thus I came to think that
although the term *Śūnyatā* is a noun and may indicate a static
state of emptiness it should be understood as a verb which
signifies 'emptying' or 'non-substantializing'. In fact, the real
meaning of *Śūnyatā* is a pure function of emptying everything
including itself. For if *Śūnyatā* is fixed and substantialized it is
no longer true *Śūnyatā*. True *Śūnyatā* is a complete emptying,
self-negating *function* without any fixation. Thus, through dialogue
with Christian colleagues, I came to emphasize 'dynamic *Śūnyatā*',
that is the dynamic nature of *Śūnyatā*.

My emphasis on 'dynamic *Śūnyatā*' indicates at least the following two points. First the emphasis on the dynamic character
of *Śūnyatā* is not necessarily new. Traditionally, Mahayana
Buddhism has strongly admonished the attachment or fixation
of *Śūnyatā* by saying that '*Śūnyatā* is *aśūnyatā* (non-*śūnyatā*); therefore it is *atyanta-śūnyatā* (ultimate *Śūnyatā*).'[3] And, as well known,
the *Prajñāpāramitā-hrdaya-Sūtra*, that is the *Heart Sutra*, states:

> Form is emptiness and the very emptiness is form; emptiness
> does not differ from form; form does not differ from empti-
> ness: whatever is form, that is emptiness, whatever is emptiness,
> that is form.[4]

However, through the dialogue with Christian thinkers I came to realize the necessity of going beyond the traditional interpretation of *Śūnyatā* and of clarifying the positive and soteriological meanings of *Śūnyatā* more explicitly. Thus recently I have been emphasizing that *Śūnyatā* indicates *boundless openness* freed from any sort of 'centrism', including egocentrism, anthropocentrism, cosmocentrism and even theocentrism. Therefore in *Śūnyatā* everything without exception is realized as it is in its suchness and yet as interrelated and interpenetrating each other. In other words, in *Śūnyatā*, everything is realized in its distinctiveness in the light of wisdom and yet in the light of compassion even a most wicked person is not eternally punished but eventually is saved.

Second, along with this dynamic understanding of *Śūnyatā* I also came to realize that the Christian notion of kenosis is very important not only within Christianity but also in Buddhist–Christian dialogue. From my student days I was deeply moved by the following passage from the Epistle to the Philippians:

> Have this mind in you, which was also in Christ Jesus: who, existing in the form of God, count not the being on an equality with God a thing to be grasped, but emptied himself, taking the form of a servant, being made in the likeness of man; and being found in fashion as a man, he humbled himself, becoming obedient even unto death, yea, the death of the cross.[5]

In this passage the self-emptying, that is kenosis of the Christ, the son of God, is impressively stated. While I was deeply moved by this image of the kenotic Christ, I also had a long-standing question, that is, when the Son of God emptied himself did God the Father just remain God without emptying Himself? In my view, if God is all loving, God the Father must have emptied Himself even while the Son of God emptied himself. In other words, without the self-emptying of God the Father, the self-emptying of the Son of God is inconceivable. The kenosis of Christ must have its origin in the kenosis of God. I want to be very clear on this point: the kenosis of God Himself is the condition of possibility of the kenosis of the Son of God. Thus at the East–West Religions in Encounter Conference in Honolulu, Hawaii, in 1983 I delivered a paper 'Kenotic God and Dynamic *Śūnyatā*'. To this presentation Hans Küng made a negative comment by saying that there is not any mention anywhere in the New Testament of the incarnation of God Himself. When I was thus reconsidering my notion of kenotic God after the conference I read Karl Rahner's book *Foundations of Christian Faith* and was surprised by his emphasis on the self-emptying of God. Rahner clearly states:

> The primary phenomenon given by faith is precisely the self-emptying of God, his becoming, the kenosis and genesis of God himself.[6]

I also found the same idea in Jürgen Moltmann's book *The Crucified God.*[7] To me the notion of the kenotic God is extremely important for our Buddhist–Christian dialogue because when we clearly realize the notion of the kenotic God in Christianity and the notion of the dynamic *Śūnyatā* in Buddhism – then without eliminating the distinctiveness of each religion but rather by deepening their respective spiritualities – we find a significant point of contact at a deeper dimension. The article, 'Kenotic God and Dynamic *Śūnyatā*' is a milestone in my participation in Buddhist–Christian dialogue.[8]

III

The second issue that has emerged in my understanding of Buddhism through the Buddhist–Christian dialogue is that of Buddhist ethics, especially the problem of justice, or at least how Buddhism should understand the notion of justice. Another question raised repeatedly in Buddhist–Christian dialogue is how are ethics and the distinction of good and evil possible in Buddhism which is based on the notion of 'Emptiness' beyond the good and evil duality? Due to its emphasis on *Śūnyatā* and the non-discriminative mind is not Buddhism indifferent to ethical issues, especially social evil? Is not Buddhism lacking the notion of justice? To answer these questions I have been led to clarify the Buddhist meaning of 'going beyond good and evil' and to try to incorporate the notion of justice in the realization of Emptiness.

In Christianity, in the light of the God who is love and justice, the distinction between good and evil is clear and good always has a priority over evil. Yet Christianity goes beyond the realm of the ethical and transcends to the realm of faith, because in the sight of God 'none is righteous, no, not one' (Rom. 3: 9), 'no one does good, not even one' (Rom. 3: 12), and we are 'the foremost of sinners' (1 Tim. 1: 15). But we can be saved through faith in Jesus Christ who is the incarnation of the Son of God. And as Jesus said, 'Why do you call me good? No one is good but God alone' (Mark 10: 18) – in Christianity God alone is good absolutely. Accordingly, in Christianity 'to go beyond good and evil' in the ethical sense is to go to God as the absolute good.

By marked contrast, in Buddhism 'to go beyond good and evil' in the ethical sense is to awaken to *Śūnyatā* which is neither good nor evil. The realization of *Śūnyatā*, however, is not indifferent to the distinction of good and evil. Being beyond the duality between good and evil *Śūnyatā* rather embraces the duality without being confined by it and grasps again the distinction between good and evil in the new light of Emptiness. In order to make this point clear for my Christian friends I have been emphasizing that, because *Śūnyatā* is not a static state of emptiness but a dynamic function of emptying, Buddhist ethics can be established dynamically on the newly grasped distinction between good and evil.

Chinese Zen master Ch'ing-yüan Wei-hsin of the T'ang dynasty clarified his enlightenment, that is, his awakening to *Śūnyatā*, as follows:

> Before I began the study of Zen, I said 'Mountains are mountains; water is water.'
>
> After I got an insight into the truth of Zen through the instruction of a good master, I said, 'Mountains are not mountains; water is not water.'
>
> But now, having attained the abode of final rest [that is Awakening], I say 'Mountains are *really* mountains; water is *really* water.'[9]

Following Ch'ing-yüan Wei-hsin we may say:

> Before I began the study of Buddhism, I said, 'good is good; evil is evil.'
>
> After I got an insight into the truth of Buddhism, I said, 'good is not good; evil is not evil.'
>
> But now, having attained Awakening, I say, 'good is *really* good; evil is *really* evil.'

This regrasping of good and evil in the realization of Emptiness, however, is not enough in the Buddhist–Christian dialogue. Buddhism must answer the problem of justice and social ethics. When I studied at the Union Theological Seminary in New York both Paul Tillich and Reinhold Niebuhr emphasized the importance of justice in relation to love. They said that love without justice is not true love, but justice without love is not true justice. At that time I realized that the Buddhist equivalent to the Christian notion of love would be the notion of compassion, *karuṇā*. But there is no Buddhist equivalent to the Christian notion of justice. Instead of justice, Buddhism talks about wisdom, *prajñā*. The Buddhist pair is not 'love and justice', but 'compassion and wisdom'.

Buddhist history shows indifference to social evil, with a few exceptions. Nichiren, for example, strongly emphasized justice against injustice. Also Pure Land Buddhists rose in revolt against feudal lords who attempted to extend political control over religious orders. With these few exceptions, the general attitude of Buddhism toward social injustice has been rather weak. We must learn from Christianity how to solve the problem of society and history at large and interpret this in terms of the Buddhist standpoint of wisdom and compassion.

If I am not mistaken the Christian notion of justice has at least two aspects: the first is justice as a kind of balancing between various human beings as they strive to actualize their potential for being.[10] The second is the justice which entails judgment and punishment. The first aspect of justice is defined by Paul Tillich as 'the form in which power of being actualizes itself in the encounter of power with power'[11] and as 'the form of the reunion of the separated'.[12] This aspect of justice is not antithetical but, I think, can be incorporated into the Buddhist notion of wisdom and compassion. But the second aspect of justice is hard for Buddhism to incorporate into itself and furthermore, in my view, it is not necessary to do so. Justice in its second aspect is a double-edged sword. On the one hand, it judges sharply what is right and what is wrong. On the other hand, judgment based on justice naturally calls forth a counter-judgment as a reaction from the side so-judged. Accordingly, we fall into an endless conflict and struggle between judge and the judged. Gautama Buddha clearly realized this endless conflict as a result of judgment within the notion of justice itself. He said that to meet resentment with resentment will fall into that endless conflict. Instead, the Buddha preached the interrelationality and the lack of any fixed self-nature of every single thing.

However, we must be careful in applying the Buddhist notion of interrelationality and compassion within the social level, because such an application may serve to cover social inequality and injustice. This is an important warning which I learned from liberation theology. Buddhists must develop 'dynamic *Śūnyatā'* and create a new notion of justice on the basis of wisdom and compassion which, clearly realizing a distinction between things and events, can actualize and maintain the balance of power.

IV

The third issue which emerged in my understanding of Buddhism through the Buddhist–Christian dialogue relates to the Buddhist view of history. If *Śūnyatā*, which is completely free from any sort of 'centrism' and in which everything, including past and future, is understood to be reciprocal, is the ultimate reality in Buddhism, what then is history? How can we talk about the novelty of things in time and the direction and end or outcome of human events? In order to answer these questions that have been repeatedly raised by Christian colleagues in our dialogues I have been urged to think about the Buddhist view of history.

I must recognize that in the Buddhist tradition a consciousness of history in the sense it is currently understood in the West has scarcely developed and there is no Buddhist equivalent of a systematically organized doctrine of history like Christian eschatology – with an exception of the '*Shōzōmatsu* view of history', which talks about the three periods after the Buddha's death and which is emphasized mainly by Pure Land Buddhism.

Buddhism, all the same, has a unique view of time.[13] Time is understood to be entirely without beginning and without end. Since time is beginningless and endless it is not considered to be linear as in Christianity or circular as in non-Buddhist Vendantic philosophy. Being neither linear nor circular, time is not understood to be irreversible but reversible, and yet time moves from moment to moment, each moment embracing the whole process of time. Due to the absence of God as the creator and the ruler of the universe, in Buddhism there is no beginning in terms of creation and no end in terms of last judgment. Accordingly we must realize the beginninglessness and endlessness of *saṃsāra*, that is the transmigration of 'living-dying'. This realization is essential because it provides a way to overcome *saṃsāra* and to turn it into *nirvāṇa*. For if we clearly realize the beginningless*ness* and endless*ness* of the process of 'living-dying' *at this moment*, the whole process of 'living-dying' is *concentrated* in this moment. In other words, this moment embraces the whole process of 'living-dying' by virtue of the clear realization of the beginninglessness and endlessness of the process of 'living-dying'. Here, in this point, we can overcome *saṃsāra* and realize *nirvāṇa* right in the midst of *saṃsāra*.

Because of this unique view of time, however, Buddhism is relatively weak in its view of history. Time is not directly history. Time becomes 'history' when the factor of spatiality (Worldhood, *Weltlichkeit*) is added to it. History comes to have meaning when time is understood to be irreversible and each moment has an unrepeatable uniqueness or once-and-for-all nature (*Einmalichkeit*). But since time is understood to be entirely beginningless and endless and thus reversible, the unidirectionality of time and the uniqueness of each moment essential to the notion of history is not clearly expressed in Buddhism.

Through the dialogue with Christian thinkers, however, I came to realize that Buddhism can develop its own view of history if we take seriously the compassionate aspect of *Śūnyatā*, that is the self-emptying of *Śūnyatā*. In the wisdom aspect of *Śūnyatā*, everything is realized in its suchness, in its interpenetration and reciprocity with everything else. Time is not an exception. Accordingly, in the light of wisdom realized in *Śūnyatā*, past and future are interpenetrating and reciprocal. Furthermore, the beginningless and endless process of time is totally concentrated in each moment. This is why in Buddhism each and every 'now' is realized as the eternal Now in the sense of the absolute present. However, in the light of compassion, also realized in *Śūnyatā*, another aspect of time comes to be realized. Although all things and all people are realized in their suchness and interpenetration in the light of wisdom *for an awakened one*, those *'unawakened' from their own side* have not yet awakened to this basic reality. Many beings still consider themselves unenlightened and deluded. Such people are innumerable at present and will appear endlessly in the future. The task for an awakened one is to help these people as well to 'awaken' to their suchness and interpenetration with all other things. This is the compassionate aspect of Śūnyatā which can be actualized only by emptying the wisdom aspect of Śūnyatā. As the generation of 'unawakened' beings will never cease this process of actualizing the compassionate aspect of Śūnyatā is endless. Here the progress of history toward the future is necessary and comes to have a positive significance.

In the light of wisdom realized in Śūnyatā, everything and everyone is realized in its suchness and time is overcome. In the light of compassion also realized in Śūnyatā, however, time is religiously significant and essential. And in the endless process of the compassionate work of an awakened one trying to awaken others, Śūnyatā turns itself into *vow* and into *act* through its self-emptying. At this point, history is no longer a 'history of *karma*' in which people are transmigrating beginninglessly and endlessly. It becomes a 'history of vow and act' in which wisdom and compassion are operating to emancipate innumerable sentient beings from transmigration. Here we do have a Buddhist view of history.

It is not, however, an eschatological or teleological view of history in the Christian or Western sense. If we use the term eschatology, the Buddhist view of history is a completely realized eschatology, because in the light of wisdom everything and everyone without exception is realized in its suchness, and time is thereby overcome. If we use the term teleology, the Buddhist view of history is an open teleology because in the light of compassion the process of awakening others in history is endless. And the completely realized eschatology and the entirely open teleology are dynamically united in this present moment, now. This is a Buddhist view of history as I have come to understand it through the Buddhist–Christian dialogue.

Notes

1. 'Buddhism and Christianity as a Problem of Today', *Japanese Religions*, Vol. 3, No. 2 and No. 3 (1963).
2. 'A Symposium on Buddhism and Christianity.' A Reply to Professor Abe by Paul Wienpahl, Charles Hartshorne, Winston King, Neles Ferre, I.T. Ramsey and Hans Waldenfels in *Japanese Religions*,

Vol. 4, No. 1 (1964), and Vol. 4, No. 2 (1966). Abe's rejoinder, including his papers, 'Christianity and Buddhism – Centering around Science and Nihilism', and 'Man and Nature in Christianity and Buddhism', in *Japanese Religions*, Vol. 5, No. 2 (1968); Vol. 5, No. 3; Vol. 7, No. 1 (1971). Further comments and criticisms by Ernst Benz, Paul Wienpahl, Winston King, Thomas J.J. Altizer, Fritz Buri, Horst Bürkle and Hans Waldenfels, in *Japanese Religions*, Vol. 8, No. 4 (1975), and Vol. 9, No. 1 (1976).

3. *Prajñāpāramitā-Sūtra*, Taishō 8: 250 b.
4. *Prajñāpāramitā-hrdaya-Sūtra*, Taishō 8: 848.
5. Phil. 2: 5–8.
6. Karl Rahner, *Foundations of Christian Faith; An Introduction to the Idea of Christianity* (New York: The Seabury Press, 1978), p. 222.
7. Jürgen Moltmann, *The Crucified God*: The Cross of Christ as Foundation and Criticism of Christian Theology. (New York: Harper & Row, 1974), pp. 197 f.
8. The revised and much enlarged version of the article has been published in book form, edited by John Cobb and Christopher Ives, including the responses by Jürgen Moltmann, Schubert Ogden, Thomas Altizer, David Tracy, Catherine Keller and others in *The Emptying God: A Buddhist–Jewish–Christian Conversation* (Maryknoll, NY: Orbis Books, 1990), 3–65.
9. *Wu-têng Hui-yüan* (Japanese: *Gotōegen*) edited by Aishin Imaeda (Tokyo: Rinrōkaku Shoten 1971), p. 335. See also Masao Abe, *Zen and Western Thought* (London: Macmillan, 1985), pp. 4 ff.
10. Christopher Ives, 'A Zen Buddhist Social Ethics', PhD dissertation, Claremont Graduate School, p. 258: revised version published as *Zen Awakening and Society* (London: Macmillan, 1992).
11. Paul Tillich, *Love, Power, and Justice* (New York: Oxford University Press, 1954), p. 67.
12. Ibid., p. 62.
13. Masao Abe, 'Kenotic God and Dynamic Śūnyatā', see note 8 above.

5

The Problem of Self-Centeredness as the Root-Source of Human Suffering*

I

Unlike plants and animals, human beings have self-consciousness, reason and free will. These characteristics unique to human beings have both a bright and a dark aspect for their lives. The bright aspect lies in the fact that human beings, unlike other creatures, can use their endowments to shape the future, develop science and technology, establish economic, social and political organizations. As a thinking animal they can create human culture and civilization. As for the dark aspect, by dint of the fact of being self-conscious existences, human beings have become separated from their original naturalness, whereas plants and animals, existing in nature, live just as they are, without reflection. Separated from their original naturalness human beings have become self-centered, alienating themselves from others, even from themselves. Such self-centeredness and the accompanying self-estrangement are what create human suffering in all aspects of their lives.

In short, human beings are a combination of these two aspects, one bright and one dark, both rooted in human self-consciousness. Although philosophies and religions have long been aware of the twofold aspect of human beings, some traditions have emphasized one aspect over the other. Ancient Greek philosophy,

* This paper was originally delivered at the World Academic Conference of the Seoul Olympiad '88 held in Seoul, Korea in August, 1988.

Confucianism and modern Western philosophy, for instance, emphasize the bright aspect of human self-consciousness, rationality and free will. By contrast, the Judeo-Christian tradition, Buddhism, Taoism and contemporary existential philosophy have dealt with the problematics of the dark aspect as seen in such terms as sinfulness, *avidyā* (ignorance), attachment, anxiety and despair. In my understanding, if we fail to give proper and adequate attention to the dark aspect of human existence we cannot appropriately and relevantly develop its bright aspect in the greater context of human existence. This cannot be emphasized enough because the self-centeredness deep-seated in human self-consciousness is precisely the root-source of human suffering. The confusion in ethics and values in contemporary society largely derives from the inadequate understanding of human self-centeredness and the lack of a thoroughgoing solution of the condition originated in self-centeredness.

In the following I would first like to discuss the problematics of self-centeredness in relation to four dimensions of human life: individual, national, anthropocentric and religious. After analyzing the problematics involved in each, I would like to suggest how each of them can be overcome to open up a spiritual horizon in which a new ethics and religion can be established. With regard to the latter point I think the Buddhist notion of *anātman* may offer very helpful insights.

II

FOUR FORMS OF SELF-CENTEREDNESS AND WAYS OF OVERCOMING THEM

Individual self-centeredness

To be a self-conscious existence is for a human being to be conscious of the distinction between self and others. From the dimension of consciousness the self regards others as objects against which the self stands as subject. Out of the subject–object dichotomy thus created, consciousness grasps everything from that dichotomous point of view. Putting itself at the centre of the world, the self regards all others from the outside, as existing peripheral to itself. This is the case not only in knowing, the self's cognitive activity, but also in doing, the self's volitional activity. In other words, from the dichotomous point of view the self regards others not only as objects of cognition, but also as objects of emotion and volition, that is, as the objects of like and dislike, love and hate, affection and detestation. In this way, the human self becomes inextricably involved in the subject–object dichotomy and the persistent self-centeredness engendered by it.

More importantly, when consciousness creates the subject–object dichotomy, this dichotomy manifests itself not only in the self–other relationship but also in the human self as such. This means that through consciousness the very human self is divided into two entities: self as the subject of consciousness and self as the object of consciousness. Self-consciousness implies the self's split into these two entities, and thereby self-attachment and self-estrangement.

We must clearly realize that along with separation from others there is always another deeper separation from ourselves. Along with attachment to others there is always another more serious self-attachment. Along with estrangement from others there is always another more invidious self-estrangement.

In self-consciousness the self objectifies itself in cognitive, emotional and volitional terms; it thereby attaches to, reifies and substantializes itself. It is through the substantiation of the self that centeredness takes place.

Buddhism insists that the notion of substantial selfhood is an illusion and emphasizes the necessity of realizing *anātman*, the no-self. This is because Gautama Buddha, the founder of Buddhism, perceived that the ego-self which is oriented by self-centeredness is an unreal entity and the root-source of human suffering. In order to be free from suffering the ego-self together with its self-centered mode of existence must be completely negated and the no-self fully realized.

The Buddhist notion of *anātman*, however, is often misunderstood to be nihilistic. Especially in the West one often encounters the question of how ethical decision and personal responsibility are possible with the realization of the no-self.

With the emphasis on the no-self, Buddhism does not deny the self-identity of the individual person. It is irrefutable that everyone has their own individual self-identity. But what we must ask is whether that self-identity is an absolute, enduring and substantial one or not. The self is the self only in relation to others; there can be no self without others, no 'I' apart from you. This is because what we call 'self' is a relative notion, not an absolute one. Nevertheless, we often absolutize the notion of self and assume that a substantial and enduring selfhood exists by saying 'I am I.' But in fact that 'I' is unreal and illusory, and does not exist in any substantial sense. When each human self insists on an absolute, substantial selfhood, serious conflict will inevitably arise. Though we have self-identity in a relative sense we have no self-identity in any absolute and substantial sense. This is the implication of the Buddhist notion of 'no-self'.

Realization of no-self naturally entails the realization of the relativity and interrelation between human selves. Self is not a closed and fixed entity, but an open and relational entity through which self and others dynamically interact without loss of their relative self-identities. This is the true nature of self. Accordingly, through the realization of the no-self, one can awaken to the true nature of self. The realization of the no-self is precisely the realization of true self. Furthermore, in the realization of true self one awakens not only to the true nature of one's own self but also to the true nature of everything else. The spiritual dimension of the true nature of all existence is revealed through the realization of one's own true nature. It is in this dimension that human ethics, far from being denied, can be properly established.

National self-centeredness

We live in an age in which nation-states, acting alone or in groups, are constantly in conflict with one another. Regional wars flare up one after another in different places around the globe, and world peace is constantly threatened by fears of total nuclear holocaust initiated by the superpowers.

A nation-state has two aspects. On the one hand, it is a historical and cultural unit with people living together in the same geographical area, and, in most cases, speaking a common language. Without the rich heritage of the nation-state, each with its own unique culture and history, the world would soon become a dull and monotonous place. On the other hand, the nation-state is also a political unit which holds claim to authority and sovereignty. To perpetrate its own existence during times of crisis, national sovereignty ultimately demands the sacrifice of the lives of the very individuals comprising it; turning outward, it does not hesitate to use military force to engage other sovereign nations in a life-and-death struggle of conquest. Once set in motion nothing is able to check the machinations of sovereign states. Sovereign states neither know nor practise the principle of self-negation, because they take as their basic position self-affirmation and self-assertion which, during crisis, predisposes them to neglect, or even willfully destroy, the position of humankind. Reflected in this is the sovereign state's essentially self-centered nature.

International organizations resulting from the compromises and agreements made between sovereign states may to a certain degree be effective when it comes to resolving international conflicts and promoting cooperation. But as long as they presuppose the sovereignty of the nation-states, due to the self-centered nature of sovereign states, basically international organizations can neither check national egoism and self-centeredness nor can they totally eliminate war. Instead, although such organizations are able to exert some control over smaller nations, there is imminent danger that organizations such as these may be transformed into magnificent edifices of hypocrisy wherein the arrogance of larger nations, the possessors of great military power, cannot help but be tacitly recognized. The plan to establish a world league of nations or a world government cannot be said to be the ultimate path to true world peace as long as the standpoint of sovereign nations goes unchallenged, and until the sovereignty is transferred from the nation-states to humankind as a single, living unit.

Terms like 'humankind' and 'global community' are so widely used these days as to form a kind of jargon. All the same, such terms as yet remain vague and largely undefined concepts. 'Humankind', for instance, is sometimes thought of as referring to the aggregate of the various races or peoples: or it may also be used to refer to human beings who as one biological species dwell on this planet in this galaxy, the latter concept having emerged with the advent of the space age. But even if the term humankind is clearly defined, it is merely a definition imposed from without; that is, it would still be regarded as a quantitative concept, rather than a qualitative one.

What is of paramount importance today is that we internalize humankind as a qualitative concept and grasp it as a single, living, self-aware entity. Unless we do so, we can never resolve the conflicts between nations which now confront us to bring true peace into the world. Nor can we expect to build a profound and rich human society based on individual freedom and the unique characteristics of the various races and cultures, that is, a human society in which all can live in harmony with one another.

From what position is it possible to grasp humankind as a single, living, self-aware entity? I believe that not only each individual but each nation-state itself must awaken to the fact that the sovereign nation-state is not an absolute and substantial entity, but a relative, non-substantial one. By renouncing self-centeredness a nation-state should recognize that true sovereignty must rest with humankind as a whole. In our global age in which all humankind shares the same fate, the nation no longer serves as the basic unit for understanding the world: the world itself, rather, has become the true unit. Accordingly we should not seek to comprehend the world in terms of the nation, but, rather, the nation in terms of the world. In this sense the term international can no longer be synonymous with the world, for the world now transcends that stage to assume trans-international dimensions. What is needed now is a sovereignty based on the principle of self-negation and guided by the virtues of wisdom and compassion rather than power and justice.

Only when humankind's sovereignty overcomes its self-centeredness by dedicating itself to the principle of self-negation guided by wisdom and compassion will a single government having all humankind as its basis be possible, creating, as it were, a true government of humankind, by humankind, for humankind.

Anthropocentric self-centeredness

Even when we overcome national self-centeredness to assume the standpoint of all humankind, we should not fall into the error of anthropocentrism. Generally speaking, in the West, nature has been understood to be subordinate to human beings. Greek philosophy and modern Western philosophy, which emphasize rationality and human reason, have regarded nature as a self-developing entity or as objective matter regulated by natural law. In the Judeo-Christian tradition it is believed that the first human beings, Adam and Eve, were given dominion over nature by God. Nature was regarded as something secondary and peripheral to humans who were the only ones among all God's creatures to be created in His image (*imago dei*) and made responsible to His Word. Western culture thus has been strongly oriented by anthropocentrism in its relation to nature and the universe.

Eastern culture in general is not anthropocentric but rather cosmological. But through the introduction of Western culture and civilization the notion of anthropocentrism has exerted great influence in present Eastern countries as well, especially in highly industrialized societies like Japan, Korea and Taiwan.

The rise of anthropocentrism is now creating in all dimensions of humankind – individual, race, class and nation – endless conflicts which have at their base ego and power. At the same time, its anti-natural character, by destroying the natural order, is now being transmuted into an anti-human character which conversely threatens to destroy the very basis of human existence. Anthropocentrism, at its limit, is plunging humankind into a trap of its own making. The opposition of sovereign superstates which need not the principle of self-negation, the grim possibility of total nuclear destruction of humankind, the strange uneasiness of a world peace achieved by a balance of terror – all of these are aspects of the self-entrapment produced by anthropocentrism in the political dimensions.

In this connection I would like to suggest the remedy Buddhism provides for anthropocentrism. In Buddhism, the world of human beings and the world of nature are understood to be *equally* subject to change, that is, both are transitory and transmigratory. Emancipation from the cycle of human birth and death is not to be achieved until a person can eliminate a more universal problem – the transience common to all things in the universe. Here we see that the *basis* for Buddhist salvation is not personalistic, as in an I–Thou relationship with God, but cosmological and thus impersonal and trans-anthropocentric.

This is not to imply, however, that human beings have no special significance among creatures. It is only humans who, endowed with self-consciousness and free will, can go beyond anthropocentrism and reach an awareness of that transience common to all things, not just to human beings.

This cosmological basis of Buddhist human salvation may

contribute to a spiritual foundation which could solve one of the most pressing problems of today's world – the ecological problem of the destruction of the natural environment which is inextricably connected with human estrangement from nature. Environmental destruction results from anthropocentrism when people regard nature merely as a means to realize selfish goals and persist in seeking new ways to exploit and conquer it. By contrast, the cosmological view does not see nature as something subordinate to humans, but sees them as subordinate to nature, more precisely as a part of nature from the standpoint of cosmos. Thus the cosmological view both allows humans to overcome estrangement from nature and to live harmoniously with nature without losing their individuality.

What is necessary for the present day is not a new humanism but a new cosmology. There must be a cosmology which is extricated from anthropocentrism and yet which can provide humankind with its proper place in the universe. It is not an objective cosmology but an existential and personalistic one.

Religious self-centeredness

When we step beyond anthropocentrism we naturally come to the threshold of religion. Though anthropocentrism is not completely absent in the Judeo-Christian tradition, the tradition, when seen as a whole, goes well beyond anthropocentrism by dint of its thoroughly theocentric concerns. In that tradition the limitations of human beings are clearly set forth in terms of their creatureliness and sinfulness, and the God Yahweh, the creator of everything, human beings included, and the ruler of the universe, is worshipped as the only God. For God commands the people, 'You shall have no other gods before me.' To go beyond anthropocentrism in the Judeo-Christian tradition is to transcend the human toward the one God; beyond anthropocentrism the religion becomes monotheistic. By contrast, in Buddhism, as discussed above, beyond anthropocentrism there opens the boundless horizons of the vast cosmos. Accordingly, Buddhism is not monotheistic but non-theistic in its religious life.

By 'non-theistic' I mean that in Buddhism there is no notion of a creator or ruler of the universe. Instead, Buddhism advances the law of dependent co-origination, that everything, being without substance, is interdependent with each other, that nothing exists independently. In Buddhism this interdependency is applied to everything, not only to what exists in this universe but also beyond it. In other words, Buddha is not self-existent but is interdependent with sentient beings; *nirvāṇa* is not self-existent, but is interdependent with *saṃsāra*; *satori* (awakening) is not self-existent, but is interdependent with illusion. This is because in Buddhism even religious and sacred entities such as Buddha, *nirvāṇa* and *satori* are understood to be non-substantial, empty, without a fixed and enduring selfhood. Everything without exception is dynamically interdependent and interacting. This complete interdependency of the universe, not one God as the ruler of the universe, is the basic principle of Buddhism and the human salvation it promises.

All religious traditions, Christianity and Buddhism included, seek to free people from self-centeredness. Religions typically share a commom message of peace, harmony and salvation to be gained by overcoming self-centeredness in its various forms. But precisely because of the fact that a religion will emphasize salvation on the basis of its own particular kind of ultimate principle, there is a strong tendency to exclusively regard its own principle as absolute and to be intolerant of what others teach. This is the self-contradiction innate to religion. The history of religion and even the religious situation in the contemporary world today remind us that long and bloody wars have had their origin in religious intolerance. Religions harbour their own special form of self-centeredness – a self-centeredness based on religious faith in one ultimate principle such as God or supernatural deity.

Religious self-centeredness is more clearly recognized in monotheistic religions such as Judaism, Christianity and Islam than it is in non-theistic religions such as Buddhism and Taoism. Although Buddhism and Taoism talk about the oneness of the basic principle of the universe, it is not a monistic or monotheistic oneness but rather a non-dualistic oneness. It is not a oneness represented by one absolute God as the ruler of the universe but a oneness realized in the complete interdependency of everything in and out of the universe. Monotheistic oneness does not include the element of self-negation and is substantial, whereas non-dualistic oneness includes self-negation and is non-substantial. Here again the denial of selfhood and the realization of the non-self is crucial.

III

In the above I have discussed four forms of self-centeredness – individual, national, anthropocentric and religious – and have tried to analyze the problematic that they involve: the self-centeredness at the root-source of human suffering. I have also tried to show how the Buddhist notion of *anātman*, or non-self, could serve as a remedy for the problems and sufferings encountered in human life. This is because through the realization of the no-self, the realization that there is no substantial and enduring egoself, the true nature of the self and its interrelation with others are clearly realized, showing a way to clear away the confusion in ethics and values in contemporary society.

6

Suffering in the Light of Our Time: Our Time in the Light of Suffering: Buddha's First Holy Truth

It is a great pleasure for me to participate in this international conference on Buddhism and Christianity at De Tiltenberg. It is a long-cherished desire for me to visit this place; I have been involved in Buddhist and Christian dialogue over a long time, but this conference is a highlight of my dialogue experience. I have been asked to talk about suffering in the light of our time; our time in the light of suffering: Buddha's first Holy Truth.

As you know there are Four Noble Truths, the fundamental teaching of Gautama the Buddha, learned as follows:

- that existence is suffering;
- that the cause of suffering is craving or thirst;
- that by the extinction of craving, *nirvāṇa* may be attained;
- that the means for the attainment of *nirvāṇa* is the practice of the Eightfold Path: right view, right intention, right speech, right conduct, right livelihood, right effort, right mindfulness and right concentration.

I think this is familiar to you.

EXISTENCE IS SUFFERING

When Gautama the Buddha says 'existence is [characterized by] suffering', he does not mean that human life is simply full of suffering without any pleasure at all. In 1966 I was a visiting professor of Buddhism at the Claremont Graduate School in Southern California, and one day I taught the students that Gautama Buddha emphasized that human life is suffering. Then a student said: 'Gautama Buddha might have said so because ancient India was very poor, without pleasure, but in America we are full of pleasure, so that such a pessimistic teaching of Buddhism is not applicable in the United States!'

But when Gautama Buddha says that human existence is characterized by suffering, he does not mean that human life is simply full of suffering, without any pleasure at all. It is obvious that there is pleasure as well as suffering in human life – in India, in the US, anywhere in the world. In daily life we distinguish between pleasure and suffering, seeking for and clinging to pleasure, while avoiding and detesting suffering. This is an inclination inherent in human nature, but according to Buddhism real suffering lies precisely in this inclination. Pleasure and suffering are in reality inseparable and intertwined – one is never found without the other. Hence the position that they are rigidly opposed to is abstract and unreal. The more we try to cling to pleasure and avoid suffering, the more entangled we become in the duality of pleasure and suffering. It is this whole process which constitutes 'Suffering' (with a capital S). When Gautama the Buddha says 'existence is characterized by suffering', he is referring to this Suffering and not to suffering as opposed to pleasure. It is the reality of this non-relative Suffering which a person must realize in his or her existential depths. Since life and death are the fundamental sources of pleasure and suffering, and human existence is entangled in attachment to life and detestation of death, human existence is understood in Buddhism to be bound to *saṃsāra*, the cycle of birth and death.

Accordingly, when Gautama the Buddha says 'the cause of suffering is craving', he means by craving not simply the attachment to pleasure but a deeper and more fundamental attachment that is rooted in human existence, that of loving pleasure and hating suffering, with its accompanying phenomenon of making a distinction between the two. According to Gautama's teaching, this fundamental attachment originates in an illusory view of life in the world which is the result of the basic ignorance innate in human nature. Craving is a human passion linked to mankind's entanglement in the duality of pleasure and suffering, and deeply rooted in the ego. It is by extinguishing this craving that *nirvāṇa* can be attained. Thus *nirvāṇa* is not a negative or *lifeless state* such as the mere annihilation of human passion would suggest, but an existential awakening to egolessness, *anattā* or *anātman*, attained through liberation from craving, liberation from attachment to the dualistic view which distinguishes between pleasure as something to be sought after and suffering as something to be avoided.

The position of the Buddha clearly emerges in his first sermon after his attainment. Gautama the Buddha says: 'Monks, these two extremes should not be followed by one who has gone forth as a wanderer. What two? Devotion to the pleasure of sense, a low practice of villagers, a practice unworthy, unprofitable, the way of the world on the one hand; and on the other devotion to self-mortification, which is painful, unworthy and unprofitable.' By avoiding the two extremes the *Tathāgata*, the Buddha, has gained knowledge, a calm, special knowledge: enlightenment, *nirvāṇa*.

In this connection the following four points are to be noted:

1. Gautama the Buddha takes the Middle Way, transcending both hedonism and asceticism. Accordingly, he does not negate human desire as such but, in avoiding these two extremes, relegates it to its proper position in human life. The Middle Way is not simply a midpoint between pleasure and suffering, but rather is the Way which *transcends* the very duality of pleasure and suffering. Thus, living the Middle Way is none other than being in *nirvāṇa*.

2. For Buddhism, the Middle Way or *nirvāṇa* is not an objectively observable state or something which can be considered merely a goal of life, but rather an existential ground from which human life can properly begin without becoming entangled in the duality of pleasure and suffering. By living the Middle Way, in *nirvāṇa*, we can be master of, and not enslaved by, pleasure and suffering. In this sense *nirvāṇa* is the source of human freedom and creative activity.

3. In his awakening to egolessness or no-self, Gautama Buddha overcame duality itself by transcending the particular duality of pleasure and suffering. In other words, he could awaken to egolessness or no-self only when he became free from duality itself. This he achieved by breaking through the particular duality which impinged upon him most as a burning existential dilemma – the duality of pleasure and suffering. Accordingly,

nirvāṇa as the existential awakening to egolessness or no-self
is beyond any kind of duality, including that of good and evil,
right and wrong, life and death, human beings and nature,
and even that of human beings and God. To attain *nirvāṇa*
in this sense is salvation. *Nirvāṇa* as the awakening to egolessness
or no-self is most clearly realized in Mahayana Buddhism. In
that tradition, to enter *nirvāṇa* is not to die one's physical
death, but to die the death of the ego and thereby to live a
new Life, to live the life of the true Self.

4. Although *nirvāṇa* is beyond duality, it is not characterized by
a monistic view. Monism is not yet free from duality, for it
is still opposed to dualism or pluralism. Being beyond duality, the view of one who has attained *nirvāṇa* is not monistic
but rather non-dualistic. This is why Buddhism does not
proclaim the one God, but speaks of *Śūnyatā* (Emptiness).
Emptiness is realized by going beyond the one God and thus
is not the relative emptiness of a mere vacuum.

Śūnyatā, which is often translated as Emptiness, sounds quite
nihilistic. Some time ago I discussed the Christian notion of the
creatio ex nihilo, creation out of nothingness. It is said that God
creates everything out of nothingness, but nothingness in this
context is negative, and God is beyond this type of nothingness.
So God creates everything out of that type of nothingness. But
the Christian mystics talk about Godhead, 'Gottheit', from which
the personal God emerges, and a Christian mystic, Jakob Boehme,
spoke about Godhead as 'Das Nichts'. So the personal God
emerged from 'Das Nichts'. That 'Das Nichts' is not nothingness
in a negative sense, but rather in a positive sense, because that
nothingness or 'Das Nichts' is a source for a personal God.
Where Buddhism talks about Emptiness, *Śūnyatā*, roughly speaking it may correspond to the Christian mystic notion of 'Das
Nichts' or 'Godhead'.

Being beyond the one God, Emptiness is identical to individual things; it makes them truly individual. In this Emptiness
everything is itself in the sense that everything is as it is, and
yet at the same time everything is equal in its as-it-is-ness. So
a dog is a dog and a cat is cat; they are very different. A pine
tree is a pine tree, an oak tree is an oak tree; they are very
different. They have their own as-it-isness. But they are equal
in terms of as-it-is-ness. So, everything and everyone has its own

distinctiveness, as-it-is-ness, and yet in terms of as-it-is-ness they are not different.

The following dialogue (*mondō*) between a monk and Joshū (778–897) illustrates the point that the universal or ultimate reality can be realized in particular things, not apart from particularity. The monk asked Joshū, 'All things are reduced to the one; where is this one to be reduced to?' Joshū replied: 'When I was in the province of Tsin I had a monk's robe made that weighed seven pounds.'

That which is ultimate or universal is not the one to which all things are reducible but a particular thing, absolutely irreplaceable, such as a monk's robe, which has a particular weight and is made in a particular place at a particular time. The universal and particular things are paradoxically one in the realization of Emptiness, which goes beyond the understanding which sees all things as reducible to the one.

Oneness as a universal principle, if substantial and self-existing, must be overcome; otherwise, we as particulars lose our individuality and cannot possibly awaken to reality. From the Buddhist point of view, this is true even for God, the 'only One'. On the other hand, if all particular things are respectively self-identical, there is no equality between them, and everything is self-centered. Both Emptiness – that is, the negation of oneness – and egolessness – that is, the negation of everything's self-centeredness – are necessary for awakening. In the realization of Emptiness, which is another term for *nirvāṇa*, all particular things are respectively just as they are and yet equal in their suchness. This is expressed in Mahayana Buddhism as: 'Difference as it is, is sameness; sameness (of things in their suchness) as it is, is difference.' This very realization is the source of wisdom and compassion in which both ignorance and self-centeredness are overcome. Just because *nirvāṇa* is in itself empty, it is full of particular things functioning freely, which neither lose their particularity nor impede one another.

What significance does Buddhist *nirvāṇa* hold for us today, East and West, with regard to contemporary thought and life, especially as it pertains to the problems of understanding ultimate reality, nihilism, the relation of man to nature, the irrational in human existence, the achieving of true community, and the understanding of the meaning of history? I want to clarify the contemporary significance of the Buddhist notion of awakening, *nirvāṇa*; I would like to deal with this problem from the standpoint of Mahayana Buddhism, a form of Buddhism developed in northern Asia, especially in China and Japan, and based on the dynamic interpretation of Gautama's teachings.

NIRVĀṆA: DYNAMIC RELATIVISM

First of all, *nirvāṇa* has relevance to the human understanding of ultimate or universal Reality in that it overcomes the major objection to monistic absolutism. The concept of the one God who is essentially transcendent, self-existing apart from everything relative, is unreal to Buddhism, in that a self-existing God cannot be spoken of without a knower. In Buddhism, mutual relativity or interdependency is the ultimate truth, and doctrines of absolute truth which exclude other views of truth as false are similarly considered unreal or illusory. In Buddhist awakening nothing is independent, self-existing or permanent; having no permanent selfhood, everything is mutually related to each and every other thing. This is not a fixed relativism simply rejecting absolutes and resulting in a form of skepticism or nihilism, but a dynamic relativism in which even the absolute and the relative, the holy and the secular, the divine and the human, are all totally interrelated. This idea of total interrelatedness of each and every thing at every moment is termed in Buddhism '*pratītya-samutpāda*', which may be translated as 'dependent co-origination'. This is dynamic relativism, beyond the opposition between relativism and absolutism. This paradoxical truth can be realized not through speculation but only through existential practice. Hence the practice of the Eightfold Noble Path and sitting meditation, *zazen*, have been emphasized.

The position of Buddhism towards other faiths is often called 'tolerant' by Western scholars. It may, however, be that the term 'tolerant' has been applied according to Western, especially Christian, standards, and is misleading in that it does not get to the heart of Buddhism. The Buddhist position, founded in *nirvāṇa*, is a 'positionless position' in the sense that, being itself entirely non-substantial, it lets every other position stand and work just as it is. Naturally, Buddhism does not exclude other faiths as false, but recognizes the relative truths which they contain. This recognition, however, is a starting point, not an end or goal, for Buddhist life. Properly speaking, Buddhists start to work critically and creatively through this basic recognition of the relative truths contained in other positions, hoping for productive dialogue and cooperation with other faiths.

The Buddhist position as realized in *nirvāṇa* may prove effective in a contemporary world which, as this world becomes more and more closely united, is witnessing the remarkable rise of a sense of pluralism and diversity of values. The dynamic relativism of *nirvāṇa* may provide a spiritual foundation for the formation of the rapidly approaching One World in which the coexistence of a variety of contrasting value systems, ways of life and ways of thinking will be indispensable.

NIRVĀṆA: BEYOND NIHILISM

Secondly, *nirvāṇa* offers a freedom beyond nihilism. One of the serious problems in the world today is the permeation of the nihilism proclaimed by Friedrich Nietzsche and others. The collapse of traditional value systems and the cry that 'God is dead' are almost universal phenomena in industrialized societies in the West. A loss of the sense of the holy and despair with regard to the corruption and impotence of the established forms of religion prevail in the world today. As a consequence of the pervasion of the scientific way of thinking, it has become increasingly difficult for modern people to believe in a personal God; nevertheless, people today are searching seriously for something to fill the vacuum which has been created in their spiritual lives. In this respect Nietzsche is a touchstone for religion for he advocated, as a prototype of future humanity, the active nihilist, the positive nihilist who, grounded in the will to power, courageously faces emptiness without God.

It is, however, unlikely that Nietzsche's active nihilism can successfully serve as a substitute for religion. I have no time to discuss this background in detail but it would seem that what is needed today and in the future is a religion *beyond* active nihilism, that is, a religion beyond 'emptiness without God'. Buddhism, which is based on *nirvāṇa*, is precisely a religion of this sort. Negating the existence of the one God, Buddhism advocates *śūnyatā* (Emptiness), which is not a nihilistic emptiness but rather a fullness of particular things and individual persons

functioning in their full capacity and without mutual impedi-
ment. In Emptiness, everything is realized as it is, in its total
dynamic reality. This radical realism involves not only liberation
from 'God' but also the overcoming of an active nihilism such
as that advocated by Nietzsche. Thus, *nirvāṇa* is a realization of
great freedom, both from theistic pietism with its dependence
on God and from nihilism in a Nietzschean sense with its
dependence on the will to power, making possible genuine self-
determination by removing the illusion of a determinator.

NIRVĀṆA, HUMANKIND AND NATURE

Thirdly, *nirvāṇa* has relevance to our understanding of the
relation of humankind to nature. Christian scholars often con-
tend that Buddhist *nirvāṇa* is impersonal. Christian personalism,
if I am not mistaken, is based on human responsibility to the
word of God. Unlike other creatures, humans are created in
God's image and can respond to the calling of God. Nature is
ruled by God through humans whom God gave 'dominion over'
other creatures. In this sense, Christian personalism is connected
with anthropocentrism among creatures. Buddhist *nirvāṇa*, on
the contrary, is based on egolessness and is not anthropocentric
but rather cosmological. In Buddhism, humans and the things
of the universe are equally subject to change, equally subject to
transitoriness or transmigration. A person cannot achieve emancipation from the cycle of birth and death until he or she can
eliminate a more universal problem: the transience common to
all things in the universe. Here we see that the *basis* for Buddhist
salvation is cosmological, not personalistic as in an I–Thou
relationship with God, and thus impersonal and trans-anthropocentric. However, it is only humans with self-consciousness and
free will who can go beyond anthropocentrism and reach an
awareness that transience is not limited to humanity but is
common to all things. As you know, Buddhism talks about
universal transience, transience in everything, including every
aspect of nature. So the realization of universal transience is one
of the key points of Buddhist awakening and it is not anthropocentric but a cosmological realization.

Furthermore, it is noteworthy that Buddhist salvation is primarily
concerned with individual persons, and is not simply concerned

with humankind in general, for as is written in a sutra: 'One is born alone, dies alone, comes alone, and goes alone.' In this sense Buddhism may also be said to be personalistic and existentialistic. Yet this does not mean that the human is understood in Buddhism in terms of a divine–human encounter in which nature is excluded, but rather that the human is grasped as a being with self-consciousness and free will on a cosmological basis which includes all of nature. Without the realization of transience and selflessness on such a cosmological basis, a human being cannot become an 'awakened one'.

Thus the following two aspects of Buddhist salvation must be noted:

1. Buddhism is primarily concerned with salvation of a human as a person who, unlike other living beings, has self-consciousness and free will and thereby alone has the potential to become aware of and emancipated from the transience common to all things in the universe. This is the existentialistic and personalistic aspect of Buddhism.
2. However, a cosmological dimension is the necessary *basis* for this Buddhist salvation: in Buddhism salvation is not from sin as rebellion against God, but emancipation from the cycle of birth and death which is part of the transience of the universe. This is the cosmological aspect of Buddhism. These two aspects are inseparable: the more cosmological the basis of salvation, the more existentially thoroughgoing the salvation. In this sense, the Buddhist cosmology which is the basis of *nirvāṇa* is an existential cosmology, not an objective scientific cosmology, and Buddhist existentialism or personalism may be called 'cosmo-existentialism' or 'cosmo-personalism'.

The Buddhist position with regard to the relation of humankind and nature may contribute a spiritual foundation out of which could arise a solution to one of the most pressing problems with which human beings are today faced, the destruction of the environment. This problem is inextricably connected with human estrangement from nature. It results from anthropocentrism whereby a person regards nature merely as a means or obstacle to the realization of selfish goals, and thus continually finds ways to utilize and conquer it. The cosmological view which is the basis of Buddhist *nirvāṇa* does not see nature as something subordinate to human beings, but sees them as subordinate to nature, more precisely as a part of nature from the standpoint of 'cosmos'. Thus the cosmological view both allows human beings to overcome estrangement from nature and to live harmoniously with nature without losing their individuality.

NIRVĀṆA AND THE IRRATIONAL

Fourthly, let us consider what significance Buddhist *nirvāṇa* may have in dealing with the irrational in human existence. Interest in mythology and primitive cultures as well as an irresistible demand to satisfy instinctive, especially sexual, desire is on the upsurge in highly industrialized societies. This phenomenon may be regarded as a reaction to the emphasis on human rationality and science which grew up in modern European culture and formed the basis for industrialization. Western thinkers such as Schopenhauer, Marx, Freud and Jung, and more recently, Camus, Marcuse and others, have emphasized the importance of the irrational aspects of human existence. Most critically, modern European culture has completely neglected the problem of death, a problem which has plagued humanity since time immemorial and is for modern people the supreme irrationality.

In short, modern European culture with its scientific orientation, pervasive as it is in highly industrialized societies, is based on human rationality and a preoccupation with life, while neglecting to deal with the irrational elements in human existence, especially the problem of death. It is not wise, however, for us simply to accept and follow present reactionary tendencies which try to counteract, by means of an influx of irrationality, this emphasis on rationalism. What is necessary today in order to deal successfully with this problem is a profound basis upon which the conflicts between the rational and the irrational, reason and desire, life and death, can be resolved. Buddhist *nirvāṇa*, or the Middle Way, in which people overcome duality and extinguish the 'craving' deeply rooted in human existence, can provide such a basis.

NIRVĀṆA AND COMMUNITY

Fifthly, let us consider what significance Buddhist *nirvāṇa* may have in the understanding and achieving of true community. It is the realization of *nirvāṇa* described previously as 'difference as it is, is sameness; sameness as it is, is difference' which provides for Buddhism an existential ground for true community. We find ourselves equal, not as children of the one God, but in the common realization of egolessness or no-self or Emptiness, which is at the same time the realization of true Self. Realization of egolessness is not something negative, like losing one's self-identity; rather it is positive in that, through this realization one overcomes one's ego-centeredness and awakens to Reality, that is, to one's own true Self as well as the true Self of others. It is in this awakening that one can live with others in true community, sharing the realization of true Self. In *nirvāṇa*, the loss of ego-self is the gain of true Self, and the sameness among individuals in their egolessness and the difference between individuals in their true Self-ness are paradoxically one.

Accordingly, in the realization of *nirvāṇa*, I am not I because I am egoless, and yet I am absolutely I because I am my true Self. Likewise, you are not you because you are egoless, and yet you are absolutely you because you are your true Self. Moreover, since I am not I, I am you, and since you are not you, you are I. Each person remains just as he or she is, yet each person is equal in that each is his or her true Self. This dynamic inter-relationship occurs in the realization of egolessness and Emptiness which is possible and in fact necessary for each human existence. This realization provides the Buddhist foundation for human beings in true community. Furthermore, this realization applies not only to human relationship to other human beings, but also to all things in nature, from dogs to mountains.

NIRVĀṆA AND THE MEANING OF HISTORY

Sixthly and finally, what significance does *nirvāṇa* have in regard to understanding the meaning of history? Since there is no God in Buddhism, there is no creation or last judgment, but rather Emptiness. Thus, for Buddhism, history has neither beginning nor end. This view of history derives from the deep realization of the *karma* of human beings. *Karma* is the universal law of an act and its consequences which is self-operating in making the world a process of perpetual becoming. Thus it is the driving force behind all action which produces various effects according to the nature of the action and which binds people to the wheel of birth and death. Unlike the Hindu concept of *karma*, however, *karma* in Buddhism is not deterministic since there is in Buddhism no idea of a God who is the controller of *karma*; rather Buddhism takes *karma* as moral power, emphasizing the possibility of final release from the round of transmigration through a free decision of the will. Accordingly, on the one hand, we are bound by our own *karma* which shares in and is inseparably linked to *karma* operating in the universe. On the other hand, however, we as beings with self-consciousness and free will have the opportunity to be liberated from *karma* through our own free act performed by our personal choice: an act which is based on the total realization within oneself of the beginningless and endless process of *karma*, that is, *karma* operating in the universe beyond oneself. In this total realization of *karma*, personal and universal, past, present and future, one is liberated from *karma* and awakens to *nirvāṇa*.

At the very moment we truly realize the beginninglessness and endlessness of history, we transcend its boundlessness and find the whole process of history from beginningless beginning to endless end intensively concentrated within the here and now. If you realize the beginninglessness and endlessness of the process of human history at this moment, the whole process is concentrated into your present being. So you are no more confined by the endless process of endless transmigration, but rather you become master of the endless process of that transmigration. Apart from the realization of the here and now, there is no history. We realize our true life and true Self at this moment in which beginning and end, time and eternity, one and many, are not seen in duality but in dynamic oneness. This is nothing other than the realization of *nirvāṇa*.

Universal *karma* can be realized not objectively but only subjectively, that is, in and through the existential realization of personal and individual *karma* – and personal *karma* can be truly transcended only when universal *karma* is subjectively overcome within oneself. Thus to one who has attained *nirvāṇa* through the total realization of *karma* the whole universe discloses itself in its reality and history as the endless process of operating *karma* ceases – eternity manifesting itself. In this sense history ends in *nirvāṇa*. This is the universal salvation of *nirvāṇa* realized by an awakened one, and constitutes the wisdom aspect of *nirvāṇa*. At the same time, though, for the *awakened one* history begins in *nirvāṇa* because those who, despite *the fact of* universal salvation realized by an awakened one, *believe themselves* to be 'unsaved' remain innumerable in the world and will appear endlessly in the future. Thus, history takes on new significance for an awakened one – it is an endless process in which he or she must try to actualize universal salvation in regard to those 'unsaved'. This constitutes the compassion aspect of *nirvāṇa*. Since the wisdom and compassion aspects are inseparable in *nirvāṇa*, history begins and ends at each and every moment in the realization of *nirvāṇa*.

In short, for an awakened one who is living in *nirvāṇa*, universal salvation is completely realized in the here and now, and yet it is to be realized endlessly in the process of history for those who think themselves to be 'unsaved'. These two aspects are dynamically united in *nirvāṇa*. Accordingly, at each and every moment of history a development toward the endless future is at once the total return to the root and source of history, which is eternity, and conversely, the total return to the root and source of history that is eternity is at once a development toward the endless future. The process of history is a succession of such moments whose dynamic structure consists of an advance which is simultaneously a return, a return which is simultaneously an advance. This Buddhist view of history leads us to a double realization: in the light of wisdom, eternity manifests itself in the here and now, and life at this moment is not a means to a future end but is the end itself, while in the light of compassion, life is an endless activity of saving others, an instrument for universal salvation.

Part Two
Buddhism in Dialogue with Tillich's Theology

7

Negation in Mahayana Buddhism and in Tillich: A Buddhist View of 'The Significance of the History of Religion for the Systematic Theologian'

In his final lecture, 'The Significance of the History of Religions for the Systematic Theologian', Paul Tillich clearly expressed a hope to write a new *Systematic Theology* in dialogue with the whole history of religion. Toward the end of that lecture he stated:

> My own *Systematic Theology* was written before these seminars [joint seminars with Mircea Eliade] and had another intention, namely the apologetic discussion against and with the secular. Its purpose was the discussion or the answering of questions coming from the scientific and philosophical criticism of Christianity. But perhaps we need a longer, more intensive period of interpenetration of systematic theological study and religious historical studies.[1]

An interest in history of religions was not new. It went back to his student days. As Mircea Eliade stated in his tribute to Tillich:

> His old interest in History of Religions was reawakened and increased by his voyage to Japan and his encounter with Buddhist and Shinto priests and scholars. The impact of his visit on Tillich's entire life and thought was tremendous. . . .

He was impressed and moved by the Shintoist, cosmic type of religion and by the Buddhist and Zen schools. (*FR*, 31–2.)

As a member of the welcoming committee when Paul Tillich visited Kyoto in 1960, I was able to witness in part his encounter with Japanese religions. Tillich's own reflections on his experience in Japan are found in his book *Christianity and the Encounter of the World Religions*.[2] But as Eliade pointed out in his tribute, Tillich's 'profound experience [in Japan], simultaneously religious and cultural, was only partially expressed' in that book (*FR*, 32). It was through his joint seminar with Mircea Eliade at the Divinity School of Chicago in 1964 that Tillich became deeply attracted by the non-Christian religions and was inspired to develop a new *Systematic Theology* in dialogue with the history of religions. In his final lecture, 'The Significance of the History of Religions for the Systematic Theologian', we can see his provocative and dynamic ideas on the subject in their full scale and depth.

As Jerald C. Brauer wrote in his Editor's Preface to *The Future of Religions*: 'The lecture . . . proved to be one of his most tightly packed and comprehensive lectures of recent years.' It includes discussions which are so tightly condensed that it is not always easy (for me at least) to grasp his exact meaning. In the following I would like to examine his final lecture and make some comments from a Buddhist point of view.

I

Tillich rejects the orthodox attitude that dismisses all religions other than Christianity as false, and rejects also a theology of the secular that posits a theology without *theos*. The former, represented in our century by Karl Barth, absolutizes one's own religion as the only true revelation and regards other religions as futile human attempts to reach God. To this attitude the history of religions has no positive significance. On the other hand, the latter, exemplified by the so-called theology-without-God language, often absolutizes the secular and tries to absorb the sacred by the secular.

Therefore Tillich insists that 'as theologians, we have to break through two barriers against a free approach to the history of religions: the orthodox-exclusive one and the secular-rejective one' (*FR*, 83).

In this regard, I see a parallel of sorts between Tillich's approach and the approach of Mahayana Buddhism. This parallel can be found particularly between their approaches to the history of religions. Mahayana Buddhism criticizes as too narrow Theravada Buddhism, which tends to venerate the historical Buddha as the supreme enlightened One beyond human being and regards *nirvāṇa* as the ultimate goal of Buddhist life. Unlike Theravada Buddhism, Mahayana Buddhism insists on the possibility or even of the actuality of attaining Buddhahood for every one of us and emphasizes the dynamic identity of *saṃsāra* and *nirvāṇa*. This attitude of Mahayana Buddhism may be regarded as the rejection of the orthodox-exclusive attitude. On the other hand, the Mahayana attitude may also be considered as rejecting the secular-rejective attitude. Its emphasis on the identity of *saṃsāra* and *nirvāṇa* does not indicate the absolutization of the secular realm of *saṃsāra* but, on the contrary, the complete negation of *saṃsāra*, a negation accompanied by the complete negation of the sacred realm of *nirvāṇa*. One can see this double negation of *saṃsāra* and *nirvāṇa* in a Mahayana admonition: 'One should not abide in *saṃsāra* in order to awaken to wisdom: one should not abide in *nirvāṇa* in order to fulfill compassion.' Accordingly, one may say that both Tillich and Mahayana Buddhism seek to overcome the two barriers against a free approach to the history of religions: the orthodox-exclusive one and the secular-rejective one.

What, then, is Tillich's approach to the history of religions? At one point in his lecture, Tillich states: 'My approach is dynamic-typological. There is no progressive development which goes on and on, but there are elements in the experience of the Holy which are always there, if the Holy is experienced.' (*FR*, 86).

With the idea of dynamic typology, Tillich clearly rejects Hegel's construction of the history of religions, calling it a one-directed dialectics in which the past of the history of religions loses its meaning: 'For Hegel [for instance] the Indian religions are long, long past, long ago finished, and have no contemporary meaning' (*FR*, 86).

Instead, his dynamic typology acknowledges a universal religious basis that is the sacramental basis of all religions. The Holy is experienced here and now within everything finite and particular.

But in religious experience there is also a critical element that resists the demonization of the sacramental, as well as an ethical or prophetic element, the element of 'ought to be'. Tillich calls the unity of these three elements, sacramental, critical and ethical, in a religion 'The Religion of the Concrete Spirit' and states, 'The inner aim [or telos] of the history of religions is to become a "Religion of the Concrete Spirit"' (*FR*, 87, 88). The unity of the above three elements gives the history of religions its dynamic character. The Religion of the Concrete Spirit, however, is not a matter of the future, but

> . . . appears everywhere [fragmentarily] in the struggle against the demonic resistance of the sacramental basis and the demonic and secularistic distortion of the critics of the sacramental basis. We can see the whole history of religions in this sense as a fight for the Religion of the Concrete Spirit, a fight of God against religion within religion. And this phrase, the fight of God within religion against religion, could become the key for understanding the otherwise extremely chaotic, or at least seemingly chaotic, history of religions'. (*FR*, 88.)

Here we see the crucial point of Tillich's understanding of the history of religions.

II

Tillich then raises a question as to 'how these dynamics of the history of religions are related to the relationship of the religious and the secular' (*FR*, 89). To Tillich the Holy is not only open to demonization but also to secularization. He states, 'These two, demonization and secularization, are related to each other, in so far as secularization is the most radical form of de-demonization' (*FR*, 89).

The Holy is open to demonization because, once it becomes dominant, it elevates something particular, such as symbols, rites or institutions, to the ultimate itself. The Holy must be open to the use of the secular as a critical tool against itself.

On the other hand, the Holy is also open to secular, rational and critical movement. The rational necessarily judges the irrationality of the Holy and thus 'the Holy becomes slowly the morally good, or the philosophically true' (*FR*, 90) and ultimately the rational eliminates the religious dimension altogether. However, when the secular fights against the domination by the Holy, it becomes empty and cannot live by itself. Tillich was well aware of this dynamic dimension of the sacred and the secular in the religious experience and emphasizes 'the Religion of the Concrete Spirit' as the telos of the history of religions and 'Dynamic typology' as the most adequate approach for the theology of the history of religions.

In his book *Christianity and the Encounter of the World Religions*, Tillich talks about the positive relation of Protestantism to the secular realm:

'[It is] due to the Protestant principle that the sacred sphere is not nearer to the Ultimate than the secular sphere. It denies that either of them has a greater claim to grace than the other: both are infinitely distant from and infinitely near to the Divine. This stems from the fact that Protestantism was largely a lay movement.'[3]

If this is the case, the Protestant principle is strikingly similar to the principle of Mahayana Buddhism. As I mentioned earlier, Mahayana Buddhism emphasizes that: 'One should not abide in *saṃsāra* in order to awaken to wisdom: One should not abide in *nirvāṇa* in order to fulfil compassion.' It is necessary for a Buddhist to overcome the attachment to the secular realm of *saṃsāra* and attain *nirvāṇa* through awakening to wisdom. As Tillich rightly points out, *nirvāṇa* is the telos of Buddhist life.[4] But, however important *nirvāṇa* may be, if one simply remains in *nirvāṇa* one cannot be said to be completely free from attachment and selfishness, since by abiding in *nirvāṇa*, enjoying one's own wisdom and salvation, one may forget the suffering of one's fellow beings still involved in the flux of *saṃsāra*. In order to be completely free from attachment and selfishness and to awaken to one's true Self which is identical with the true Self of all others, one must not abide in *nirvāṇa* and return to the realm of *saṃsāra*; that is, one must overcome the attachment to *nirvāṇa* and identify oneself with suffering fellow beings. It is this that constitutes the fulfilment of compassion.

Unlike Theravada Buddhism, Mahayana Buddhism characteristically emphasizes the overcoming of the sacred realm of *nirvāṇa* by saying, 'in order to fulfil compassion one should not abide in *nirvāṇa*.' In Mahayana Buddhism, both attachment to the secular realm of *saṃsāra* and attachment to the sacred realm of *nirvāṇa* must be overcome, and that which is neither *saṃsāra* nor *nirvāṇa*, that which is neither secular nor sacred, must be fully realized. This is the realization of *śūnyatā*, which is often translated as 'emptiness'.

But *śūnyatā* is not a nihilistic emptiness, it is a dynamic fullness. For *śūnyatā* is realized only through the double negation of *saṃsāra* and *nirvāṇa*. This implies that one must move freely from *saṃsāra* to *nirvāṇa*, from *nirvāṇa* to *saṃsāra* without attaching to either. This dynamic free movement between *saṃsāra* and *nirvāṇa*, between the secular and the sacred, is *nirvāṇa* in the true Mahayanic sense. *Śūnyatā* is simply another term for *nirvāṇa* in this dynamic sense. This is the reason that Mahayana Buddhism, based on the realization of *śūnyatā*, emphasizes that '*saṃsāra* as it is, is *nirvāṇa*; *nirvāṇa* as it is, is *saṃsāra*.' The ultimate in Mahayana Buddhism is *śūnyatā* as a dynamic fullness that is both *saṃsāra* and *nirvāṇa* as neither *saṃsāra* nor *nirvāṇa* at one and the same time.

I would like to call *śūnyatā* in this dynamic sense the 'Mahayana principle'. It is strikingly similar to Tillich's Protestant principle in which 'the sacred sphere is not nearer to the Ultimate than the secular sphere. It denies that either of them has a greater claim to grace than the other: both are infinitely distant from and infinitely near to the Divine.' The Mahayana principle may be traced to the fact that, like Protestantism, Mahayana Buddhism was largely a lay movement.

III

I am not, however, sure that Tillich's Protestant principle and my Mahayana principle are exactly the same. Rather, I detect a very subtle but essential difference between them. And this difference, it seems to me, entails a different approach to the history of religions between Christianity, as understood by Tillich, and Buddhism, as I understand it.

In both Tillich and Mahayana Buddhism the secular and the sacred are understood to be dynamically identical. In Mahayana Buddhism, however, this dynamic identity is realized only through the realization of *śūnyatā* (emptiness), which is realized by the double negation of the secular and the sacred. Since this double negation is not partial but complete and thoroughgoing, it is at the same time a double affirmation. That is to say, negation of negation is nothing but affirmation of affirmation; absolute negation is itself absolute affirmation. And without the realization of absolute negation there can be no realization of absolute affirmation. These statements should not, however, be taken objectively or conceptually, as they do not simply indicate a logical problem, but rather an existential and religious self-realization that can be grasped only in a non-objective manner. To return to our original issue, in the realization of absolute negation *qua* absolute affirmation, the secular as it is, is sacred; the sacred as it is, is the secular. As I mentioned shortly before, this dynamic identity is possible only through the realization of *śūnyatā*. Although Tillich talks about a similar dynamic identity between the secular and the sacred in terms of the Protestant principle, in my point of view, the realization of *śūnyatā* is lacking. For Tillich, the Ultimate is God, not *śūnyatā*.

I am not concerned now with the terms or concepts themselves, rather with the reality behind them.

Tillich's notion of God is very different from the traditional theistic notion of God. To him God is the ground of being and the infinite power of being that conquers non-being. God is viewed as a polarity of being and non-being. However, Tillich's notion of mutually dependent polarity of being and non-being is not a thoroughgoing and perfect one. To Tillich being and non-being, though consisting of a polarity, do not represent a symmetrical correlation. This we can see from statements he makes in *Systematic Theology*. 'Being precedes nonbeing in ontological validity as the word "nonbeing" itself indicates.' Elsewhere he says 'being embraces itself and nonbeing' while 'nonbeing is dependent on the being it negates.'[5] If in Tillich God as the Ultimate is understood as being itself or the ground of being on the presupposition of an asymmetrical polarity of being and nonbeing, the identity of the secular and the sacred must be said to lack sufficient dynamic force to enable it to reach *complete* fulfillment of the Protestant principle where 'the sacred sphere is not nearer to the Ultimate than the secular sphere'. It must be said to lack enough dynamic force to fully realize 'a mutual judging' between Christianity and secularism 'which opens the way for a fair valuation of the encountered religions and quasi-religions'.[6]

On the other hand, if the Ultimate is understood, not as God, but as *śūnyatā*, the dynamic identity between the secular and the sacred is fully and thoroughly realized. For *śūnyatā* is not being-itself realized on the presupposition of the asymmetrical polarity of being and non-being; it is absolute nothingness (or absolute negation *qua* absolute affirmation) which is realized by overcoming the symmetrical polarity of being and nothingness (I use the term *nothingness* as a stronger form than *non-being*) in that *śūnyatā* is neither being nor nothingness and yet both being and nothingness.[7]

In the realization of *śūnyatā*, Tillich's 'Religion of the Concrete Spirit' as the telos of the history of religions is fully realized and we can see the whole history of religions as a fight for the Religion of the Concrete Spirit; however, not as a fight of God against religion within religion, as Tillich suggests (*FR*, 88), but as a fight of *śūnyatā* against religion within religion. That this is the case in Buddhism, particularly in Mahayana Buddhism, is seen by the previously mentioned Mahayana admonition: 'One should not abide in *nirvāṇa*, one should not abide in *saṃsāra*,' as well as by other emphasis in Mahayana Buddhist scriptures. We read, for instance, that 'all the trees, grasses, and lands attain Buddhahood' and that 'the sounds of the streams are Buddha's speech: the shapes of the mountains are Buddha's body.' These phrases do not, as is sometimes thought, indicate nature mysticism. Nature mysticism is lacking in the realization of *śūnyatā*, emptiness, which is the essential ground of these Mahayana statements. Such secular entities as trees, lands, streams and mountains are non-substantial and empty, without any enduring nature and, precisely because they are so, they are dynamically identical with the sacred. Or we can say the same thing from the opposite side, that since the Buddhist Ultimate is *śūnyatā*, non-substantial emptiness, it can penetrate or be identical with trees, lands, streams and mountains.

Quoting Bonhoeffer and other contemporary theologians Tillich states:

'[According to them] Christianity must become secular, and God is present in what we do as citizens, as creative artists, as friends, as lovers of nature, as workers in a profession, so that it may have eternal meaning. Christianity for these men has become an expression of the Ultimate meaning in the action of our daily life. And this is what it should be.'[8]

However, in order to fully realize this dynamic identity between the secular and the sacred, the very notion of God must be overcome and be replaced by the notion of *śūnyatā* or absolute nothingness. This is not a fight of God against religion within religion, but a fight of *śūnyatā* against religion within religion. This is the reason why Zen Buddhism emphasizes:

> *Encountering a Buddha, killing the Buddha;*
> *Encountering a patriarch, killing the patriarch;*
> *– Only thus does one attain liberation and disentanglement*
> *from all things, thereby becoming completely unfettered and free.*[9]

In the Japanese tradition not only painting and calligraphy but also such mundane activities as drinking tea, arranging flowers, martial arts and so on, have been transformed into ritual, religious practice under the influence of Zen. They are non-religious religious practice. The Tea ceremony, for instance, is performed beyond God, or through 'killing the Buddha'. The Ultimate is fully expressed in such actions of daily life.

Tillich advances the idea of 'God above God' in order to demythologize the idea of God and to transcend the theistic notion of God to give a new valuation to secularism. But as I also said in my response to Langdon Gilkey:

> If Tillich's phrase 'God above God' still implies yet another 'God' that is above God, as the term is normally understood, then this 'God' cannot really be *above* God at all. If the phrase 'God above God' is truly to signify that which is *above* God or *beyond* God, then what is signified cannot be spoken of as a 'God' at all. In my point of view what is signified must be absolute Nothingness or *śūnyatā*.'

IV

I referred before to Tillich's notion of dynamic typology which he believed to be the most adequate approach to the history of religions. I share that belief because, unlike Hegel's progressive view of history, Tillich's dynamic typology grasps religions in their particularity and contrasting polarity on the universal religious basis – the experience of the Holy. He also emphasizes that under the method of dynamic typology one religion judges not only other religions but also itself in the light of its encounter with other religions. This is an extremely important issue in understanding the significance of the history of religions for the systematic theologian. In my remaining remarks, I would like to make a critical observation of Tillich in this regard.

To Tillich as a systematic theologian the criterion of judging other religions as well as Christianity itself is the event of the Cross, the image of Jesus as the Christ. I well understand this. As Tillich unambiguously states: 'It is natural and unavoidable that Christians affirm the fundamental assertion of Christianity that Jesus is the Christ and reject what denies this assertion.'[10]

My question in this connection, however, is how this fundamental Christian assertion can be reconciled with the notion of dynamic typology. Since dynamic typology by definition presupposes the plurality of and interrelationality among various types of religion, it cannot accommodate itself to the Christian assertion of the event of Jesus as the ultimate criterion of judging all religions. And to thoroughly maintain the Christian assertion of the event of Jesus Christ as the ultimate criterion of judging all religions undermines the position of dynamic typology.

Of course, Tillich tries to resolve this issue. On the one hand, he emphasizes that in addition to the interfaith dialogue among various types of religions, the dynamic typological approach includes self-reflection on the part of each religion: 'Under the method of dynamic typology every dialogue between religions is accompanied by a silent dialogue *within* the representatives of each of the participating religions.'[11] This emphasis is directly linked with another emphasis, that of the importance of self-judgment within Christianity in the light of its encounter with other religions.

On the other hand, Tillich tries to reduce the uniqueness or particularity of the event of Jesus Christ as much as possible to the extent it does not distort the fundamental Christian assertion of Jesus as the Christ:

'What is particular in him [Jesus] is that he crucified the particular in himself for the sake of the universal. This liberates his image from bondage both to a particular religion [Judaism] and to the religious sphere as such . . . With this image, particular yet free from particularity, religious yet free from religion, the criteria are given under which Christianity must judge itself and, by judging itself, judge also the other religions and the quasi-religions.'[12]

This is a unique interpretation of the event of the Cross that beautifully reconciles the fundamental assertion of Christianity with the notion of dynamic typology. Speaking from the Buddhist point of view, however, I still see a difficulty in agreeing completely to his interpretation of the event of the Cross as the criterion for judging all religions.

If I am not mistaken, the event of the Cross is the one and only historical event which is, to use Tillich's terminology, the 'final revelation', the last, genuine, decisive and unsurpassable revelation. And the sole way for us to approach this event is through participation. This means that 'particular yet free from particularity, religious yet free from religion' – the dialectical identity of particularity and universality, immanence and transcendence, humanity and divinity – is fully realized *only* in Jesus as the Christ and other people only *participate* in that dialectical identity, without fully realizing it. This requires that the event of the Cross be central not only to Christians but to followers of all other religions as well. This is the implication of the idea that the event of the Cross is the criterion for judging all religions. It also implies that, as Tillich himself states, 'that which has happened there [in the event of the Cross] in a symbolic way, happens *fragmentarily* in other places, in other moments, has happened and will happen even though they are not historically or empirically connected with the Cross.'[13]

This notion of the event of the Cross as the criterion for judging not only Christianity but also all non-Christian religions is, I am afraid, not compatible with the dynamic typology of world religions which presupposes the experience of the Holy in everything finite and particular; nor is it possible for Buddhism to accept such a position.

V

The basic principle of Buddhism is *pratītya-samutpāda*, dependent co-origination. This principle indicates that everything in and out of the universe is interdependent, co-arising and co-ceasing; nothing exists by itself, independent of other things. This is the reason Gautama Buddha, the founder of Buddhism, did not accept the age-old Vedantic notion of Brahman believed to be the ultimate sole ground of all beings, eternal, unchangeable and substantial. Instead, he advocated the principle of dependent co-origination, based on the realization of the impermanence and non-substantiality of all things. Under the principle of dependent co-origination, good and evil, being and nothingness, one and many, God and nature, are *completely* interdependent, co-arising and co-ceasing. *Bonum ipsum*, that is, the good itself, Being itself with a capital B, the absolute One as the source of the many, and even God above God are, due to their self-existing nature, regarded from the Buddhist point of view as unreal, conceptual constructions. The key to the realization of dependent co-origination is to overcome the notion of absolute oneness. Buddhism is neither dualistic nor monistic.

Buddhists have another term for the ultimate reality embodied in the notion of 'dependent co-origination': *tathatā*, which means 'suchness' or 'as-it-is-ness'. Under the principle of dependent co-origination, everything is realized truly as it is in its suchness or distinctiveness, yet everything is interrelated on the common basis of the realization of the non-substantiality or emptiness of all things – even the absolute One is not an exception to this realization.

I believe this Buddhist principle of dependent co-origination provides the best foundation for dynamic typology as an approach to the history of religions. For under the principle of dependent co-origination each and every type of religion is grasped as it is in its suchness or distinctiveness. And yet this does not occur in a confused or chaotic state but in close interrelatedness or typological structure on the common universal basis of emptiness.

In this connection one may then ask: What is the Buddhist criterion of judging itself and other religions? In one sense there is no criterion in Buddhism because Buddhism does not establish any monistic or monotheistic principle such as God, the event of the Cross or Brahman. It tries to overcome *any and all* discrimination in order to attain non-discrimination, that is, complete equality. Non-discrimination as the mere negation of discrimination is, however, called in Buddhism false equality, for that would not be true non-discrimination. Sheer non-discrimination as the negation of discrimination is still not free from a higher form of discrimination, that is, a discrimination between discrimination and non-discrimination. True non-discrimination can be realized only through the negation of non-discrimination. Here again we need the double negation, the negation of discrimination and the negation of non-discrimination. Through this double negation, and the realization of *śūnyatā*, we arrive at absolute affirmation. That is to say, we come to a clear and definite discrimination through the negation of non-discrimination. That is the discrimination of non-discrimination or the discrimination based on non-discrimination. At that point discrimination as it is, is equality, and equality as it is, is discrimination. The Buddhist criterion for judging itself and all other religions can be found in this dialectical notion of the discrimination of non-discrimination.

In order to help understand the Buddhist standpoint of the discrimination of non-discrimination I would like to quote a statement made by a Chinese Zen master, Ch'ing-yüan Wei-hsin, who lived in the T'ang dynasty:

'Before I began to study Zen, I said, 'Mountains are mountains; water is water.' After I got an insight into the truth of Zen through the instruction of a good master, I said, 'Mountains are not mountains; water is not water.' But now, having attained the abode of final rest [that is, Awakening], I say, 'Mountains are *really* mountains; water is *really* water.'[14]

The master's first understanding, 'Mountains are mountains; water is water,' represents a discrimination through objectification. In his second understanding, 'Mountains are not mountains; water is not water,' he overcomes objectification and discrimination and realizes the non-discrimination of mountains and water. At this point, however, he is still not completely free of discrimination, for by negating discrimination he remains in non-discrimination. In order to attain the final state of awakening he must overcome non-discrimination and thereby attain the third understanding, 'Mountains are really mountains; water is really water.' Here in this final understanding mountains and water are clearly discriminated in their distinctiveness on the basis of non-discriminative equality. This is the starting point of Buddhist activity and creativity.

Of course, this dynamic principle of the discrimination of non-discrimination applies not only to mountains and streams, but to all things, including various world religions. By applying this principle to Christianity and Buddhism in their interfaith dialogue, we might say:

> Before I practised Buddhism I said, 'Christianity is Christianity, Buddhism is Buddhism,' because I was caught in discrimination.
>
> After I had an insight into the truth of Buddhism I said, 'Christianity is not Christianity; Buddhism is not Buddhism' because I broke through the limitation of the particularity of Christianity and Buddhism through the realization of non-discriminative equality.
>
> But now, by overcoming this non-discriminative equality in awakening, I say, 'Christianity is really Christianity and Buddhism is really Buddhism.'

This is a picture of dynamic typology in a Buddhist perspective. If you extend this to other religions you may understand the significance that the history of religions has for the Buddhist systematic theologian.

Notes

1. Paul Tillich, *The Future of Religions* (New York: Harper & Row, 1966), p. 91 (hereafter cited in text as *FR*).
2. I wrote a review article of this book shortly after its appearance in 1966. The article is included in my book *Zen and Western Thought* (London: Macmillan; Honolulu: Univ. of Hawaii Press, 1986), pp. 171–85.
3. Paul Tillich, *Christianity and the Encounter of the World Religions* (New York: Columbia Univ. Press, 1963), pp. 47–8.
4. Ibid., p. 64.
5. Paul Tillich, *Systematic Theology* (Chicago: Univ. of Chicago Press, 1951), pp. 1: 189; idem, *The Courage to Be* (New Haven: Yale Univ. Press, 1957), pp. 34, 40.
6. Tillich, *Christianity and the Encounter*, op. cit., p. 94.

7. Masao Abe, 'Non-Being and *Mu* – the Metaphysical Nature of Negativity in the East and West', in *Zen and Western Thought*, op. cit., pp. 121–34.
8. Tillich, *Christianity and the Encounter*, op. cit., p. 94.
9. *Lin-chi lu*. See Masao Abe, 'God, Emptiness, and the True Self', in *Eastern Buddhist*, Vol. 2, No. 2 (1969), p. 16.
10. Tillich, *Christianity and the Encounter*, op. cit., p. 29.
11. Ibid., p. 57.
12. Ibid., pp. 81–2.
13. Ibid., p. 89; italics added.
14. *Wu-têng Hui-yüan* (Japanese: *Gotōegen*), edited by Aishin Imaeda (Tokyo: Rinrōkaku Shoten, 1971), p. 335. See also Masao Abe, 'Zen Is Not a Philosophy, but . . .' in *Zen and Western Thought*, op. cit., pp. 4–24.

8

Double Negation as an Essential for Attaining the Ultimate Reality: Comparing Tillich and Buddhism

Robert Scharlemann states, 'It might be argued that the polarity of being and nonbeing in Tillich's ontological structure is not meant to be the same as the polarity of being and nothing' in Buddhism. He also points out that 'there seems to be a clear difference in the predications being made' in these two cases. So far, I understand that Scharlemann agrees with me in making a distinction between God and śūnyatā in terms of being and nothingness. However, in this connection we must clarify what that difference really means and what is the cause of the difference. These are crucial points of the present discussion.

Second, assuming that they – the polarity of being and nonbeing in Tillich and the polarity of being and nothing in Buddhism – are the same and that some theologian were to understand 'God' to mean one who 'is neither being nor nothingness and yet both being and nothingness', Scharlemann raises a question: 'Would the names "God" and "śūnyatā" then be equivalent in meaning?'

In order to elucidate these issues properly I would like to clarify the following six points.

(1) The polarity of being and non-being in Tillich's ontological structure and the polarity of being and nothing in Buddhism are categorically different in their nature and role. In Tillich's ontological structure, as seen in his words 'Being precedes nonbeing in ontological validity, as the word "nonbeing" itself indicates'

and 'being "embraces" itself and nonbeing,' while 'nonbeing is dependent on the being it negates. "Dependent" points first of all to the ontological priority of being over nonbeing.'[1] Nonbeing is understood to be ontologically subordinate to being. By contrast, in Buddhism 'nothing' is not subordinate to being, but being and nothingness are understood to be of completely equal force in relation to each other. As I state elsewhere:

> They [being and nothingness] are entirely relative, complementary, and reciprocal, one being impossible without the other. In other words, *mu* (nothing) is not one-sidedly derived through negation of *u* (being). *Mu* (nothing) is the negation of *u* (being) and vice versa. One has no logical or ontological priority to the other. Being the complete counter-concept to *u* (being), *mu* (nothing) is more than privation of *u* (being), a stronger form of negativity than 'nonbeing' as understood in the West.[2]

Accordingly, the term *non-being* cannot be properly used in Buddhism to indicate the negative side of reality. In order to indicate the negative side of reality, the terms *nothing* or *nothingness* are more appropriate in Buddhism. Thus we must know that, although equally indicating polarity, the polarity of being and non-being in Tillich and the polarity of being and nothing in Buddhism are essentially different from each other; the former is an asymmetrical polarity whereas the latter is a symmetrical polarity.

(2) The Christian notion of God indicates the ultimate reality beyond the polarity and opposition of being and non-being, whereas the Buddhist notion of *śūnyatā* refers to the ultimate reality equally beyond the polarity and opposition of being and nothing. So far there is a sort of parallel between the two religions. However, since the nature of the polarity of positive and negative principle in these two religions is categorically different, the nature of the ultimate reality (God and *śūnyatā*) to be realized by overcoming that polarity is also essentially different. In Tillich, God is conceived as being-itself, and 'being "embraces" itself and non-being. Being has nonbeing "within" itself as that which is eternally present and eternally overcome in the process of the divine life.'[3] God does not exclude non-being but indicates a sort of dialectical relation of being and non-being. To

use the term of Scharlemann, God is a 'third in which being and nonbeing are united' or fused.

By contrast, in Buddhism the ultimate reality is realized as *śūnyatā*, which is not being-itself nor absolute Being but absolute nothingness. However, the absolute nothingness is not negative or nihilistic but most positive and dynamic. For *śūnyatā*, another term for absolute nothingness, is beyond the *symmetrical* polarity and opposition of being and nothing and thereby embraces being and nothing in their polarity and opposition. Unlike God, who – to use Scharlemann's phrasing of Tillich – 'is' being-itself and 'is not' nothing, *śūnyatā* 'is' and 'is not' being and 'is' and 'is not' nothingness.

(3) This difference between God and *śūnyatā* is not a difference in degree but in quality. The polarity of being and non-being in Tillich is based on being, as we see in his words 'Being embraces itself and nonbeing.' On the other hand, the polarity of being and nothing in Buddhism is based neither on being nor on nothing in their relative sense but upon absolute nothingness, that is, nothingness in the absolute sense. Although we equally see polarity of being and nothing in both Tillich and Buddhism, the basis of polarity is radically different. In Tillich the ultimate reality (God) is conceived as the third in which being and non-being are united, whereas in Buddhism the ultimate reality (*śūnyatā*) is not the third nor the first nor the second. This means that in Buddhism ultimate reality is realized through the complete turning over of the original horizon of the polarity of being and nothing. In other words, not only the complete negation of nothing but also the complete negation of being; that is, the double negation of two poles is necessary for the realization of ultimate reality as emptiness.[4]

(4) This qualitative or categorical difference in the nature of the polarity of being and nothing in Tillich and Buddhism indicates the different role of the polarity in attaining the ultimate reality in the respective religions. In Tillich, since the polarity of being and nothing is an asymmetrical polarity with being's superiority over nothing, the overcoming of this asymmetrical polarity leads us *obliquely* on the side of being to reach the ultimate point of being, that is, Being or being-itself. By contrast, in Buddhism, since the polarity of being and nothing is a symmetrical polarity, with equal weight for being and nonbeing, the overcoming of this symmetrical polarity entails us

straightforwardly to go beyond the horizon of polarity itself to attain a new horizon which is neither being nor nothing – that is, to a realization of *śūnyatā*.

However, if *śūnyatā* is simply regarded as the end or goal of straightforward transcendence, it is neither true *śūnyatā* nor true emptiness because it is objectified and reified as the end. The objectified or reified emptiness is not true emptiness. Emptiness must be emptied. Transcendence must be transcended. True emptiness is the ever self-emptying activity that is incessantly turning into being. Thus true Emptiness is neither being nor nothing, and both being and nothing at one and the same time. This is why true Emptiness is called Wondrous Being.

This true Emptiness and Wondrous Being is the ultimate reality in Buddhism, which is realized only by transcending straightforwardly the horizon of polarity of being and nothing (and by returning to the original plane through transcending the transcendence). This straightforward transcendence is possible because the polarity of being and nothing is realized not as asymmetrical with being's superiority over nothing but as symmetrical, with equal weight of being and nothing. This means that in Tillich the polarity of being and non-being plays a role as the springboard for slantwise transcendence, whereas in Buddhism the polarity of being and nothingness plays a role as the springboard for straightforward transcendence.

(5) When Tillich conceives God as the dialectical relation of being and non-being, he indicates that God as the power of being overcomes the shock of non-being, conquers non-being, and finally fulfills being itself. Although this understanding of the relation of being and non-being is dialectic, is not the whole dialectical movement taking place within the framework of being? It is true that in *The Courage to Be* Tillich emphasizes that non-being opens up the divine self-seclusion: 'Nonbeing (that in God which makes his self-affirmation dynamic) opens up the divine self-seclusion and reveals him as power and love. Nonbeing makes God a living God. Without the No he has to overcome in himself and in his creature, the divine Yes to himself would be lifeless.' Here we can see that in Tillich the divine self-seclusion (the framework of being itself) is opened up through the dialectical movement of non-being. In this understanding, however, is the divine self-seclusion *completely* opened up, and is the framework of being itself *fundamentally* broken through?

To answer these questions it would be helpful to look at another quotation from *The Courage to Be*:

> We could not even think 'being' without a double negation: being must be thought as the negation of the negation of being. This is why we describe being best by the metaphor 'power of being.' Power is the possibility a being has to actualize itself against the resistance of other beings. If we speak of the power of being-itself we indicate that being affirms itself against nonbeing.[5]

In this passage Tillich clearly talks about a double negation and stresses that 'being must be thought as the negation of the negation of being.' However, from his theological stance can he equally stress 'nothingness must be thought as the negation of the negation of nothingness'? Only when this statement is clearly realized together with the statement 'Being must be thought as the negation of the negation of being' is the double negation as the key factor to attain the ultimate reality fully realized and the divine disclosure completely opened up. Here in Tillich we still see a superiority of being over nothingness. What is the ontological ground of this persistent superiority of being over nothingness?

As Tillich suggests, double negation is necessary to attain ultimate reality. In order to attain ultimate reality not only double negation concerning being (that is, being as the negation of the negation of being), but also double negation concerning nothingness (that is, nothingness as the negation of the negation of nothingness) is necessary. In Tillich double negation concerning being (that is, being as the negation of negation of being) is clearly realized, but double negation concerning nothing (nothingness as the negation of negation of nothingness) is lacking. This is the reason why, to Tillich, ultimate reality is God as being-itself or the power of being.

On the other hand, in Mahayana Buddhism double negation is carried out thoroughly to the extent that the horizon of the polarity of being and nothingness itself is overcome. In Mayahana Buddhism not only double negation concerning being – being as the negation of the negation of being – but also double negation concerning nothingness – nothingness as the negation of the negation of nothingness – is clearly realized. For instance, *Mulamādhyamāka Kārikās* (13: 7–8), an important writing of the Mādyamika

School, emphasizes that 'Emptiness too is empty', and '*śūnyatā* – *śūnyatā*', and 'Emptiness – emptiness' is stressed. These phrases indicate that emptiness must be negated to attain true Emptiness. This true Emptiness as the negation of emptiness is ultimate reality in Buddhism because this true Emptiness is nothing but Wondrous Being and true fullness. In order to attain Wondrous Being (absolute being), the double negation of being and nothingness is essential. Here the divine seclusion is completely opened up.

As we see above in Tillich, although the relation of being and non-being is grasped quite dialectically and being is realized through the double negation of non-being, in the final analysis being is given priority over non-being and God is conceived as Being itself. This concept of God cannot be accepted by Buddhists as the ultimate reality because to a Buddhist the ultimate is the complete non-dual dynamism that is neither being nor nothingness and yet both being and nothingness. This dynamism has been traditionally expressed as 'whatever is form, that is emptiness, whatever is emptiness, that is form' (*Heart Sutra*) and '*Saṃsāra* as it is, is *nirvāṇa; nirvāṇa* as it is, is *saṃsāra*.'[6]

(6) There is still another important point in understanding the difference between Tillich and Buddhism in terms of the polarity of being and nothing. In Tillich, the question of being is produced by the 'shock of nonbeing'. The shock of non-being is inescapable to human existence due to human finitude. 'Finitude unites being with dialectical nonbeing. Man's finitude, or creatureliness, is unintelligible without the concept of dialectical nonbeing.'[7]

To Tillich the existential awareness of non-being is anxiety, which can be overcome only through faith as the courage to be. This is so because courage is the self-affirmation of being in spite of non-being. 'Faith is the state of being grasped by the power of being-itself.'[8] This is Tillich's solution of the basic anxiety innate in human existence. Here again we see that, although the relation of being and non-being is understood dialectically, being and non-being (nothingness) are not grasped as opposing each other in a contradictory manner but in a way in which non-being is subordinate to being. How can this subordination of non-being (nothingness) to being be ontologically validated? I well understand that the courage to be in Tillich, and faith and hope in Christianity, are entirely an existential and personal experience that is beyond the ontological dimension. But however existential and personal faith as the courage to be may appear, it needs to be ontologically verified in our time, when the *raison d'être* of religion, Christianity and Buddhism included, is questioned by various forms of anti-religious ideologies such as scientism, Marxism, traditional Freudian psychoanalytic thought and nihilism in the Nietzschean sense.[9] So my question, 'How can the subordination of non-being (nothingness) to being be ontologically validated?' is not merely an ontological but an existential question essentially related to our religious life.

In Buddhism, on the other hand, the polarity of being and nothingness (not non-being) is grasped in a thoroughly dialectical manner in that being and nothingness are not only opposing but also contradictory with each other. Since being and nothingness, or, more broadly, positivity and negativity, are essentially different and antagonistic principles, they consist of a fundamental antinomy or an existential dilemma. Buddhism understands human existence as a self-contradictory existence. The realization of one's own self-contradictory existence is called great death, which is not death as a counterpart of life but death as a fundamental conflict between life and death as the two antagonistic principles. A Buddhist solution of the human problem is realized by breaking through great death and attaining *nirvāṇa*, a blissful freedom from life and death.

In the above, I have tried to clarify how different the understanding of the polarity of being and nothing is between Tillich and Buddhism. Now I would like to deal briefly with the second issue raised by Scharlemann.That is to say, if the assumption is made that the polarity of being and nothing or non-being is understood in the same way in Tillich and Buddhism and that some theologian understands 'God' as one who 'is neither being nor nothingness and yet both being and nothingness,' Scharlemann raises a question: 'Would the names "God" and "*śūnyatā*" then be equivalent in meaning?'

My answer is, yes. That which is neither being nor nothingness and yet both being and nothingness indicates ultimate reality, which is the unobjectifiable non-dualistic dynamism transcending and yet embracing all existing conflict and opposition. The Buddhist notion of *śūnyatā* or Emptiness which is at the same time Fullness and thereby is called Wondrous Being, indicates the non-dualistic dynamism. But we need not cling to the term *śūnyatā*, As I stated earlier, *śūnyatā* or Emptiness must be emptied. What is important is not the term *śūnyatā* but the ultimate reality indicated by it. If 'God' indicates ultimate reality in the above dynamic sense, 'God' and '*śūnyatā*' are perfectly equivalent in meaning. Although Tillich's interpretation of God as being does not, as discussed above, indicate the ultimate reality in the above sense, Christian tradition is not lacking in such a non-dualistic dynamic interpretation of God. For instance, Dionysius the Areopagite characterized God as 'dazzling darkness'. God is dazzling and yet dark: God is dark and yet dazzling. This, however, does not mean that God is *half* dazzling and *half* dark but that God is *fully* dazzling and yet at the same time *fully* dark: *fully* dark and yet at the same time *fully* dazzling. This is because to Dionysius the Areopagite, God as the ultimate reality is precisely the unobjectifiable, non-dualistic dynamism. To him God is neither dazzling nor dark and yet both dazzling and dark. 'God' as dazzling darkness is equivalent to '*śūnyatā*' in which *saṃsāra* as it is, is *nirvāṇa*: *nirvāṇa* as it is, is *saṃsāra*.

Notes

1. Paul Tillich, *Systematic Theology* (Chicago: Univ. of Chicago Press, 1951), 1: 189; idem, *The Courage to Be* (New Haven: Yale Univ. Press, 1957), pp. 34, 40.
2. Masao Abe, *Zen and Western Thought*, (London: Macmillan; Honolulu: Univ. of Hawaii Press, 1986), p. 127.
3. Tillich, *The Courage to Be*, op. cit., p. 34.
4. Abe, 'Non-Being and *Mu*', in *Zen and Western Thought*, op. cit., pp. 121–34; Tillich, *The Courage to Be*, op. cit., p. 180.
5. Ibid., pp. 180, 179.
6. *Mahā-samnipata-sūtra*, Taishō, 397 (in Vol. 13).
7. Tillich, *Systematic Theology*, op. cit., 1: 189.
8. Tillich, *The Courage to Be*, op. cit., p. 172.
9. Masao Abe, 'Kenotic God and Dynamic Sunyata', in John Cobb and Christopher Ives (eds), *The Emptying God: A Buddhist-Jewish-Christian Conversation* (New York: Orbis Books, 1990), pp. 3–9.

9

A Response to Professor Langdon Gilkey's Paper, 'Tillich and the Kyoto School'

In his paper, 'Tillich and the Kyoto School', Professor Langdon Gilkey compares Paul Tillich with two of the most distinguished figures of the Kyoto School, Nishitani Keiji and Tanabe Hajime, and presents a penetrating analysis and discussion of their affinities and differences. Such an intellectual endeavour, by a leading American theologian, of comparing a Western theologian to a Japanese philosopher, would have been almost inconceivable until approximately a decade ago. I, as a member of the Kyoto School, greatly appreciate Professor Gilkey's ground-breaking efforts in this regard. The paper covers many important issues pertaining to the East–West or Buddhist–Christian encounter. I am most eager to deal with all of these issues in full detail from my own point of view, but due to time restriction, I must confine myself to discussing only the most crucial points.

I

Gilkey first compares Nishitani with Tillich. After pointing out the remarkable similarities between the two, Gilkey states that for Nishitani 'will is an undialectical category: it stands inexorably for finitude and so for *this* finite reality'. Therefore the answer to the problem caused by the principle of will is the cessation of will or non-attachment rather than the transformation of will. By contrast, Gilkey continues, 'for Tillich, as for most Christian theologians, will is a dialectical category: that is, it is to be both affirmed and negated, for it can be the bearer and initiator of both good and of evil'. And the fallen will can be transformed and restored by courage and grace. A transcendent ground for this restoration is the New Being, not the Nothingness emphasized by Nishitani. Thus, Gilkey says, 'Tillich would say of Nishitani – that Nishitani has correctly analysed the will as it appears in existence, but he has overlooked will in essential humanity and in the New Being'. Whether this is the case or not must be carefully scrutinized.

Then, in the second half of his paper, Gilkey compares Tanabe with Tillich. Gilkey recognizes greater and more surprising similarities between Tillich and Tanabe than he does between Tillich and Nishitani, especially by referring to Tanabe's notion of 'metanoesis' which includes the breakdown of the self-power, followed by repentance and faith in other-power. Gilkey also says, 'We have in Tanabe's thought the most explicit and elegant – along with that of Tillich – exposition and defense in our time of the concept of "theonomy"'.

Yet, Gilkey does not fail to detect the subtle and essential differences between Tanabe and Tillich. For Tanabe, Gilkey argues, the theonomy is possible only if Other Power is Nothingness and not Being, whereas for Tillich, it is not Nothingness but Being-Itself that is a theonomous power and imparts a theonomous meaning. This is because Being-Itself is a dialectical category. Due to this dialectical character of Being-Itself, God as Being-Itself is dialectically related to non-being, and is viewed as a polarity of being and non-being. God is the theonomous ground of the autonomy, freedom and creativity of relative beings and their common history. Thus Gilkey emphasizes:

> If, therefore, Tanabe wishes as he does to stress the restoration of the self into action in the world, he needs to admit as much 'Being' in his concept of Nothingness, as Tillich, in order to be theonomous, needs to inject 'Non-being' into his symbol of God.

Whether this suggestion does hit the mark or not must be carefully examined.

Up to this point, I have raised two questions: one concerning Gilkey's comparison of Nishitani and Tillich, particularly in regard to the understanding of the problem of will; the other concerning Gilkey's comparison of Tanabe with Tillich, particularly about the character of Other Power. And I have reserved immediate answers to these two questions. For, in my view, these two questions are ultimately rooted in a more fundamental, basic problem, that is the problem of God and non-being, or the Power of being and non-being, or more precisely: How should we understand being, non-being and nothingness as the religious principles for human salvation and freedom? Without a clear and authentic understanding of this problem we cannot properly answer the above two questions.

II

As I noted earlier, for Tillich, Being-Itself is a dialectical category: Being is dialectically related to non-being and God is viewed as a polarity of being and non-being. As Gilkey has stated in another paper 'The Symbol of God', which he delivered at the Tillich Centennial Meeting at Hope College, Michigan, last year, God and non-being are not understood in Tillich merely as opposites but as a mutually dependent polarity. For Tillich being and non-being present a major polarity, not only in relation to the finite but even more so in relation to God.

> For Being and Non-Being, affirmation and negation are inextricably and surprisingly interwoven in the whole texture of Tillich's thought so it cannot be understood without grasping this fundamental pattern. Tillich defines a polarity as mutually related contrast, a coincidence of opposites such that they depend on each other and that they rise and fall together: the more there is of one, the more possibility there is of the other. This is precisely the case with God as the Power of Being and Non-Being. Strangely these two form a mutually dependent polarity rather than the radical opposition which seems at first to be the case.

This understanding of being and non-being is strikingly similar to the Buddhist standpoint. However, when I closely examine Tillich's thought, I cannot help but find at least two important differences between the understanding of Tillich and Buddhism. First, I am ready to recognize Tillich's idea of a mutually dependent polarity of being and non-being. However, I must ask whether or not this mutually dependent polarity is a thoroughgoing and perfect one. My answer is negative, because towards the end of his presentation, in referring to Tanabe's notion of the infinite Nothingness which is dependent as much on the finite as the latter is on the former, Gilkey went on to say that:

> He [Tillich] would shy away from Tanabe's explicit affirmation of a symmetrical correlation between infinity and finitude, a symmetrical dependence of the divine ground on its creatures equivalent to their dependence on the divine ground.

As I quoted some years ago in my paper 'Non-Being and *Mu* – The Metaphysical Nature of Negativity in the East and West',[1] Tillich says in Vol. I of his *Systematic Theology*, 'Being precedes nonbeing in ontological validity as the word nonbeing itself indicates,'[2] and 'Being "embraces" itself and nonbeing'[3] while 'nonbeing is dependent on the being it negates. "Dependent" points first of all to the ontological priority of being over nonbeing.'[4]

A Buddhist will want to raise a question about the ontological ground of Tillich's so-called 'ontological priority' of being over non-being. Although we hope that there is ontological priority of being over non-being, there is, in reality, no ontological ground on which being has priority over non-being.

Thus I stated:

> It is assumed that being embraces *both* itself *and* non-being. But the very basis on which *both* being *and* non-being are embraced must not be 'Being' but that which is neither being nor non-being.[5]

This 'that which is neither being nor non-being' and which embraces being and non-being is precisely absolute Nothingness or *Śūnyatā* in the Buddhist sense. And even when we take nothingness in the relative sense, we should be clearly aware of the difference between non-being and nothingness – because nothingness is more than non-being.

Second, in Tillich, negativity as a polar element with positivity is understood in terms of non-being as a polar element with being. This implies that in Tillich and in the West in general, from the outset, negativity is understood to precede positivity in ontological validity. Accordingly, in the West it is generally assumed that death must be and can be overcome by life, attaining the eternal life; evil must be and can be conquered by good, attaining the supreme good. Although it is our hope to overcome death by the power of life and it is an ethical imperative to conquer evil by the power of good, whether it is possible in actual human life is another question. Although Tillich recognizes the polarity of being and non-being, to him God as the power of Being is the unconditional power that conquers the non-being that threatens us by the shock of nothingness. His notion of 'courage' is the self-affirmation of a finite being over against the resistance of the non-being surrounding and permeating it. 'God is the answer to the anxiety of finitude, the Power of Being that "conquers" non-being: thus God is existenced and defined as the answer, *as* that which *resists* and *overcomes* non-being.'[6]

By contrast, Buddhism does not recognize any superiority of positivity over negativity. Ontologically and religiously speaking, positivity and negativity are completely interrelated and inseparable. Life and death, good and evil are not two different entities, but are completely interrelated and inseparable. Accordingly the fundamental issue for Buddhism is not to overcome death by life, to conquer evil by good, but to be liberated from the endless conflict between life and death, good and evil, and attain *nirvāṇa*, a blissful freedom from this conflict innate in human existence. When Nishitani discusses the problem involved in will and emphasizes the awakening to *Śūnyatā* as the solution of that problem, he takes will as the root and source of the above endless conflict between life and death and good and evil innate in human existence. In one sense he takes the notion of will more dialectically than Tillich. Accordingly, as the solution to the problem Nishitani does not *talk* about mere cessation of will or non-attachment, but the realization of 'Emptiness' which is dynamically Fullness at one and the same time, and in which self is restored as the true Self through the realization of no-self.

As I said earlier, Gilkey insists that Tillich's notion of Being-Itself is a dialectical category. Being is a close relative of Nothingness in so far as Being-Itself is a theonomous power and imparts a theonomous meaning. Non-being in the divine creative life is necessary if there is to be ontological 'room' for finitude at all. The polarity of being and non-being in God, the self-negation as well as the finite self-affirmation of God, is the presupposition for the polarity of the divine absoluteness and concreteness, of divine ground and plural world – and so for the theonomy of ultimate ground and autonomous plural world (p. 15).

According to Gilkey, in New Being the power of being is dialectically also the power of non-being in the finite – that it may represent the divine ground as both Being and Non-Being (p. 16). God is apparently both being and non-being, the power of being united with the strange and paradoxical 'power' of non-being.

I have been deeply moved by this interpretation of God by Tillich and greatly appreciate it. At the same time, I have a serious question about his interpretation of the dialectical character of God as Being-Itself. That is, if the negative pole of the polarity of being and non-being is understood in terms of 'non-being', which is ontologically subordinate to the positive pole, being, that polarity is not a symmetrical but an asymmetrical one. In this case, God as Being-Itself, is perhaps not a perfect answer to the anxiety of finitude which is deeply rooted in the persistent struggle between positivity and negativity. What we must overcome in order to find out the answer to the anxiety of human finitude is not a struggle based on an asymmetrical polarity of positivity and negativity but a struggle that emerges from a symmetrical polarity of positivity and negativity. Accordingly, the answer is not God as Being-Itself which participates in the non-being while ultimately conquering it. Instead it must be absolute Nothingness which, by overcoming a symmetrical polarity between positivity and negativity, is itself, neither positive nor negative, neither being nor nothingness.

III

In this connection it may be helpful to consider what is the true absolute. The absolute is essentially different from the relative. The absolute is realized by negating the relative. This is the necessary condition for the absolute. The absolute in this sense, however, is not truly absolute, because it is distinguished from and is standing against the relative, and thus is still involved in the *relative* relationship to the relative. It is the absolute in the relative sense. In order to attain the *true* absolute, the absolute in the relative sense must be overcome, must be negated. Here we need another negation. We need the negation of the relative and the negation of the absolute. Here that which is neither relative nor absolute is reached through the negation of negation. That is the absolute Nothingness. Since this absolute Nothingness is freed from all types of the relative, including the relativity between the relative and the absolute, this is the true absolute. This argument indicates that the true absolute is the absolute Nothingness, not the absolute Being, and that only the absolute Nothingness is the true absolute. This is the reason philosophers of the Kyoto School, including Tanabe Hajime, take the absolute Nothingness as the ultimate Reality.

The absolute Nothingness is, however, not nihilistic. Since negation of negation is an affirmation – not an affirmation in the relative sense, but in the absolute sense – the negation of negation is precisely a great affirmation. Unlike the relative nothingness which stands opposite to being, the absolute Nothingness is dynamically identical with the absolute Being through the negation of negation. As a great affirmation and the absolute Being the Absolute Nothingness can be religiously the principle of salvation. A Great Affirmation can be attained only through the negation of negation. The absolute Being can be realized only through the absolute Nothingness. In other words, the absolute Being without the realization of the absolute Nothingness is not the true absolute Being. I wonder if Tillich's notion of Being-Itself, however seemingly dialectical, in so far as it is realized by overcoming an asymmetrical polarity of positivity and negativity and is lacking in a clear realization of the absolute Nothingness, is not true Being-Itself.

Let me conclude my response to Gilkey's paper by my comment on Tillich's well-known phrase, 'God above God'.[7] If Tillich's phrase, 'God above God' still implies yet another 'God' that is above God as the Word is normally understood, then this 'God' cannot really be *above* God at all. If the phrase 'God above God' is truly to signify that which is *above* God or *beyond* God, then what is signified cannot be spoken of as a 'God' at all. What is signified must be Absolute Nothingness.

Notes

1. Masao Abe, *Zen and Western Thought* (Honolulu: Univ. of Hawaii Press, 1985), pp. 121–34.
2. Paul Tillich, *Systematic Theology*, Vol. I (Chicago: Univ. of Chicago Press, 1951), p. 189.
3. Paul Tillich, *The Courage to Be* (New Haven: Yale Univ. Press, 1957), p. 34.
4. Ibid., p. 40.
5. Abe, op. cit., p. 121.
6. Paul Tillich, *Love, Power, and Justice* (New York: Oxford University Press, 1954), pp. 36–41.
7. Tillich, *The Courage to Be*, op. cit., pp. 186–90.

10

In Memory of
Dr Paul Tillich

Not only is the death of Dr Paul Tillich on 22 October 1965, a great loss for Christianity but for Buddhism as well, for Buddhism has lost in him a dialogue companion and a co-searcher for human truth. Tillich was an outstanding Christian theologian who open-mindedly confronted non-Christian religions and who particularly exerted himself to engage in a searching conversation with Buddhism. It may not be too much to say that Paul Tillich was the first great Christian theologian in history who tried to carry out a serious confrontation between Christianity and Buddhism at their depths.

I first met Dr Tillich one mid-September day in 1955 when I visited the Union Theological Seminary prior to my study there. Shaking hands with me, he appeared to me like a huge rock because of his broad shoulders and massive frame. Upon greeting him, however, I felt a kind of restlessness in him. Unlike his stout constitution, his eyes moved restlessly. This gave me an incomprehensible feeling.

Paul Tillich and Reinhold Niebuhr were two theologians with whom I particularly had wanted to study, so when I heard of Dr Tillich's transfer from Union to Harvard Divinity School that academic year I was disappointed. However, while at Union I occasionally visited Harvard to attend his lectures; and during my two years in America I never missed the sermons, lectures and the like that he often delivered in New York.

At his lectures his attitude was commanding and dignified; but when sitting on stage behind a speaker, as for example during a panel discussion, his eyes would wander and I would receive that same impression of uneasiness. From listening to him at various opportunities I came to think that the restlessness was perhaps related to his emphases on 'the risk of faith', 'doubt as an element of faith', 'courage to be' and the *'in spite of* nature of Christian faith'. It seemed the apparent restlessness had taken root deeply in his soul, an *esprit de finesse* involved in faith as 'courage to be'.

Tillich's *Systematic Theology* is as magnificent as a Gothic cathedral, yet is built strongly coloured with existential elements peculiar to the present day. It is built not on the basis of *analogia entis*, but through the method of *correlation* working in polar tension between existential questions and theological answers.

As Professor Jerald Brauer mentioned in his tribute given at a memorial service, and published in *Criterion*, Tillich was, as he described himself, a man who always lived on the boundaries, between the holy and the profane, philosophy and theology, religion and culture, Europe and America, and being and nonbeing. His faith, in terms of 'courage to be', and his *esprit de finesse*, somewhat coloured with restlessness, were inseparably connected with his own existential life. Polar tension and dynamic synthesis were characteristic of Paul Tillich both in his life and in his theology. It was this characteristic that drove him into an encounter between East and West and also led him to visit Japan, where he confronted Buddhism with his whole existence.

During his Japanese visit in 1960, he lectured at various universities and visited many Buddhist temples and Shinto shrines; he conversed with Buddhist scholars and Buddhist and Shinto priests as well as with Christian leaders and missionaries. For three weeks he stayed in Kyoto; during this time his conferences and meetings with Buddhist scholars, and his various temple visits, were carefully planned by Professors Nishitani, Takeuchi and other members of Kyoto University. As a member of the reception group I took Dr and Mrs Tillich to Daitokuji Temple, one of the head temples of the Rinzai Zen School, and to Tōji Temple of the Shingon School. At Daitokuji Dr Tillich seemed particularly to enjoy the tea ceremony performed by a Zen priest in a quiet tea-room of the temple. At Tōji he was apparently very much impressed by the esoteric atmosphere and the demonic expressions in the paintings and statues of that school. Under Dr Shin'ichi Hisamatsu's guidance he visited the rock garden of Ryōanji Temple and the monastery of Myōshinji Temple.

In his visits to Buddhist temples his attention was much attracted to the nature of Buddhist truth which he found expressed in Buddhist fine arts. His interest in the actual power of Buddhism in contemporary Japan, which was to him a most serious subject, was reflected in questions to Buddhist scholars on various occasions. At the meeting he had with Buddhist scholars at Otani University, for instance, he raised the following three questions: 'If some historian should make it probable that a man named Gautama never lived, what would be the consequence for Buddhism?' 'How is Buddhism "at the top", represented by the founders, priests, monks, theologians and so on, related to the popular beliefs of the ordinary adherents or followers of Buddhist teachings?' and 'To whom does a Buddhist pray, if he prays instead of meditating?'

The first question was asked from his long-standing concern about the problem of the historicity of Jesus. The second and third questions were directly connected with the actual religious experience in Buddhism. They referred to problems concerning the superstitious, mechanized and demonized experiences in Buddhism: they lead to the question: 'Is there in Buddhism any event which is comparable to the Reformation in Christianity, an attempt which bridges the gap between popular believers, who easily become superstitious, and the leading Buddhists, who have a clear realization of Buddhist truth?' Although Tillich discussed various theological, philosophical and practical problems, one of his basic interests was clearly this problem of demonization and its overcoming in Buddhism.

He was always open-minded and searching in his questions and discussions and Buddhist scholars responded to him wholeheartedly. My own impression, however, was that the communication was not always successful. He seemed to have felt he was not receiving satisfactory answers to his questions. Buddhists could not satisfactorily convey their basic ideas to him. Thus – as he expressed at a meeting in Kyoto – he was inclined to think that Buddhism, having had no experience of reformation, was therefore not liberated from demonization, a view which, I think, was not altogether correct. This probably stems partly from an insufficiency of communication through translation and partly from the fact that the Buddhist participants often represented different standpoints within Buddhism.

It surprised me to learn that after his return to America, he had talked about the impact he had received from Buddhism to the extent that he was sometimes suspected of having become a Buddhist. His deep and positive appreciation of Buddhism –

which if I am not mistaken was rather different from his evaluation of Buddhism in Kyoto – may be in part owing to his tender mind, whose quality was impressively expressed in words spoken in Kyoto: 'This is my analysis up until today, but it might be different tomorrow because the impressions come upon me like waves, and I may be wrong in this analysis.' The truth, though, might be that the experience of immersing himself in an actual Buddhist environment led him to become aware, in the last part of his stay in Japan and especially after his return to the United States, of the Buddhist reality.

His book *Christianity and the Encounter of the World Religions*, based on his Bampton Lectures at Columbia University, was the first publication expressing his encounter with Buddhism in a systematic way. I read it with great sympathy and appreciation in regard to his methodology as well as to his attempt at a 'Christian–Buddhist Conversation'. I also found him in this book going beyond the view he had expressed about Buddhism in Kyoto. Yet at the same time I noticed that in his 'Christian–Buddhist Conversation' Buddhism was still understood from a Christian perspective.

Professor Mircea Eliade's tribute, presented at the same memorial service for Dr Tillich, and later published in *Criterion*, struck me because in it he disclosed that Tillich had wanted to write 'a new *Systematic Theology*, oriented toward, and in dialogue with, the whole history of religions', and that this intention, combined with his renewed interest in History of Religions, emanated chiefly from his recent voyage to Japan. Indeed, with the death of Paul Tillich, Buddhism, and all world religions, have lost an irreplaceable dialogist and a truly great Christian theologian.

Part Three
Buddhism and Contemporary Theology

11

Beyond Buddhism and Christianity – 'Dazzling Darkness'

In his response 'God's Self-Renunciation and Buddhist Emptiness: A Christian Response to Masao Abe',[1] which is directed to my article 'Kenosis and Emptiness',[2] Hans Küng raises a number of crucial issues for Buddhist–Christian dialogue. Due to the restriction of space, however, I would like to limit myself to answering the following three issues which I believe to be the most essential. First, is Abe's approach a true dialogical hermeneutic? Second, is the idea of the kenosis of God Himself truly Christian? Third, is Śūnyatā the central concept of Buddhism?

I

In response to the first question, Hans Küng argues:

> There is no question: Masao Abe's basic intention is dialogic. He isolates key concepts from Christian texts which he then transplants into a Buddhist context, where the concept of kenosis is understood not simply as ethical, exemplary humiliation, but is recast as ontological emptying, an emptying of God, Himself, yes, ultimately as Emptiness in general, Śūnyatā. In this manner, as a Buddhist, he discovers his own world – even on the foreign, Christian soil. Just as the Christian authors earlier gave a Christian exegesis of Greek or Buddhist texts, so also Abe gives a Buddhist exegesis of the Christian texts.[3]

Hans Küng concludes that my interpretation of the kenotic passage in Philippians is 'a Buddhist exegesis of the Christian texts' in that it isolates key concepts from Christian texts and transplants them into a Buddhist context. Is this understanding of my interpretation of the hymn in Philippians (and the subsequent discussion of the kenosis of God) a fair and pertinent one? My basic intention in this regard is not to impose Buddhist categories upon the Christian context, then to give a 'Buddhist' exegesis of the Christian texts. Instead, I have tried to understand the Christian texts, in the present case the concept of kenosis, from within a Christian framework, as much as this is possible. Nevertheless, I have offered a new interpretation that differs from the traditional orthodoxy (a) because I cannot be completely satisfied with the traditional interpretation, and (b) because, in order to cope with the challenge by contemporary anti-religious ideologies, a new interpretation is urgently needed today. In this connection, I have tried to understand the Christian notion of kenosis by deepening the spirituality of Christianity without at the same time distorting Christianity. Careful readers of my interpretation,[4] I hope, will not fail to recognize this intention.

Although I am a Buddhist, I hope my readers will dispel the presupposition that my discussion and interpretation of Christianity is a 'Buddhist' exegesis. I sincerely hope that my discussion of Christianity will be judged not in terms of whether it is Buddhistic or not, but in terms of whether or not it is in accord with Christian spirituality. The interreligious dialogue may adequately and effectively take place if both sides of the dialogue try to grasp the other side's spirituality from within, without imposing its own ontological and axiological categories.

In my article 'Kenotic God and Dynamic *Śūnyatā*', which considers the Epistle to the Philippians (2: 5–8), I emphasized that 'Christ's kenosis (self-emptying) signifies a transformation not only in appearance but in substance, and implies a radical and total self-negation of the Son of God.'[5] I also argued that 'in the kenosis of Christ, it is not that the Son of God *became* a person through the process of his self-emptying, but that fundamentally Christ *is* a true human being and true God at one and the same time in his dynamic activity of self-emptying.'[6]

Taking one step further, I insisted that if Christ the Son of God empties himself, should we not consider the possibility of the self-emptying of God – that is, the kenosis of God the Father? Is it not that the kenosis of Christ – that is, the self-emptying of the Son of God – has its origin in God 'the Father' – that is, the kenosis of God? Without the self-emptying of God 'the Father', the self-emptying of the Son of God is inconceivable. This is why I stated:

> In the case of Christ, kenosis is realized in the fact that one who was in the form of God emptied 'himself' and assumed the form of a servant. It originated in the Will of God and the love of God which is willing to forgive even the sinner who has rebelled against God. It was a deed that was accomplished on the basis of God's *will*. On the other hand, in the case of God, kenosis is implied in the original *nature* of God, that is, 'love'.[7]

Criticizing Karl Rahner's understanding of the self-emptying of God as still leaving behind traces of dualism, I argued:

> If God is really unconditional love, the self-emptying must be total, not partial. It must not be that God *becomes something else* (Rahner's words) by partial self-giving, but that in and through total self-emptying God *is* something – or more precisely, God *is* each and every thing. This emphasis, however, should not be taken to signify pantheism. (See the following section.) On the contrary, only through this total kenosis and God's self-sacrificial identification with everything in the world is God truly God. Here we fully realize the reality and actuality of God, which is entirely beyond conception and objectification. This kenotic God is the ground of the kenotic Christ. The God who does not cease to be God even in the self-emptying of the Son of God, that is, the kenosis of Christ, is not the true God.[8]

This is the point of my understanding of the kenotic God. Does this understanding indicate, as Hans Küng suggests, that I take the concept of kenosis 'not simply as ethical, exemplary humiliation, but as *ontological* emptying, an emptying of God, Himself, yes, ultimately as Emptiness in general, *Śūnyatā*'?[9] Since the *nature* of God is *love*, an emphasis on the self-emptying of God as His dynamic nature does not necessarily indicate an 'ontological' interpretation at the expense of the 'ethical' meaning of the Son of God's self-emptying. And, in my understanding, I am *not* trying to 'replace'[10] the kenotic God of Christianity 'by the all-inclusive (dynamic) Emptiness (*Śūnyatā*) of Buddhism'[11] as Hans Küng suggests.

Everything in my understanding and interpretation of the idea of kenosis is based on the most fundamental tenet of Christianity, namely that 'God is love' (1 John 4: 8). If God is really all-loving, God does not have the Son of God emptying himself without God Himself ceasing to be God the Father. Again, if God is really an all-loving God, He is not self-affirmative but self-negating, not self-assertive but self-emptying, and becomes *das Nichts* by completely identifying Himself with everything in the universe, including the most sinful man. This understanding may not be the same as the traditional Christian understanding, but it is not correct to characterize it as a 'Buddhist' interpretation, as Hans Küng suggests, because my understanding arises from reflection on this central Christian definition, 'God is love.'

II

Secondly, is the kenosis of God Himself truly Christian?

Rejecting the notion of the kenosis of God as unbiblical, Hans Küng strongly maintains that:

> In the entire New Testament . . . nowhere is there mentioned an incarnation or a renunciation (kenosis) of God Himself; the Philippian hymn only speaks of a kenosis of Jesus Christ, the Son of God. Furthermore, this kenosis is not understood as a permanent status, position, relationship but as a humiliation occurring in a unique, historical life and death on the cross.[12]

It is clear that an explicit literal reference of kenosis can be found only in the Philippians passage. This does not, however, mean that the concept of kenosis is a limited or special one in the New Testament. 2 Corinthians 8: 9 conveys the same idea as the Philippians in its own words:

> For you know the grace of our Lord Jesus Christ, that though he was rich, yet for your sake he became poor, so that by his poverty you might become rich.

This idea of kenosis or condescension can also be found in John 3: 13, 16: 28, 17: 5, and Romans 15: 3. A New Testament scholar states, 'We should recognize that the *kenosis* motif is not confined to any one or two, or more passages, but is the underlying theme

of the New Testament. The very incarnation assumes a condescension.'[13]

The crucial issue of our present dialogue is not, however, the
kenosis of the Son of God, but the kenosis of God Himself. In this
regard, Hans Küng argues:

> Certainly, the self-sacrifice of the Son does not occur against the
> will of the Father. God desires the redemption of humanity and
> so also the self-sacrifice of Jesus. Still, God the Father does not
> give Himself up but His Son (the Church condemns the
> monophysitic 'patripassianism'), and so God the Father (*ho
> theos*) does not die upon the cross, but the man, Jesus of
> Nazareth, the Son of God. Only He, not God Himself, is (ac-
> cording to the dying words of Jesus quoting Psalm 22: 1
> [Vulgate 21: 1]) forsaken by God! Jesus being forsaken by God
> is, according to the New Testament, no divine 'paradox', but
> human agony crying to heaven.[14]

Thus Hans Küng's attitude toward the kenosis of God is basically
the same as that of the early Church. With this understanding of
God who is impassible and immutable how does Hans Küng
understand the problem of evil, especially the problem of the
Holocaust at Auschwitz? Due to the contemporary human pre-
dicament, the theological climate has been considerably changed.
In this regard we should not overlook the following remarks by
Karl Rahner, a leading Catholic theologian of our time.

> If it is said that the incarnate Logos died only in his human
> reality, and if this is tacitly understood to mean that this death
> therefore did not affect God, only half the truth has been stated.
> The really Christian truth has been omitted . . . Our 'possessing'
> God must repeatedly pass through the deathly abandonment
> by God (Matthew 27: 46; Mark 15: 4) in which alone God
> ultimately comes to us, because God has given himself in love
> and as love, and thus is realized, and manifested in his death.
> Jesus' death belongs to God's self-utterance.[15]

Through a uniquely trinitarian interpretation of the Christ event,
Jürgen Moltmann also emphasizes the death of God's Fatherhood
in the death of the Son.

When one considers the significance of the death of Jesus for God himself, one must enter into the inner-trinitarian tensions and relationship of God and speak of the Father, the Son and the Spirit.[16] The Christ event on the cross is a God event, and conversely, the God event takes place on the cross of the risen Christ. Here God has not just acted externally in his unattainable glory and eternity. Here he has acted in Himself and has gone on to suffer in Himself. Here He Himself is love with all His being. So the new Christology which tries to think of the death of Jesus as the death of God must take up the elements of truth which are to be found in *kenoticism* (the doctrine of God's emptiness of himself).[17]

In the forsakenness of the Son the Father also forsakes himself, though not in the same way . . . The Son suffers dying, the Father suffers the death of the Son. The grief of the Father here is just as important as the death of the Son. The fatherlessness of the Son is matched by the Sonlessness of the Father, and if God has constituted himself as the Father of Jesus Christ, then he also suffers the death of his Fatherhood to the death of the Son. Unless this were so, the doctrine of the trinity would still have a monotheistic background.[18]

Although I have some disagreement with and criticisms of Karl Rahner's and Jürgen Moltmann's interpretation of the kenosis of God (cf. pp. 15–26 in *The Emptying God*), I deeply sympathize with them because to me the kenosis of God as understood by them deeply accords with the spirituality of Christianity. In this regard, Hans Küng raises a very crucial question to the notion of the kenotic God, one which must be properly answered by a kenotic theologian.

The stumbling-block of a (Buddhist or Christian) Christology (and Trinitarian Doctrine) which completely identifies Jesus with God and brazenly declares Jesus' death to be the death of God is made strikingly clear in the case of the resurrection: such a Christology cannot explain who brought this supposedly dead God back to life.[19]

The answer is dependent on how the notion of kenosis is to be understood. If kenosis is merely understood as a humiliation or condescension in terms of self-emptying, the question that Küng raises above is naturally inevitable and its answer must be negative, i.e. there is no living God who could have brought Christ back to life. But the Philippian hymn clearly shows that kenosis includes not only the humiliation of the Son of God but also the *exaltation* of the Son of God. Precisely as a result of his humiliation, Christ was raised to a place higher than before. Thus, quoting the following words from *Interpreter's Bible*, Vol. 5, p. 50:

> The way he took was that of self-denial and entire obedience, and so acting he won his sovereignty.

I clearly recognized the inseparability of the state of humiliation and the state of exaltation in the event of Christ's death on the cross. Self-emptying is nothing but self-fulfilment. Thus my answer to the above question is affirmative: God the Father and God the Son glorify each other through an inverse correspondence, through an 'other-self affirmation via own-self negation'.

In this connection, we must not overlook the following passages in the book of Colossians, about which it is unclear how much attention Hans Küng pays in his current discussion.

> For in him (Christ) all the fullness (*pleroma*) of God was pleased to dwell. (1: 19.)

> For in him the whole fullness (*pleroma*) of deity (*theotetos*) dwells bodily. (2: 9.)

These passages clearly show the fullness of God dwells in Christ, especially in bodily form. It was God's pleasure that all of his fullness should dwell in Christ in order that through Christ, God might 'reconcile to himself all things, whether on earth or in heaven, making peace by the blood of his cross' (1: 20).

As I said earlier, in Jesus Christ the state of humiliation and the state of exaltation are inseparable; kenosis and pleroma are inseparable. Now the most crucial question is *how* they are inseparable. Does the state of humiliation come first and then the state of exaltation follow afterwards? Is kenosis a cause and pleroma an effect or result? Such a temporal or causal understanding of the inseparability of these twin sides of the same reality is nothing but a conceptualization or an objectification of the two

sides without existentially and religiously committing oneself to
the midst of the event. It is an outsider view, not an insider view.
For an insider, committing oneself religiously to faith in Jesus
Christ, the state of humiliation and the state of exaltation are not
two different states but a single, dynamic one; that is, humiliation
as it is is exaltation, and exaltation as it is is humiliation; kenosis
as it is is pleroma, and pleroma as it is is kenosis. Each pair in
these two sets of biconditional terms is dynamically non-dual
through mutual and simultaneously reciprocal negation. How is
this dynamic identity of the 'as-it-is-ness' of humiliation and
exaltation, kenosis and pleroma, possible? It is possible because
the dynamic identity is based on the kenotic God the Father, who
is self-emptying and unconditional love, and ultimately on the
Godhead who is neither *essentia* nor *substantia*, but *Nichts* or
Ungrund.[20]

Thus in my article 'Kenotic God and Dynamic *Śūnyatā*', in
concurrence with Moltmann, I stated as follows:

> The death of Jesus on the cross is not a divine-human event,
> but is most certainly a trinitarian event of the Father, the Son,
> and the Spirit. What is important in this regard is the total,
> personal aspect of the sonship of Jesus. The sonship of Jesus,
> however, is ultimately rooted in *Nichts* or *Ungrund* as the
> Godhead in 'the unity of three persons in one God.' Only
> here ... can we say with full justification – as Moltmann states
> – that 'in the Cross, Father and Son are most deeply separated
> in forsakenness and at the same time are most inwardly one
> in their surrender' (Moltmann: *The Crucified God*, p. 244). Again,
> only here – when the sonship of Jesus is understood to be
> ultimately rooted in *Nichts* as Godhead – can the event of the
> cross of Jesus be understood truly as the event of an uncon-
> ditioned and boundless love fully activated for the Godless or
> the loveless in this law-oriented society.[21]

In this way I understand Godhead as *Nichts* or *Ungrund* which
is exemplified by Christian mystics such as Meister Eckhart and
Jakob Böhme. Is my interpretation of God as *Nichts* 'a Buddhist
exegesis of the Christian texts',[22] or 'the renunciation of God
Himself in Buddhist *Śūnyatā*',[23] or a replacement of the kenotic
God 'by the all-inclusive (dynamic) Emptiness (*Śūnyatā*) of Bud-

dhism',[24] as Hans Küng suggests? (I also came to understand God as *Nichts* through my critique of Hans Küng's statement 'God in the Bible is subject and not predicate: it is not that the love is God, but that God is love – God is one who faces me, whom I can address' [cf. *The Emptying God*, pp. 25–6].)

III

At this point we must turn to the third question, that is, is *śūnyatā* the central concept of Buddhism? In this connection, Hans Küng raises (a) the question of Being and Nothingness, then (b) the problem of *śūnyatā* as Buddhism's ultimate Reality, and finally (c) the issue of an Eastern-Western understanding of God.

The question of being and nothingness

Referring to Hegel and Heidegger, Hans Küng points out an affinity and difference between them and Buddhism (cf. *Buddhist Emptiness and Christian Trinity*, pp. 35–7). Unfortunately, his point of discussion is not so clear to me. So I would like to present my own view of this question as follows: as Hans Küng correctly points out, for Hegel neither pure Being nor pure Nothing is true, and only Becoming as their unity (*Einheit*) or unseparatedness (*Ungetrenntheit*) is their truth. In his *Science of Logic*, Hegel argues:

> The truth is not their lack of distinction, but they are not the same, that they are absolutely distinct, and yet unseparated and inseparable, each disappearing immediately in its opposite. Their truth is therefore this movement, this immediate disappearance of the one into the other, in a word, Becoming: a movement wherein both are distinct, but in virtue of a distinction which has equally immediately dissolved itself.[25]

This is strikingly similar to the Buddhist understanding of Being and Nothing. However, as I pointed out elsewhere:[26]

> Despite Hegel's emphasis on the unseparatedness and material passing over (*übergehen*) of Being and Nothing, it cannot be overlooked that in his system Being is prior to Nothing. In

Hegel the beginning (*Anfang*) of everything is Being as such, and his dialectical movement develops itself in terms of Being (thesis), Nothing (antithesis) and Becoming (synthesis). In this way, Being as such is the supreme principle of Hegel's metaphysical logic. In so far as Being is thus given priority over Nothing, however dialectical 'Becoming' as the unity may be, it is not a genuine Becoming but a quasi-Becoming which is after all reducible to Being because in Hegel Becoming is a synthesis of Being and Nothing in which 'Being' is always the thesis. In addition, by asserting that there is a final synthesis, his system cuts off all further development: it swallowed up the future and time itself. For all its dynamically fluid, dialectical character, his system is consistently formulated in an irreversible, one-directional line with Being as the beginning.

By contrast, in Buddhism Being has no priority over Nothingness; Nothingness has no priority over Being. There is no irreversible relation between Being and Nothingness. Thus 'Becoming' – to use this term – in Buddhism is not a *synthesis* which presupposes duality of Being and Nothingness with priority given to Being, but is instead a complete *inter*dependence and *inter*penetration among everything in the universe – that is, *pratītya-samutpāda* or dependent co-origination. 'Becoming' in Buddhism is grasped in terms of *pratītya-samutpāda* and, as such, is completely free from irreversibility and from any sort of priority of either contrary, being or non-being, over the other. Dependent co-origination is not *Werden* in Hegel's sense, which is a synthesis of Being and its conceptual contrary, Nothing. Dependent co-origination is neither Being nor Nothing, nor even Becoming.

The problem of *Śūnyatā* as Buddhism's ultimate Reality

Hans Küng raises a very basic question which any Buddhist thinker must answer, that is, 'What is actually the highest truth, what is the ultimate Reality in Buddhism? Is it *śūnyatā* for all schools of Buddhism?'[27] Then he points out various paradigm shifts in the history of Buddhism from primitive Buddhism to the Mādhyamika and Yogācāra schools in which such key notions as *nirvāṇa*, *śūnyatā*, and *dharma-kāya* have been interpreted differently. This historical fact makes the question 'What is the ultimate Reality in Buddhism?', difficult.

In this connection we must first clearly realize an essential difference between Christianity and Buddhism in understanding 'ultimate Reality'. Christianity also underwent various paradigm shifts in its history, but the ultimate Reality has always been believed to be 'God'. And as Paul emphasizes, 'One God and Father of us all, who is above all and through all and in all' (Eph. 4: 6), God is believed to be 'one' absolute God. This monotheistic character of God is the underlying theme of all forms of Christianity regardless of their historical diversity. By contrast Buddhism is fundamentally free from having a monotheistic character. Rejecting the age-old Vedantic notion of Brahman as the sole reality underlying the phenomenal world, Gautama Buddha advanced the teaching of *pratītya-samutpāda*, that is, dependent co-origination in which everything in and out of the universe, without exception, is interdependent, co-arising and co-ceasing, and nothing exists independently. Even the ultimate does not exist by itself. Rather, this complete interdependency itself among everything in the universe is understood as 'ultimate Reality' in Buddhism. It is often called 'not one, not two' because it is neither monotheistic nor dualistic. The diversity within Buddhism is bigger than that in Christianity, because Buddhism has no single volume of canon like the Bible in Christianity, and instead of talking about one absolute God, Buddhism takes *pratītya-samutpāda* and *śūnyatā*, i.e. Emptiness, as the ultimate Reality.

The diversity of understanding of ultimate Reality in Buddhism should not be judged by Christian standards. It is rather natural in Buddhism that even such key concepts as *pratītya-samutpāda*, *nirvāṇa*, *śūnyatā* and *tathatā* (suchness) have been grasped differently.

Buddhism, and particularly Mahayana Buddhism, based on the idea of *śūnyatā* or *anātman*, developed itself freely and richly according to the spiritual climate of the time and place into which it was introduced. Thus, throughout its long history in India, China and Japan, Buddhism produced many divergent forms which are radically different from the original form of Buddhism preached by Śākyamuni. Nevertheless, they were not driven out from the Buddhist world, but became spiritual foundations from which new expressions of Buddhism emanated. In this connection it may be interesting to note that one Buddhist scholar regards the history of Buddhism as 'a history of heresy', meaning by this that Buddhism has developed itself by means of heresy and by continually embracing various heresies.

In the West, where Mahayana Buddhism in China and Japan is relatively unknown, people are apt to judge the whole of Buddhism by taking the 'original' form of Buddhism preached by Śākyamuni as their standard. Such a static view fails to appreciate the dynamic development of Buddhism. The diversity and profundity of the history of Buddhism, especially of Mahayana, is no less rich than the whole history of Western philosophy and religion. It is a development coming out of the inexhaustible spring of *śūnyatā* or *tathatā* (suchness). Yet, this 'history of heresy' in Buddhism has evolved without serious bloody inquisitions or religious wars. There is no equivalent to the European Crusades in the history of Buddhism.

Even though, as I said earlier, it is rather natural for Buddhists to employ such key concepts as *pratītya-samutpāda, nirvāṇa, śūnyatā* and *tathatā* differently at different times in the history of Buddhist thought, we must fully realize with Hans Küng that:

> there is no stifling the critical question – what is a Buddhist supposed to make of talk about an Ultimate Reality, when each and every thing is 'empty' and emptiness is somehow everything. Can we talk concretely, or do we have to go around in circles?[28]

Hans Küng correctly emphasizes that *śūnyatā* has to be seen in the context of the macroparadigm changes'[29] of Buddhist thought. Thus he refers to Nagarjuna's *Mādhyamaka-kārikā* and to the Yogācāra doctrine as the two main trends in the history of Mahayana Buddhism. In this connection, Hans Küng severely criticizes my approach to the issue of the Buddhist ultimate Reality.

> If I am not mistaken, Masao Abe did not propose Buddhist Ultimate Reality as all Buddhists would understand the term, but as it is understood in a very specific Buddhist paradigm: in the Mādhyamika as interpreted by a specific Zen philosophy.[30]

I admit the precision of his criticism and the limitation of my approach to the issue. I did not pay due attention to the Yogācāra doctrine and other schools of Buddhism particularly when I discussed *śūnyatā* as ultimate Reality in Buddhism. This is because I thought (and still do think) that with respect to the Buddhist–Christian dialogue in which we are now engaged, what is needed is not a detailed discussion of the doctrine of, say, *śūnyatā* within the various schools of Buddhism, but (a) a self-critical view of *śūnyatā* as the ultimate Reality underlying Mahayana Buddhism as a whole, and (b) that each participant in the Buddhist–Christian dialogue represent his or her own religion, not merely intellectually or as based on doctrine, but existentially as well. By doing so, each participant may spiritually clarify the essence of his/her religion through a personal existential commitment. Without speaking from such an existential commitment, the interfaith dialogue may be apt to be merely conceptual and superficial. A self-critical existential commitment on the part of each dialogue partner is essentially necessary because interfaith dialogue today must take place not merely between the two religions in question, but in the face of challenge by the current anti-religious ideologies prevailing in our society which seriously question the *raison d'être* of religion itself. My existential, and not merely intellectual, approach to interfaith dialogue probably gives Hans Küng the impression that 'Masao Abe did not propose Buddhist Ultimate Reality as all Buddhists would understand the term, but as it is understood in a very specific Buddhist paradigm: in the Mādhyamika as interpreted by a specific Zen philosophy.'[31]

Now, we must answer Hans Küng's basic question, what is ultimate Reality in Buddhism? Hans Küng himself rightly mentions two Buddhist options with regard to ultimate Reality. According to him, the first option is to understand 'Emptiness' with Nagarjuna and the Mādhyamikas as primarily *negative*, whereas the second option is, with the Yogācāra school, to interpret 'Emptiness' *positively*. It is true that Mādhyamika and Yogācāra understand 'Emptiness' differently, but I am afraid that it is an oversimplification to state, as Hans Küng does, that Mādhyamika understands Emptiness negatively whereas Yogācāra understands it positively.

In his book *Mādhyamika and Yogācāra*, Gadjin M. Nagao, a renowned Buddhologist of Japan today, states

Presently (by modern scholars) the Mādhyamika philosophy . . . is believed to be wholly inherited by Maitreyanātha, Asanga, and other Yogācāras. The *Prajñāpāramitā sūtras* are equally revered as authentic by both schools, and further, the doctrine of emptiness occupies an important position in the Yogācāra school.[32]

Of course Nagao recognizes the difference between Mādhyamika and Yogācāra in their understanding of *śūnyatā*:

... Is it proper to speak of the logical process involved in establishing *śūnyatā* as the same in both schools? Isn't it that, although the name *śūnyatā* is shared by both, what is intended by this name is entirely different in the two schools? For one thing, their points of departure differ: the Mādhyamika starts from *pratītya-samutpāda*, while the Yogācāra starts from *abhūta-parikalpa* (unreal imagination). Another remarkable difference is that the Yogācāra speaks of the 'existence of non-existence' when defining *śūnyatā*. We must also pay attention to the fact that, although both the Mādhyamikas and the Yogācāras are thought to base their idea of *śūnyatā* on the *Prajñāpāramitā sūtras*, the Yogācāras also place importance on the *Cūlasuññata-sutta* of the *Majjihima-nikāya*.[33]

Before becoming involved in the detailed discussion of the difference between Mādhyamika and Yogācāra, it is important for our purpose of answering the question, 'what is ultimate Reality in Buddhism?', to explore the true meaning of '*śūnyatā*' underlying both schools, Mādhyamika and Yogācāra, in contrast to Abhidharma's view of *śūnyatā*, which the Mahayana Buddhists tried to overcome.

In early Buddhism, the theory of dependent co-origination and the idea of emptiness were still naively undifferentiated. It was Abhidharma Buddhism which awakened to a particular philosophical understanding of emptiness and set it up in the heart of Buddhism. But the method of its process of realization was to get rid of concepts of substantiality by analyzing phenomenal things into diverse elements and thus advocating that everything is empty. Accordingly, Abhidharma Buddhism's philosophy of emptiness was based solely on *analytic* observation – hence it was later called the 'analytic view of emptiness'.[34] It did not have a total realization of the emptiness of phenomenal things. Thus the overcoming of the concept of substantial nature or 'being' was still not thoroughly carried through. Abhidharma fails to overcome the substantiality of the analyzed elements themselves.

But beginning with the *Prajñāpāramitā-sūtra*, Mahayana Buddhist thinkers transcended Abhidharma Buddhism's analytic view of emptiness, erecting the standpoint which was later called the 'view of substantial emptiness'.[35] This was a position which did not clarify the emptiness of phenomena by analysing them into elements; rather, it insisted that all phenomena were themselves empty in principle and that the nature of phenomenal existence itself is empty of substantial, perduring content. With respect to everything that is the *Prajñāpāramitā-sūtra* emphasizes: 'not being, and not not being'. 'Isness' is not to be equated with 'being', nor yet with the negation of 'being'. This sutra clarified not only the negation of being, but also the position of the double negation – the negation of non-being as the denial of being – or the negation of the negation. It thereby disclosed 'Emptiness' as free from both being and non-being. That is, it revealed *prajñā* – wisdom.

It was Nagarjuna who gave this standpoint of Emptiness as found in the *Prajñāpāramitā-sūtra* a thorough philosophical foundation by drawing out the implications of the mystical intuition seen therein and developing it into a complete philosophical realization. Nagarjuna criticized the proponents of substantial essence of his day who held that things really exist in a one-to-one correspondence with concepts. He said that they had lapsed into an illusory view which misconceived the real state of the phenomenal world. He insisted that with the transcendence of the illusory view of concepts, true Reality appears as *animitta* (no-form, or non-determinate entity). But Nagarjuna rejected as illusory not only this 'eternalist' view, which took the phenomena to be real just as they are, but also rejected the opposite 'nihilistic' view that emptiness and non-being are true reality. Nagarjuna thereby took the standpoint of Mahayana Emptiness, an independent standpoint liberated from every illusory point of view connected with either affirmation or negation, being or non-being, and called that standpoint the *Middle Way*.[36]

Nagarjuna's idea of the Middle Path does not indicate a mid-point between the two extremes as the Aristotelian idea of *to meson* might suggest. Instead, it refers to the way which *transcends every possible duality* including that of being and non-being, affirmation and negation. Therefore, his idea of Emptiness is not a mere emptiness as opposed to fullness. Emptiness as *śūnyatā* transcends and embraces both emptiness and fullness. It is really formless in the sense that it is liberated from both 'form' and 'formlessness'. Thus, in *śūnyatā*, Emptiness as it is, is Fullness, and Fullness as it is, is Emptiness, formlessness as it is, is form, and form as it is, is formless.[37]

Hence, the well-known passage in the *Prajñāpāramita-hrdaya-sūtra* – the *Heart Sutra*:

Form is emptiness and the very emptiness is form; emptiness does not differ from form; form does not differ from emptiness; whatever is form, that is emptiness; whatever is emptiness, that is form.[38]

As the *Heart Sutra* clearly indicates, the realization that 'form is emptiness', however important and necessary it may be, is not sufficient; it must be immediately accompanied with the realization that 'the very emptiness is form' and those two realizations are one, not two. In later Chinese Buddhism one encounters the saying 'True Emptiness is Wondrous Being'. This phrase indicates not only the dynamic identity of non-being and being, negation and affirmation, but also the recovery and re-establishment of being out of non-being.

In this connection, there are two more points which are important for adequately understanding the notion of *śūnyatā*. First, although *śūnyatā* is an ontological or metaphysical concept established by Nagarjuna to indicate the ultimate Reality, it is also unmistakably a practical and religious ideal. In Nagarjuna and Mādhyamika, as in Buddhism in general, meditation is of cardinal importance, and *Śūnyatā* or Emptiness was recognized as an object of meditation. The same is the case with respect to Yogācāra. As Nagao argues, 'The Yogācāra who, as the name suggests, was greatly concerned with yoga-praxis, inherited the Nagarjunian notion of Emptiness, and, when they elucidated features of yoga-praxis such as the six pāramitās, the ten bhūmis, and so on, Emptiness seems to have been the basis of their theories.'[39] Second, although the realization of Emptiness is essential one should not *cling to* Emptiness as Emptiness. This is why Mahayana Buddhism has throughout its long history rigorously rejected the attachment to Emptiness as a 'confused understanding of Emptiness', a 'rigid view of nothingness', or a 'view of annihilatory nothingness'. In order to attain true Emptiness, Emptiness must empty itself: Emptiness must become non-Emptiness (*aśūnyatā*). Since Emptiness is non-Emptiness it is ultimate Emptiness (*atyanta-śūnyatā*).[40]

Precisely because true Emptiness is Emptiness which 'empties' even itself, true Emptiness is absolute Reality which makes all phenomena, all existents, truly *be*, and stand forth. This is a

Buddhist answer to the question, 'Why is there anything at all, rather than nothing?'[41]

The existential realization that true Emptiness 'empties' itself indicates that ultimate Reality is not a static state which is objectively observable but a dynamic activity of *emptying* in which everyone and everything is involved. Indeed, there exists nothing whatsoever outside of this dynamic whole of *emptying*. You and I are involved in this dynamic whole of *emptying*. You are Emptiness and Emptiness is you.

Although the term *Śūnyatā* or Emptiness sounds negative, the true meaning of *Śūnyatā* is positive and affirmative. So *Śūnyatā* is regarded as the synonym for *Mahayamā pratipad* (The Middle Path), *Tathatā* (Suchness), *Dharma-kāya* (Body of Truth), and so forth. In the *Prajñāpāramitā-sūtra*, ultimate Reality is called *prabhāsvaram cittam* (the spotless, luminous, pure mind) and, in the latter Mādhyamika and Yogācāra Schools, *Śūnyatā* is compared with *prabhāsvaram cittam*.[42] I myself use the term 'boundless openness'[43] to make the point that *Śūnyatā* is completely free from any kind of centrism – not only from egocentrism but also from anthropocentrism, cosmocentrism and even theocentrism.

Boundless openness is unobjectifiable; 'it' cannot be thought to have a centre that occupies a position relative to other points on a perimeter, for there is no perimeter, and therefore no centre relative to a perimeter. It is like a circle whose centre is everywhere but whose circumference is nowhere, to borrow a well-known metaphor from Christian mysticism. The state of boundless openness is the state of complete emptyingness. When realized existentially, this state or standpoint is a complete emancipation from any kind of bondage resulting from discrimination based on any kind of centrism.

An Eastern-Western understanding of God

At the end of his response, 'God's Self-Renunciation and Buddhist Emptiness', Hans Küng seeks for a structural similarity between Buddhist 'Emptiness' and Christian 'pleroma' under the title 'An Eastern-Western Understanding of God'. I highly appreciate and share his *intention*, but I cannot completely agree with his *conclusions*.

Correctly understanding that *nirvāṇa*, Emptiness, and *Dharma-kāya* are parallel terms for the Buddhist conception of ultimate Reality, Hans Küng argues as follows:

Their function is analogous to that of the term 'God.' Would it, then, be wholly impermissible to conclude that what Christians call 'God' is present, under very different names, in Buddhism, insofar as Buddhists do not refuse, on principle, to admit any positive statement?[44]

I have no objection to this argument and, because I do not refuse, on principle, to admit any positive statements, I fully admit that 'what Christians call "God" is present, under very different names, in Buddhism.' But I have some reservation with respect to the remainder of his argument:

What is, according to Christianity, *the one infinite reality* [my emphasis] at the beginning, in the middle, and at the end of the world and humanity? . . . If God is truly the 'Ultimate Reality,' then God is *all these things in one*.[45]

Thus he mentions *nirvāṇa, Dharma, Emptiness* and *the primal Buddha* as Buddhistic parallels to the Christian notion of God. I must part from Hans Küng when he talks about God as 'the one infinite reality at the beginning, in the middle, and at the end of world and humanity', however. For it seems to me that Hans Küng believes that infinite or ultimate Reality must be *one*. (Elsewhere he talks about 'the question of the one true Ultimate Reality').[46] His Judeo-Christian understanding of Ultimate Reality is monistic or monotheistic. In Buddhism, however, the ultimate does not begin with a conception of *one* infinite reality but rather with the *denial* of the conception of one infinite reality. This is clearly seen from the fact that Gautama Buddha did not accept the age-old Vedantic notion of *Brahman* as the sole reality underlying the phenomenal universe and which is identical with *Ātman* as the unchangeable substantial self. Instead, the Buddha advocated *pratītya-samutpāda* or dependent co-origination and *Anātman* (no-self). The Buddha's doctrines constitute a rejection of monism or monotheism and imply an epistemic awakening to the boundless openness in which everything, including the one and the many, the divine and the human, is grasped as completely interdependent and interpenetrating. Because the Buddha was dissatisfied with monotheism as an expression of the nature of ultimate Reality, it is quite natural that the realization of *Śūnyatā* or Emptiness arose from this Buddhist context as the ultimate Reality beyond a monotheistic standpoint.

Buddhism is neither monistic nor monotheistic, neither poly-theistic nor pantheistic. Buddhism may be called *panentheism*, however, because immanence and transcendence are dynamically identical. The key point in this respect is that immanence and transcendence are identical through the negation of negation, that is the negation of immanence and the negation of transcendence. Transcendence and immanence, the one as opposed to the relative many, the finite and infinite, are diametrically opposed to each other and yet through the negation of negation, they are realized as dynamically identical. Ultimate Reality relates to itself through the bottomless ground of its own ultimacy or unconditionality by negating itself from within itself, by emptying itself of its own infinite unrelatedness and embracing the form of its own self-negation. The form of ultimate Reality's own unconditional self-negation exists or stands forth as its own mirror image and opposite, that is, as the relative many. This dynamic identity of the finite and infinite, of the transcendent and immanent, etc., is realized through the function of ultimate Reality's relating to itself through its own boundless openness or *Ungrund*. This func-tion is the principle of self-emptying of Emptiness itself, both within and through itself. This self-relating function is the unobjectifiable principle of the self-negation of ultimate Reality within and through its own timeless unobjectifiability. It is this dynamic principle of the self-negation of the boundless Whole within itself that sets up an 'inverse correspondence' between the two faces of this self-interrelating Whole, between, namely, the finite and infinite, or the primal one and the relative many. The dynamic identity of the finite and infinite, of the transcendent and immanent, etc., is realized through the inverse correspondence made possible through the realization of Emptiness that is beyond and yet inclusive of all conceptual binaries.

Inverse correspondence is not in any way a pantheistic concept; rather, it is a concept belonging to a functionalist ontology and takes its full meaning only alongside of the notion of the principle of self-transcendence *via* internal self-negation, or self-affirmation through self-negation, of the unobjectifiable Whole itself. This is what is meant by *dynamic Śūnyatā*.

Quoting Nicholas of Cusa's notion of *coincidentia oppositorum*, Hans Küng suggests a structural similarity between the Buddhist 'Emptiness' and the Christian 'pleroma'.[47] However, unless the Christian notion of 'pleroma' is freed from the monotheistic structure, I do not see 'a structural similarity' between 'Emptiness' and 'pleroma', even though both concepts can be said to transcend and embrace all opposites in their respective manner. As I said before, 'Emptiness' as the ultimate Reality in Buddhism is not monotheistic, nor pluralistic, nor pantheistic. But the Buddhist notion of ultimate Reality is panentheistic in that immanence and transcendence are totally and dynamically identical through mutual negation. Through 'trans-descendence', ultimate Reality is at once inter-relational and boundlessly open in all directions. There is no single centre in any sense – even in the theocentric sense – and thus '*coincidentia oppositorum*' is fully and completely realized. 'Emptiness' is not the one infinite reality nor one absolute God but *Nichts* in the sense of the absolute Nothingness which is beyond and yet embraces both being and nothingness. It is right here that everything, including all of nature, human, non-human and divine, is realized just as it is, each in its individual and relational suchness.

On the other hand, in Christianity, the real 'pleroma' or 'fullness' of God is identical with the real 'kenosis' or 'self-emptying' of God Himself, a kenosis which is total, not partial. Only through the realization of the total kenosis of God Himself is the real 'pleroma' of God fully realized.

Only in the kenotic God can kenosis as-it-is be dynamically one with pleroma, and pleroma as-it-is be dynamically united with kenosis. Only in the kenotic God can humiliation as-it-is be exaltation, and exaltation as-it-is be humiliation. I believe that this dynamic identity of kenosis and pleroma indicates the ultimate Reality in Christianity. However, if the notion of kenosis is applicable only to the Son of God, but not to God Himself, that is to say, if God is understood *not* to empty Himself even in the self-emptying of the Son of God, then the above dynamic identity of kenosis and pleroma, humiliation and exaltation, cannot be fully realized. 'Ultimate Reality' is then only realized to a limited sense, unless grasped in its essential activity of total self-abnegation or self-immolation for the sake of being 'all-in-all'. Otherwise, 'ultimate Reality' still retains a monotheistic sense and is only one-sidedly transcendent. However, if one breaks through the monotheistic framework and realizes the kenosis of God Himself, the ultimate Reality as the dynamic identity of kenosis and pleroma is fully realized. It is right here that the basic tenet of Christianity, 'God is love', is completely fulfilled. Once freed from its monotheistic and theocentric character, Christianity not only becomes more open to interfaith dialogue and cooperation without the possibility of falling into exclusivism, but it also becomes compatible with autonomous reason that is peculiar to modern humanity and it will be able to cope with the challenge presented by Nietzschean nihilism and atheistic existentialism. The future task of Christianity is to open up the monotheistic framework through the full realization of the kenosis of God Himself and to realize the ultimate Reality as the dynamic unity of kenosis and pleroma.

The dialectic identity of kenosis and pleroma, self-emptying and self-fulfilment, may be compared with 'dazzling darkness', a term employed by Pseudo-Dionysius the Areopagite.[48] It does not mean that God as the ultimate Reality is half dazzling and half dark. Instead, it indicates that God is fully dazzling and fully dark at one and the same time. That is to say, being dazzling as-it-is is darkness; being dark as-it-is is dazzling. This dialectical identity as the ultimate Reality is possible only when God is understood to be completely kenotic or self-emptying and not One as a monotheistic unity, nor one nor two nor three but as *Nichts* or *Ungrund*.

Now with respect to Buddhism, the traditional static view of *śūnyatā* must also be broken through and interpreted dynamically – not as the static *state* of emptiness, but as the dynamic *activity* of emptying everything, including itself. In *śūnyatā*, form is ceaselessly emptied, turning into formless emptiness, and formless emptiness is ceaselessly emptied, and therefore forever freely taking form. For this reason the *Prajñāpāramitā-sūtra* emphasizes:

Form is Emptiness and the very Emptiness is form.

Here we may also quote the Mahayana Buddhist expression: '*Saṃsāra* as-it-is is *nirvāṇa; nirvāṇa* as-it-is is *saṃsāra.*' These statements are nothing but verbal expressions of the Buddhist ultimate Reality which may very well be compared with 'dazzling darkness'. Darkness (*saṃsāra*) as-it-is is dazzling (*nirvāṇa*); the Dazzling (*nirvāṇa*) as-it-is is darkness (*saṃsāra*). Again, in order to properly understand to Buddhist ultimate Reality as 'dazzling darkness', one must clearly realize 'self-emptying Emptiness' by breaking through the traditional static view of *Śūnyatā*. The future task of Buddhism is to realize how this self-emptying Emptiness concentrates itself into a single centre in the boundless openness, a centre which is the locus of the real manifestation of a personal deity and the ultimate criterion of ethical judgment and value judgment in general.[49] As Hans Küng rightly states, 'every statement about Ultimate Reality would . . . have to pass through the dialectic of negation and affirmation. Every experience of Ultimate Reality would have to survive the ambivalence of nonbeing and being, dark night and bright day.'[50] In full agreement with his statement, I would like to present the idea of 'dazzling darkness' as the common symbol of the ultimate Reality in Buddhism and Christianity, the meaning of which can be realized only by going beyond the traditional formulations of the doctrines and practices of both Buddhism and Christianity.

God is 'dazzling darkness'
because in God, who is the infinite love,
self-emptying as-it-is is self-fulfilment,
self-fulfilment as-it-is is self-emptying.

Śūnyatā is 'dazzling darkness'
because in *Śūnyatā*, which is boundless openness,
saṃsara as-it-is is *nirvāṇa*,
nirvāṇa as-it-is is *saṃsara*.

Notes

The author is grateful to Mr David Cockerham, who revised the manuscript and gave valuable suggestions at its final stage.

1. Hans Küng, 'God's Self-Renunciation and Buddhist Emptiness: A Christian Response to Masao Abe', in Roger Corless and Paul F. Knitter (eds), *Buddhist Emptiness and Christian Trinity* (New York: Orbis Books, 1990), pp. 26–43.
2. Masao Abe, 'Kenosis and Emptiness', in *Buddhist Emptiness and Christian Trinity*, op. cit., pp. 5–25.
3. Küng, *Buddhist Emptiness and Christian Trinity*, op. cit., p. 34.
4. Masao Abe, 'Kenotic God and Dynamic Sunyata', in John Cobb and Christopher Ives (eds), *The Emptying God: A Buddhist-Jewish-Christian Conversation* (New York: Orbis, 1990), pp. 3–65. 'Kenotic God and Dynamic Sunyata' is a revised and expanded version of 'Kenosis and Emptiness.'
5. *The Emptying God*, op. cit., p. 10.
6. Ibid.

7. Ibid., p. 14.
8. Ibid., p. 16.
9. Küng, *Buddhist Emptiness and Christian Trinity*, op. cit., p. 34.
10. Ibid., p. 33.
11. Ibid.
12. Ibid.
13. Jennings B. Reid, *Jesus, God's Emptiness, God's Fullness: The Christology of St. Paul* (New York: Paulist Press, 1990), p. 67.
14. Küng, *Buddhist Emptiness and Christian Trinity*, op. cit., pp. 33–4.
15. Karl Rahner, *Sacramentum Mundi*, Vol. 2 (London: Burns & Oates, 1969), pp. 207f.
16. Jürgen Moltmann, *The Crucified God: The Cross of Christ as Foundation and Criticism of Christian Theology* (New York: Harper & Row, 1974), p. 204.
17. Ibid., p. 205.
18. Ibid., p. 243.
19. Küng, *Buddhist Emptiness and Christian Trinity*, op. cit., p. 34.
20. *The Emptying God*, op. cit., p. 26.
21. Ibid., p. 25.
22. Küng, *Buddhist Emptiness and Christian Trinity*, op. cit., p. 34.
23. Ibid.
24. Ibid., p. 33.
25. *Science of Logic*, trans. by W.H. Johnston and L.G. Struthers (London: G. Allen & Unwin, 1929), Vol. I, p. 95 (*Wissenschaft der Logik*, herausgeben von Georg Lasson (Leipzig: Felix Meiner, 1923), p. ß, Erster Teil, p. 67).
26. Masao Abe, *Zen and Western Thought* (Honolulu: Univ. of Hawaii Press, 1985), p. 53.
27. Küng, *Buddhist Emptiness and Christian Trinity*, op. cit., p. 37.
28. Ibid., p. 39.
29. Ibid.
30. Ibid.
31. Ibid.
32. Gadjin M. Nagao, *Mādhyamika and Yogācāra* (New York: SUNY Series on Buddhist Studies, 1991), p. 189.
33. Ibid., p. 199.
34. In the T'ién-t'ai Sect, the view of emptiness of Hinayana Buddhism is called the 'analytic view of emptiness', and the view of emptiness in Mahayana Buddhism is called the 'view of substantial emptiness'.
35. See note 34 above.
36. The above passages on Abhidharma and Mahayana philosophy are taken from Abe, *Zen and Western Thought*, op. cit., pp. 93–4, with some adaptation.
37. Abe, *Zen and Western Thought*, op. cit., p. 127.
38. *Prajñāpāramitā-hrdaya-sūtra*, Taishō, 8:848.
39. Nagao, op. cit., pp. 51–2.
40. *Prajñāpāramitā-sūtra*, Taishō, 8:250b.
41. Küng, *Buddhist Emptiness and Christian Trinity*, op. cit., p. 40.

42. *Madhyānta vibhāga*, 1.22c.
43. Abe, *The Emptying God*, op. cit., p. 30.
44. Küng, *Buddhist Emptiness and Christian Trinity*, op. cit., p. 42.
45. Ibid.
46. Ibid., p. 41.
47. Ibid., pp. 42–3.
48. *Pseudo-Dionysius, the Complete Works*, trans. by Colm Luibheid (New York: Paulist Press, 1987), pp. 135–7. Evelyn Underhill, *Mysticism* (New York: New American Library, 1974), p. 347.
49. Abe, 'Free Will and the Ultimate Criterion of Value Judgment in Sunyata', in *The Emptying God*, op. cit., pp. 55–9.
50. Küng, *Buddhist Emptiness and Christian Trinity*, op. cit., p. 43.

12

Thomas J.J. Altizer's Kenotic Christology and Buddhism

I

At the second conference on East-West Religious Encounter, 'Paradigm Shifts in Buddhism and Christianity', held in Honolulu, January 1984, I delivered a paper entitled 'Kenotic God and Dynamic *Śūnyatā*'. In that paper, referring to Paul's christological hymn in Philippians 2: 5–11 I stated that the kenosis or self-emptying of Christ Jesus is a key notion expressing well the loving God in Christianity and providing a point of contact with the Buddhist notion of *śūnyatā*. At the same time I also stated that, properly speaking, the kenosis of the Son of God is inconceivable without the kenosis of God the Father. If God is truly the all loving God, He, God the Father, must be self-emptying. The kenosis of Christ has its origin in the kenosis of God. On the other hand, the Buddhist notion of *śūnyatā* should not be understood to indicate a static state of everything's emptiness, but should be taken to signify the dynamic activity of emptying everything including itself. *Śūnyatā* in Mahayana Buddhism is no less than formless emptiness taking form freely through emptying itself. My suggestion was that if we interpret the Christian notion of Christ's kenosis and the Buddhist notion of *Śūnyatā* in such a way, Christianity and Buddhism would come to a point of much closer contact, not by losing their self-identities but rather through deepening their spirituality. After the Hawaii Conference I considerably enlarged and developed the paper by discussing Karl Rahner's notion of the self-emptying God and Jürgen Moltmann's notion of the crucified God.

In this presentation I would like to discuss Thomas J.J. Altizer's notion of kenotic Christology from my Buddhist point of view in the hope that my discussion will make a little clearer how a point of contact between Christianity and Buddhism is possible through the notions of kenosis and *śūnyatā*. First, I will try briefly to explain Altizer's notion of kenotic christology. And then, secondly, I would like to elucidate his appreciation and criticism of Buddhism and to present my own response to his critique.

II

First, let us consider Altizer's notion of kenotic Christology. In his early book, *The Gospel of Christian Atheism*,[1] Altizer criticizes Christian Scholasticism which following Aristotle defined God as *actus purus* or *causa sui*, and strongly rejects 'a distant and nonredemptive God who by virtue of his very sovereignty and transcendence stands wholly apart from the forward movement and historical presence of the Incarnate Word'. He takes Nietzsche's words 'God is dead' as the point of departure for his kenotic theology and states:

> Only by accepting and even willing the death of God in our own experience can we be liberated from a transcendent beyond, an alien beyond which has been emptied and darkened by God's self-annihilation in Christ.

This means that Altizer understands the 'death of God' as signifying the act of kenosis whereby God fully 'empties Himself' into the world such that he pours out His total transcendence into total immanence.

In this regard Altizer himself states:

> The Incarnation and Crucifixion are understood as a dual process, a kenotic or negative process whereby God negates his primordial and transcendent epiphany thereby undergoing a metamorphosis into a new and immanent form.

Second, let us consider Altizer's appreciation and critique of Buddhism. The distinctiveness of Thomas Altizer as a theologian lies in the fact that since the time of his doctoral work he has focused upon Mahayana Buddhist philosophy to reconstruct

Christian theology. In the preface of his most recent book, *History as Apocalypse*,[2] he states:

> If [Mahayana Buddhist philosophy] provided an initial arena for exploring a persuasion that I then adopted and have never abandoned, the conviction that Christian theology can be reborn only by way of an immersion in Buddhism, perhaps no principle offers a deeper way into our lost epic and theological tradition than does the Mahayana Buddhist dialectical identification of Nirvana and Samsara.

We should, however, not overlook that, despite this great appreciation of Mahayana Buddhism, Altizer is highly critical of certain aspects of Buddhism. His critique of Buddhism and Oriental mysticism is most clearly articulated in the first chapter of his book, *The Gospel of Christian Atheism*, entitled 'The Uniqueness of Christianity'. He states:

> Whereas the prophetic faith of the Old Testament and the primitive faith of Christianity were directed to a future and final end, and thus are inseparable from a forward-moving and eschatological ground, the multiple forms and Oriental mysticism revolve about a backward movement to the primordial totality, a process of cosmic and historical involution wherein all things return to their pristine form.

In his relatively recent book *The Descent into Hell*,[3] Altizer also emphasizes, 'If Buddhism is a way back to a full recovery and total embodiment of a primordial All, then Christianity is a way forward to a final and eschatological realization of that All.'

III

When Altizer contrasts Buddhism and Judeo-Christian tradition in terms of backward movement and forward movement he seems to presuppose a linear view of time and history. Hence he talks about the primordial beginning and the eschatological end. Buddhism is grasped by Altizer on the basis of that linear view of time and history and as involving a backward-moving process of returning to a primordial beginning or original paradise. In

Buddhism, however, time and history are understood entirely without beginning and without end. Since time is beginningless and endless it is not considered to be linear as in Christianity or circular as in non-Buddhist Oriental mysticism. Being neither linear nor circular, time is understood in Buddhism to be not irreversible, but reversible, and yet time moves from moment to moment, each moment embracing the whole process of time.

This view of time is inseparably linked with the Buddhist view of life and death. Buddhism does not regard life and death as two different entities, but one indivisible reality, that is 'living-dying'. For if we grasp our life not objectively from the outside, but subjectively from within, we are fully living and fully dying at each and every moment. There is no living without dying and no dying without living. Accordingly we are not moving from life to death, but are involved in the process of living-dying, that is, *saṃsāra*.

Further, the process of our living-dying is without beginning and without end. The process extends itself beyond our present life both into the direction of the remote past and into the direction of the distant future. (This is the reason, for example, that Zen raises the traditional question: 'What is your original face before your parents were born?' as well as the question: 'When your physical body is decomposed, where do you go?') Due to the absence of God as the creator and the ruler of the universe, in Buddhism there is no beginning in terms of creation and no end in terms of last judgment. Accordingly, we must realize the beginninglessness and endlessness of *saṃsāra* as 'death' in the absolute sense, not as a relative death, but as *Great Death*. This realization of Great Death is essential because it provides a way to overcome *saṃsāra* and to turn it into *nirvāṇa*. For if we clearly realize the beginning*less*ness and endless*ness* of the process of living-dying *at this moment*, the whole process of living-dying *is concentrated in this moment*. In other words, this moment embraces the whole process of living-dying by virtue of the clear realization of the beginninglessness and endlessness of the process of living-dying. Here, in this point, we can overcome *saṃsāra* and realize *nirvāṇa* right in the midst of *saṃsāra*. Hence, *saṃsāra* and *nirvāṇa* are dynamically identical.

Though often misunderstood, Buddhism, especially Mahayana Buddhism, does not teach one to escape from living-dying and to enter into *nirvāṇa* by not dwelling in *saṃsāra*, but to return to the world of *saṃsāra* by *not dwelling even in nirvāṇa*. To enter into *nirvāṇa* and yet not remain there, but to sojourn in the garden of living-dying, that is free movement from *saṃsāra* to *nirvāṇa*, from *nirvāṇa* to *saṃsāra* – that is *true nirvāṇa*.

Accordingly, the Mahayana emphasis that '*saṃsāra* is *nirvāṇa*' does not mean that *saṃsāra* is simply identical with *nirvāṇa*. Rather, *saṃsāra* is thoroughly *saṃsāra*; *nirvāṇa* is thoroughly *nirvāṇa*. When it is, however, truly subjectively or existentially realized that *saṃsāra* is living-dying at each and every moment, and that no moment can be objectified or substantialized, then *saṃsāra* is transcended from within and turns into *nirvāṇa* at each and every moment. Just as *saṃsāra* is essentially '*saṃsāra* of the moment', *nirvāṇa* is fundamentally '*nirvāṇa* of the moment'. If that were not the case, then *nirvāṇa* itself would be substantialized. *Saṃsāra* ceaselessly turns into *nirvāṇa* because it is *saṃsāra* of the moment. *Nirvāṇa* ceaselessly returns to *saṃsāra* precisely because it is *nirvāṇa* of the moment. *Saṃsāra* and *nirvāṇa* are thus united and interpenetrated through mutual negation at each moment. The moment is the place where we are born and die in actual reality and wherein the infinite past and the infinite future are self-consciously included and self-consciously transcended. All of the past, present and future are transcended precisely in the moment of the 'now'. Yet, as long as the moment is the moment, there is transition from moment to moment. While each moment is thoroughly independent in itself, there is endless passage. That, however, is not a simple immediate continuity but a discontinuous continuity, that is, a continuity through the realization of discontinuity at each moment.

IV

This is the Buddhist view of time and history, and Buddhist movement is based on this view. Accordingly, Thomas Altizer's view of Buddhism revolving about a backward movement to primordial totality is, unfortunately, a gross misunderstanding. Buddhism does not simply move backward or forward. It transcends the very dimension of backward and forward movement by realizing the beginninglessness and endlessness of the process of time and history. This realization of the beginninglessness and endlessness of time and history is no less than the realization of the emptiness or non-substantiality of time and history. Not only all being, but also all time, is self-emptying. If I am not mistaken, in Christianity secular time is understood to be empty and without substance. But sacred time, in which God works, is understood not as empty or non-substantial but as real. Accordingly, *kairos* at a particular point of history is emphasized, for example creation as the sacred beginning, redemption on the cross as the centre of history, and the last judgment as the divine end. It is thus natural for Christian faith to be directed to a future and final end, and Christianity is inseparable from a forward-moving and eschatological ground.

From the Buddhist point of view, however, not only secular time but also sacred time is empty, that is, without substance, without its own being. This is why Mahayana Buddhism strongly rejects attachment to *nirvāṇa*, which would entail substantialization of *nirvāṇa* by emphasizing 'Do not dwell in *nirvāṇa*', however sacred *nirvāṇa* may be. When the sacred time is substantialized somewhat apart from the secular time, as in Christianity, and *kairos* is realized only at particular points of time, the total dialectical identification of transcendence and immanence emphasized by Altizer is inconceivable. Furthermore, an emphasis on forward-movement to a final eschatological ground may cause each moment of time to be a mere step or means toward the future end, losing its independent uniqueness. As I said before, in Mahayana Buddhism, the dynamic identification of *saṃsāra* and *nirvāṇa* is realized at each and every moment and it is so realized by the clear realization of the emptiness of *nirvāṇa* (sacred time) as well as the emptiness of *saṃsāra* (secular time). If Altizer recognizes and appreciates the identification of *saṃsāra* and *nirvāṇa* from his kenotic christological point of view, as he proposes to do, how is it possible for him to talk about Buddhism as a backward movement to a primordial beginning? If his characterization of Buddhism as a backward movement to a primordial beginning is clearly and seriously intended, then his appreciation of the identification of *saṃsāra* and *nirvāṇa* is undercut.

V

If Altizer's kenotic Christology intends to be as consistent as possible in terms of God's self-emptying, it must realize the emptiness of even sacred time and overcome the forward movement toward the eschatological ground. Then how is the forward movement toward the future that is essential to time and history realized in Buddhism?

The Buddhist notion of *śūnyatā* has two aspects, wisdom and compassion. In the wisdom aspect of *śūnyatā*, everything is realized in its suchness, in its fullness, and time is overcome. This realization is possible by returning to the ontological origin of history. However, in the light of compassion, also realized in *śūnyatā*, time is religiously significant and essential. This is because, although all things and all people are realized in their suchness and fullness in the light of wisdom *for an awakened one,* those who are *'unawakened'* have not yet realized this basic reality. Many beings still consider themselves unenlightened and deluded. Such people are innumerable at present and will appear endlessly in the future. The task for an awakened one is to help these people also to 'awaken' to their suchness and fullness. This is the compassionate aspect of *śūnyatā* which can be actualized only by emptying the wisdom aspect of *śūnyatā*. As the generation of 'unawakened' beings will never cease, this process of actualizing the compassionate aspect of *śūnyatā* is endless. Here the forward movement of history toward the future is necessary and comes to have a positive significance.

In the Buddhist *śūnyatā*, these two aspects of wisdom and compassion are inseparable. Accordingly in any moment of the beginningless and endless process of history, to move forward toward the future is nothing but to return to the ontological origin of history, and to return to the ontological origin of history is identical with moving forward toward the future.

Accordingly, the Buddhist view of history based on the realization of *śūnyatā* is not eschatological or teleological in the Christian or Western sense. If we use the term eschatology, the Buddhist view of history is a completely realized eschatology, because in the light of wisdom everything and everyone without exception is realized in its suchness and fullness, and time is thereby overcome. If we use the term teleology, the Buddhist view of history is an open teleology because in the light of compassion the process of awakening others in history is endless. And a completely realized eschatology and an entirely open teleology are dynamically united in this present moment, now. This is the view of history of a kenotic Buddhology.

Notes

1. Thomas J.J. Altizer, *The Gospel of Christian Atheism* (Philadelphia: Westminster, 1966).
2. Altizer, *History as Apocalypse* (Albany: SUNY Press, 1985).
3. Altizer, *The Descent into Hell: A Study of the Radical Reversal of Christian Consciousness* (Philadelphia: Lippincott, 1970).

13

Zen Buddhism and Hasidism – Similarities and Contrasts

It is a great pleasure and honour for me to have been invited by the Hillel Council to talk on Zen Buddhism and Hasidism for my Jewish friends. The first Jewish Rabbi whom I met in my life was Rabbi Polyeff who at that time, in 1954, was a chaplain of the United States forces in Otsu near Kyoto, and who lived next door to my house. For more than one half year, Chaplain Polyeff and I visited with each other every week, teaching Judaism and Buddhism to each other. In 1955, he returned to the US and I also came to this country to study at Columbia University and Union Theological Seminary for two years. In New York I became acquainted with many Jewish people. The most important event in this connection was that I was invited to attend the week-long seminar at Columbia on Judaism and Christianity at which Martin Buber was a key speaker. After the seminar was completed, I visited Martin Buber at his apartment with D.T. Suzuki, my teacher, who was then lecturing on Zen Buddhism at Columbia. It was really an unforgettable evening for me because I could join in this illuminating conversation between two great religious thinkers of our time. In my personal contacts with Martin Buber, though brief, I was strongly impressed by a lively spirit of Hasidism embodied in Buber's own personality. Because of these unforgettable impressions of Martin Buber and this fifteen years of friendship with Jewish people I gladly accepted the invitation extended to me by Dr Benjamin Weininger and Rabbi Henry Rabin to talk on Zen and Hasidism as interpreted by Martin Buber.

I would like to talk about similarities and contrasts in Hasidism (interpreted by Buber) and Zen as honestly and precisely as I am able. In his book *The Way of Man* Martin Buber says:

159

Some religions do not regard our sojourn on earth as true life. They either teach that everything appearing to us here is mere appearance, behind which we should penetrate, or that it is only a foretaste of the true world, a gate through which we should pass without paying much attention to it. Judaism, on the contrary, teaches that what a man does now and here with holy intent is no less important, no less true – being a terrestrial indeed, but none the less factual, link with divine being – than the life in the world to come. This doctrine has found its fullest expression in Hasidism.[1]

These words, just as they are, can, in my view, be applied to Zen. This view seems to be supported by Buber himself when he says in another book, *The Origin and Meaning of Hasidism*:

We must consider afresh what seemed most clearly to us to be common to Zen and Hasidism, the positive relationship to the concrete. We have seen that in both the learning and developing man is directed to things, to sensible being, to activity in the world.[2]

Here Buber points out the 'positive relationship to the concrete' as the clearest thing in common to Zen and Hasidism. I think his idea of 'the positive relationship to the concrete' implies at least the following two points: first, everyone should begin by depending on him or herself rather than others; second, everyone must live here and now in this world rather than anticipating a more real life beyond this world. When we carefully examine Hasidism and Zen in respect to these two points we will, I hope, clearly see similarities and contrasts between the two religious traditions. Due to the limitation of time I will discuss only the first point. Let me discuss the theme that everyone should begin with him or herself.

All of you will remember the story of Rabbi Eizik who travelled to Prague to look for the treasure revealed to him in a dream. You recall how, after much effort, he dug up the treasure from beneath the stove of his own home. Buber, commenting on this story, said:

There is something that can only be found in one place. It is a great treasure, which may be called the fulfillment of existence. The place where this treasure can be found is the place on which one stands.

Then Buber goes on to say:

We nevertheless feel the deficiency at every moment, and in some measure strive to find – somewhere – what we are seeking. Somewhere, in some province of the world or of the mind, except *where we stand*, where we have been set – but it is there and nowhere else that the treasure can be found.

Zen says exactly the same thing. It says 'That which comes in from the outside is not a home-treasure.'

Zen often stresses that one should not seek Buddha externally. In the *Discourse on the Direct Lineage of the Dharma*, attributed to Bodhidharma, we read:

Topsy-turvy beings do not know that the Self-Buddha is the True Buddha. They spend the whole day in running to and fro, searching outwardly, contemplating Buddhas, honoring Patriarchs, and looking for the Buddha somewhere outside of themselves. They are misdirected. Just know the Self-Mind! Outside of this Mind there is no other Buddha.

In Buddhism, Buddha means 'an Enlightened One' or 'an Awakened One'. Accordingly, Buddha does not mean something supernatural, nor something heavenly. Buddha is nothing but one who becomes enlightened or awakened to *Dharma*, that is, the Truth. The historical Buddha, Śākyamuni Buddha, was the *first* one who awakened to the Truth. However, anyone can become a Buddha, just as Śākyamuni did, if one follows the same path. Zen asserts emphatically that the *Dharma* to which one should awaken is not simply universal truth, but one's own true nature, i.e., one's true Self. In Zen true Buddha means true Self. Now, when Zen stresses that one should not seek Buddha externally what does it really mean? In this respect is Zen exactly the same as Hasidism? The words 'Do not seek for Buddha externally' seem to mean one should seek Buddha internally, i.e. inside of one's mind. Also, we ourselves may, in fact, try to do so. It a sense, it is a necessary and required direction. Even when, however, Buddha is sought for internally or inside of oneself, in so far as Buddha *is sought for*, it must be said that Buddha is looked for externally. For, whether outside or inside of ourselves, the very act of 'seeking for' has, in its essence, the nature of an external act. 'Seeking for' itself already presupposes something external. Therefore the words 'Do not seek Buddha externally' may be understood in the following two ways.

First, the words 'Do not seek Buddha externally' do *not* simply mean 'Seek Buddha internally rather than externally,' because here one is still confined by the distinction of internal and external. The internal as discriminated from the external cannot be said to be the true internal. The true internal is the internal which is beyond the distinction between the internal and the external and which is liberated from that distinction itself. It is not the internal as the counterconcept to the external, but *the internal of the internal*. To realize the internal of the internal is to realize one's true Self through that complete negation of one's ego which Zen calls Great Death.

Secondly, the words 'Do not seek Buddha externally' really mean no less than 'do not seek Buddha at all' because 'externally' in this case is not 'externally' in a spatial or relative sense, but in the entirely essential or absolute sense. 'To seek for' implies 'to objectify'. The Buddha as an object to be attained, even sought for inside ourselves, is not, for Zen, the true Buddha. As soon as you seek for the Buddha, externally or internally, you go astray. The true Buddha can never be found as the goal of the act of 'seeking for'. From the very beginning it *is* and is working at the ground of the very act of 'seeking for'. Prior to the act of seeking, the true Buddha is here and now. This is the Zen meaning of the fact that a great treasure can be found where we stand.

Can you see the ground on which you are standing? You may see and point it out saying 'This is my ground' by moving one step backward. The ground thus seen is not the one on which you are presently standing but the one on which you *were* standing. The basis of your *present existence* cannot be seen nor can it be objectified by your self simply because it is the basis of your present existence. Exactly the same is the case for our 'true Self'. The real ground for our existence is not the point from which we take a step backward but from which we should move step by step forward. Here a complete *turnabout* must take place. However, the turning can take place only by awakening to our true 'Self', which cannot be objectified. To reach Reality all kinds of objectification must be overcome. By realizing the unobjectifiable as one's true 'Self' one turns from ego-centeredness to true Self as Reality. In Zen this turning is inseparable from the turning as seen in the following passages by Ch'ing-yüan Wei-hsin, a Chinese Zen master:

> Before I began the study of Zen, I said, 'Mountains are mountains; water is water.' After I got an insight into the truth of Zen through the instruction of a good master, I said, 'Mountains are not mountains; water not water.' However, when I reached the abode of final rest I say, 'Mountains are *really* mountains; water is *really* water.'

In his first realization that mountains are mountains and water is water, he objectified and discriminated mountains, rivers and so forth. When he overcame objectification, discrimination disappeared and he realized that mountains are not mountains, water is not water. Everything is empty. This is, however, the second and not the final realization. For in this understanding emptiness is still seen. In his final realization, however, mountains are realized just as they are, water is realized just as it is. This is possible by the realization of true Emptiness through overcoming mere objectified emptiness. This turning from the first to the third realization is, as I said, inseparable from the turning from ego-centeredness to the true Self. When we realize our true Self we realize everything as it is. When we realize that mountains are really mountains, and water is really water, we realize that I am really I, and you are really you.

Buber also emphasizes 'turning' by saying that 'turning stands in the centre of the Jewish conception of the way of man.'[3] According to Buber 'turning' means not only repentance but also that by a reversal of his whole being, a man who had been lost in the maze of selfishness, where he had always set himself as his goal, finds a way to God, that is, a way to the fulfillment of the particular task for which he has been destined by God.[4]

After pointing out the similarity of Zen and Hasidism in regard to the positive relationship to the concrete, Buber says:

> But the motive force thereto is fundamentally different in each. In Zen the intensive pointing to the concrete serves to divert the spirit directed to knowledge of the transcendent from

discursive thought. . . . It is not things themselves that matter here, but their non-conceptual nature as symbol of the Absolute which is superior to all concepts. Not so in Hasidism. Here the things themselves are the object of religious concern, for they are the abode of the holy sparks that man shall raise up. The Things are important here not as representations of non-conceptual truth but as the exile of divine being.[5]

Here I see Buber's limited understanding of Zen as well as crucial points concerning both Zen and Hasidism. Buber understands that Zen is concerned, not with things themselves, but with their non-conceptual nature as a symbol of the Absolute. The non-conceptual nature of things, however, can be realized only when we awaken to our true Self as the unobjectifiable. It is not, in Zen, a symbol of the Absolute. The non-conceptual nature of things as symbolic of the Absolute is still something objective. As we see in the final realization of Ch'ing-yüan Wei-hsin that mountains are really mountains and rivers are really rivers, in the Zen experience of *satori* things manifest themselves through one's realization of true Emptiness.

On the other hand we must ask whether in Buber and in Hasidism the subject–object structure is completely overcome. If things are the abode of the holy sparks and the human–divine relationship is understood as the I–Thou relationship, a kind of subject–object duality still remains. If God is addressed as 'Thou' is it not the case, strictly speaking, that one does not begin with oneself? If we take seriously the principle of beginning with oneself should we not overcome even the objectivity of God as Thou? Is it not the case that only in a realization of the unobjectifiable as the true Self, not as God, can we reach Reality?

Let me conclude by quoting, for further consideration by followers of both Hasidism and Zen, questions and answers from each tradition.

First from Hasidism:

'Where is the dwelling of God?'

This is the question with which the Rabbi of Kotzk surprised a number of learned men who happened to be visiting him. They laughed at him: 'What a thing to ask: Is not the whole world full of his glory?' Then he answered his own question: 'God dwells wherever man lets him in.'

Next, Zen questions and answers:

A monk asked, 'Where is the abiding place for the mind?'
'The mind,' answered the master, 'abides where there is no abiding.'
'What is meant by "there is no abiding"?'
'When the mind is *not abiding* in any particular object, we say that it abides where there is no abiding.'
'What is meant by no abiding in any particular object?'
'It means not to be abiding in the dualism of good and evil, being and non-being, thought and matter; it means not to be abiding in emptiness or in non-emptiness, neither in tranquillity nor in non-tranquillity. Where there is no abiding place, this is truly the abiding place for the mind.'

Notes

1. Martin Buber, *The Way of Man* (New York: Citadel Press, 1959), p. 39.
2. Martin Buber, *The Original Meaning of Hasidism* (New York: Horizon Press, 1960), p. 238.
3. Buber, *The Way of Man*, op. cit., p. 35.
4. Ibid.
5. Buber, *The Original Meaning of Hasidism*, op. cit., pp. 238–9.

14

The Interfaith Encounter of Zen* and Christian Contemplation: A Dialogue between Masao Abe and Keith J. Egan

I

Our task in this interfaith dialogue is to discuss the similarities and differences of practice, particularly meditation and contemplation, between Christianity and Buddhism. Such a dialogue is not an easy one because in both Christianity and Buddhism practices such as meditation and contemplation are beyond purely theoretical or theological understanding since they can be grasped only through personal commitment and penetrating inner experience. I don't think I am qualified to grasp the existential significance of Christian and Buddhist practice sufficiently. In order to develop a Christian–Buddhist dialogue, however, I will try, with the guidance of Professor Egan, to elucidate the religious meaning of practice in Christianity and Buddhism in so far as I understand them.

Referring to my question, 'What happens when Christians pray?', Prof. Egan points out in his paper for our dialogue, 'Christians at Prayer: Meditation and Contemplation', that 'any response to this question is a journey into mystery' and that an adequate

---

* In the discussion of Zen the author is largely indebted to the writings of D. T. Suzuki, especially *Essays in Zen Buddhism, First Series*.[1] The author is also grateful to Professor Donald Mitchell for his revisions and valuable suggestions.

answer requires one to 'explore the mystery of the relationship between the human and the divine in Christian prayer'. He also suggests that 'perhaps we most nearly touch upon the mystery of Christian prayer when we explore the tradition of meditation and contemplation.' Then Prof. Egan presents the historical development of the practice of meditation in Christianity which is very illuminating and helpful for me.

What is most important for me to understand is the distinction between meditation and contemplation. In his paper Prof. Egan suggests that meditation is 'what the human person can do with grace' whereas contemplation is 'what only God can do'. He also describes contemplation as 'a loving union with God that is entirely God's gift' whereas he describes meditation as 'the ordinary way one prepares oneself for the gift to contemplation'. Although meditation and contemplation can be distinguished from one another in this way, they are intimately related in Christian prayer. In Prof. Egan's words, 'To follow Teresa of Jesus, all prayer whether meditation or contemplation is directed toward love of God and love of neighbor with the latter being the only genuine sign of the presence of the love of God. I think this is the quintessence of Christian prayer.'

Now, let me present a historical sketch of Buddhism in order to prepare the ground to elucidate the affinity and difference between practice in Christianity and practice in Buddhism.

II

The early Buddhist way to deliverance consists in a threefold discipline: moral rules (*sila*), tranquillization (*samādhi*) and wisdom (*prajñā*). By *sila*, one's conduct is regulated externally, by *samādhi* quietude is attained, and by *prajñā* real understanding takes place. Hence the importance of meditation in Buddhism.

Samādhi and *dhyāna* (meditation) are to a great extent synonymous and interchangeable, but strictly *samādhi* is a psychological state realized by the exercise of *dhyāna*. The latter is the process and the former is the goal. The Buddhist scriptures make reference to so many types of *samādhi* realized through *dhyāna*. The scriptures record that before delivering a sermon, the Buddha generally entered into a *samādhi*, but never I think into *dhyāna*. but frequently in China *dhyāna* and *samādhi* are combined to make one word, *ch'an-ting*, meaning a state of quietude attained by the exercise of meditation or *dhyāna*.

Also from the Chinese tradition, the term 'Zen' (*Ch'an* in Chinese) is an abbreviated form of *Zenna* or *Ch'anna*, which is the Chinese rendering of *dhyāna*. From this fact alone, it is evident that Zen has a great deal to do with this practice which has been carried on from the early days of the Buddha, indeed from the beginning of Indian culture. *Dhyāna* is usually rendered in English as 'meditation', and, generally speaking, the idea is to meditate on a truth, religious or philosophical, so that it may be thoroughly comprehended and deeply engraved into the inner consciousness. This is practised in a quiet place away from the noise and confusion of the world. It was due to Bodhidharma (died 532) that Zen came to be the Buddhism of China. It was he who started this movement which proved so fruitful among a people given to the practical affairs of life. When he declared his message, it was still tinged with Indian colours; he could not be entirely independent of the traditional Buddhist metaphysics of the time.

Since the beginning of Buddhism, there have been two currents of thought concerning the meaning of meditation. Following Ārade and Udraka, who were the two teachers of the Buddha, one view takes meditation as a method for suspending all psychic activities or for wiping consciousness clean of all its modes. The other view regards meditation simply as the most efficacious means for coming in touch with the ultimate reality. This fundamental difference of views with regard to meditation was a cause of the initial unpopularity of Bodhidharma among the Chinese Buddhists, scholars, and *dhyāna* masters of the time. Hui-nêng, the sixth patriarch, came out as a strong advocate of intuitionalism and refused to interpret the meaning of *dhyāna* statically. For the Mind, according to him, at the highest stage of meditation, was not a mere being, a mere abstraction devoid of content and work. He wanted to grasp something which lay at the foundation of all his activities, mental and physical, and this something could not be a mere geometrical point, it must be the source of energy and knowledge. Hui-nêng did not forget that the will was after all the ultimate reality and that enlightenment was to be understood as more than intellection, more than quietly contemplating the truth. The Mind or Self-nature was to be apprehended in the midst of its working or functioning. The object of *dhyāna* was thus not to stop the working of Self-Nature but to make us plunge right into its stream and seize it in its very action. His intuition-alism therefore was dynamic.

According to Hui-nêng, Zen was the 'seeing into one's own Nature'. This was the most significant phrase coined in the development of Zen Buddhism. Around this phrase, Zen is now crystallized, and we know where to direct our efforts and how to represent it in our consciousness. He says, 'We talk of seeing into our own Nature, and not of practicing *dhyāna* or obtaining liberation.' By 'Nature' he understood Buddha-Nature, or *prajñā* (wisdom). He says that this *prajñā* is possessed by every one of us, but owing to the confusion of thought we fail to realize it in ourselves. However, when we open a spiritual eye we can by ourselves see into this true Nature.

There are some people who regard Zen as consisting in sitting quietly with an empty mind devoid of thoughts and feelings. These people do not know what *prajñā* is, what Mind is. It fills the universe, and never rests from work. It is free, creative, and at the same time it knows itself. It knows all in one and one in all. This mysterious working of *prajñā* issues from your own Nature. Do not depend upon words and letters but let your own *prajñā* illuminate within yourself. This is the message of Hui-nêng.

The thirteenth-century Japanese Zen master Dōgen is unique in his strong emphasis on 'the Oneness of practice and attainment'. He argues:

> To think practice and realization are not one is a heretical view. In the Buddha Dharma, practice and realization are identical. Because one's present practice is practice in realization, one's initial negotiation of the Way in itself is the whole of original realization. Thus, even while one is directed to practice, he is told not to anticipate realization apart from practice, because practice points directly to original realization. As it is already realization in practice, realization is endless; as it is practice in realization, practice is beginningless.

This statement shows that awakening is not subordinate to practice, attainment to discipline, Buddha-nature to becoming a buddha, or vice versa. Both sides of such contraries are indispensable and dynamically related to each other. Unless one becomes a buddha, the Buddha-nature is not realized as the Buddha-nature, and yet at the same time one can become a buddha only because one is originally endowed with the Buddha-nature. It is at this point that the dynamic truth of the simultaneous realization of the Buddha-nature and its attainment can be seen.

Shin'ichi Hisamatsu (1889–1980) is an outstanding Zen philosopher of modern Japan. He strongly emphasizes 'awakening to our true Self' as the essence of Zen. Hisamatsu argues as follows:

> Zen does not rely on any authority. If we are to speak of any authority in Zen, its basic authority is the true self, that is the true person. This authority, however, is to be called the authority of no-authority. Accordingly, the method of Zen is to get oneself – and to get others – to awaken to the True Self, which all men are in their primal nature. This is what is meant by 'directly pointing to man's Mind'. Zen takes its occasions or opportunities to come to this awakening not simply from within the teaching but freely and directly from life itself in its every aspect and action, such as walking, abiding, sitting, lying, hearing, seeing, etc. Thus, according to the time and place, Zen makes use of any of the innumerable phenomena of life as the occasion to awaken oneself or to awaken others to man's true Self-Nature.

How can we awaken to our True Self? There is a saying, 'In the practice of Zen there are three essentials.' The first is the great root of faith. Great faith is to try and give ourself to truly sitting by sitting through anything. We must have this great conviction. As the second essential thing we must have a great tenacity of purpose. And the third essential thing is the Great Doubt which is spoken of with regard to the practice of *kōans*. In this connection Hisamatsu especially emphasizes the importance of 'Great Doubt' as the necessary moment for self-awakening.

Although ordinary doubts are intellectual, the Great Doubt in the Zen sense – and particularly in Hisamatsu's sense – is not mere intellectual doubt. It is qualitatively different from the 'doubt' in Descartes' *de omnibus dubitandam* (concerning the necessity of doubting everything). It means something total in which emotional anguish and volitional dilemma as well as intellectual doubting are one fundamental subject. It is the realization of the fundamental antinomy of good and evil, life and death innate in human existence. In the Great Doubt what is being doubted is the very doubter himself. The doubter and the doubted are not two but one. When this Great Doubt, often called 'great-doubting-mass', is overcome, the bottom of man is broken through and the True Self is awakened. Here is a leap. The ordinarily antinomic self cannot *become* the True Self. Only when the ordinary self which is ultimately antinomic breaks up does the True Self of Oneness awake to itself. In this connection Hisamatsu argues as follows.

Therefore, we must say that there is a leap, a discontinuity. Moreover, this does not mean that one is saved by someone else or that redemption comes from God or Buddha. The self of life-death nature breaking up and becoming the Self without life-and-death means that the self of life-death nature becomes awakened to its original self. In this sense the Self without life-and-death has continuity with the self of life-death nature. In this Self-awakening, as between the doubter and the doubted, there is no separation between the awakened and what one is awakened to. While the doubting-mass breaks and the true self is awakened the former is related to the latter in a very special manner as the darkness of night which is dark through and through is related to the brightness which prevails after sunrise.

III

Now, I would like to compare 'meditation and contemplation' in Christian prayer and Buddhist practice. First of all, I recognize *a sort of* parallel between them. To begin with, meditation in Christianity has some affinity with meditation in Buddhism. And the relation between meditation and contemplation in Christianity has some correspondence to that in Buddhism.

In Buddhism, *dhyāna*, that is meditation, means to holds one's thoughts in a collected manner, not to let thought wander away from its legitimate path. That is, it means to have the mind concentrated on a single subject of thought. Therefore, when *dhyāna* is practiced, all the outer details are to be so controlled as to bring the mind into the most favourable condition in which it will gradually rise above the turbulence of passion and sensualities. This *dhyāna* has some similarity with Christian meditation in which, originating in Jewish meditation, *haga*, Christians meditate day and night on the Law of the Lord.

In Buddhism, however, *dhyāna* is not the end of Buddhist life. For the tranquillization resulting from *dhyāna* alone may lead one to a state of self-complacency and destroy the source of sympathetic motivation. Going beyond tranquillization, *dhyāna* must lead us to the awakening of wisdom, that is enlightenment. Without this awakening of wisdom (*prajñā*), *dhyāna*, however exalting, has no ultimate import to the perfection of Buddhist life. Thus the *Dhammapāda*, one of the earliest Buddhist literatures, (V, 372) states:

Without wisdom (*prajñā*) there is no meditation (*dhyāna*).
Without meditation there is no wisdom.

This mutual dependence of *dhyāna* and *prajñā* is what distinguished Buddhism from the rest of Indian teachings at the time. *Dhyāna* must issue in *prajñā* (wisdom) and *karuṇā* (compassion). It must develop into seeing the world as it really is and acting to save the suffering world. This was the reason why the Buddha was dissatisfied with the teaching of his teachers. And it is why after attaining enlightenment, he did not stay in meditation but left the seat of enlightenment to begin preaching to save sentient beings for his entire remaining years. To him, *prajñā* was the most essential part of his doctrine and it had to grow out of *dhyāna*. Any *dhyāna* that did not terminate in *prajñā* was not at all Buddhistic.

This identity of *dhyāna* and *prajñā* (meditation and enlightenment) is most clearly realized and most strongly emphasized in Zen. Zen is not a system of *dhyāna* as practised in India and by other Buddhist schools in China. In Zen, awakening to one's true self, that is *satori*, is crucial. *Zazen* (its Sanskrit equivalent being *dhyāna*) means sitting crosslegged in quietude and in deep contemplation. It is the practice which originated in India and which has spread all over the East. It has been going on through many centuries now, and the modern followers of Zen still strictly observe it. In this respect *zazen* is the prevailing practical method of spiritual discipline in the East, but when it is used in connection with the *kōan* it assumes a special feature and becomes the monopoly of Zen.

Hui-nêng, the Sixth Patriarch, is an important figure in the history of Zen who strongly emphasized the non-duality of *dhyāna* and *prajñā*. Hui-nêng declares:

In my teaching there is no distinction between *dhyāna* and *prajñā*: *dhyāna* is the body of *prajñā* and *prajñā* is the function of *dhyāna*; when you have *prajñā*, *dhyāna* is in *prajñā*: when you have *dhyāna*, *prajñā* is in *dhyāna*. They are one and not two.

The mere sinking into a deep meditative abyss was not the object of Zen discipline; unless *dhyāna* culminated in an immediate intuition there was no Zen in it.

Now, let us turn to Christianity. In Christianity as well, meditation alone is not sufficient for prayer. Although meditation (*hoga*) on the Law is entry into the presence of God, it is not completely free from human effort. In order to bring one's heart and mind within God's fuller presence contemplation as the gift of union with God in love is needed.

In this regard, the following statement in Egan's paper is extremely important for me in understanding meditation and contemplation in Christianity. He states:

In early Christianity as in Old Testament Judaism, meditation and contemplation (Greek *theoria*) are intimately connected with encountering God by coming into the divine presence through the Word of God in the scripture . . . The Word of God acts as a metaphor for God's presence, a metaphor for what cannot be described by human language . . . In the Christian tradition the Word of God as Scripture is intimately connected with prayer.

As clearly described in this statement, in Christianity (a) prayer is intimately connected with the Word of God; (b) the Word of God is a metaphor for God's presence; and (c) the Word of God is revealed in the scripture. Accordingly, one may conclude that the Word of God is most crucial in Christian prayer. In this regard we realize a significant difference between Zen and Christianity.

The basic expression of Zen to characterize its fundamental teaching is as follows:

Not relying on words or letters.
An independent self-transmission apart from the doctrinal teaching.
Directly pointing into one's Mind.
Awakening one's Original Nature, thereby actualizing Buddhahood.

'Not relying on words or letters' does not necessarily mean a simple negation of words or letters but indicates to return to the source *prior to* words or letters, that is to return to Buddha's Mind as the source of the Buddhist scripture. Since the Buddhist scripture is nothing but an outcome of Buddha's Mind, that is, Buddha's enlightenment, Zen requires us to go beyond the scripture and to return to the Buddha Mind directly. However, in so far as the Buddha Mind is regarded as an object to be attained, we cannot attain it. This is because the Buddha Mind cannot be objectified and the objectified Buddha Mind is not true Buddha Mind. The true Buddha Mind can be attained only through our own attainment of our own Buddha Mind, that is, our own original Nature. Only when we awaken to our own true Nature do we attain the Buddha Mind as the source of Scripture. This is what is meant by the basic expression of Zen, that is, 'An independent self-transmission apart from the doctrinal teaching. Directly pointing to one's Mind. Awakening to one's original Nature, thereby actualizing Buddhahood.'

In Christianity, is the Scripture absolutely necessary to know the Word of God? Cannot Christians hear the Word of God apart from the Scripture – for instance in the flowers blooming, the wind blowing or the bird singing? A further question: Is the Word of God the only metaphor for God's presence? Can we not encounter God in 'wordless silence' or in the 'boundless openness' of the universe?

In this regard, Zen finds more affinity with the apophatic experience than the cataphatic experience. Unlike the cataphatic theology which has as its object the intelligible names of God revealed in Scripture, the apophatic theology, originated in Clement of Alexandria and Origen and represented by Gregory of Nyssa, emphasizes the basic unknowability of God even in the Scripture. Evagrius Ponticus speaks of the highest union with God as 'pure prayer'. Pure prayer is communion with God without words or images of any kind, in which a person is rendered unconscious of anything except the God who lies beyond all that is created.[2]

As I mentioned earlier, Egan states the difference between meditation and contemplation by elucidating the former as 'what the human person can do with grace' and the latter as 'what only God can do'. At another place referring to the influence of John of the Cross and Carmelite Teresa of Jesus, Egan again states that in medieval Catholicism a sharp distinction between meditation and contemplation was established. That is, meditation was understood as imaginative and discussive, thinking about spiritual things, whereas contemplation was understood as the rare mystical experience – special graced experience, the gift of union with God in love.

In one sense, there may be said to be a sort of parallel between the Christian distinction of meditation and contemplation and the Buddhist distinction of meditation and enlightenment. That is, meditation both in Christianity and Buddhism is generally regarded as a human endeavour. And both contemplation in Christianity and enlightenment in Zen are regarded as being a higher stage than meditation and as being beyond human effort.

Such a generalization, however, can be misleading without the following clarification. First, meditation in Zen is not discursive, but is free from the activity of human consciousness. Second, in Zen enlightenment can be regarded as a higher stage than meditation in an entirely different sense than contemplation in Christianity. In Christianity, contemplation is not only beyond human effort, but a divine 'gift' given through the work of the Holy Spirit. In Zen, on the other hand, enlightenment is also beyond meditation but Zen enlightenment is *not* regarded as a divine gift of union with God in love, but it is the self-awakening to one's true self. Enlightenment in Zen is not seeing God but seeing into one's own true nature.

Another difference between Zen and Christianity is found in the fact that Zen has no authoritative scripture, *nor* does it have an authoritative Buddha. The freedom for which Zen seeks is a complete emancipation from everything, even from the notion of a Buddha in order to awaken to one's True Nature. This is the reason *The Discourse on the Direct-Lineage of the Dharma*, attributed to Bodhidharma, states as follows:

> Topsy-turvy beings do not know that the Self-Buddha is the True Buddha. They spend the whole day in running to and fro, searching outwardly, contemplating Buddha, honoring patriarchs, and looking for the Buddha somewhere outside of themselves. They are misdirected. Just know the Self-Mind! Outside of this Mind there is no other Buddha.

Ma-tsu, a Chinese Zen master (707–786), also declares:

Outside of the Mind, no other Buddha;
Outside of the Buddha, no other Mind.

Zen does not, however, arbitrarily reject the authoritative Buddha nor declare that one's Mind is the Buddha. As I stated earlier, one can attain the awakening to one's True Self only by breaking through the Great Doubt in which one's total existence becomes problematical. Enlightenment does not take place without the Great Doubt. Traditionally it is said 'Under the Great Doubt there is Great Enlightenment'. When one's ordinary understanding of selfhood is burned up in this Great Doubt, the deeper True Self that is the True Buddha can awaken.

This Great Doubt reminds me of the 'Darkness' (*gnophos*) in the Christian contemplative tradition described by such people as Gregory of Nyssa, Dionysius Areopagite and others. In this mystical Christian tradition, 'darkness' serves as a metaphor both for the unfathomable transcendence of God and for the blindness of the ordinary human understanding when confronted by God.[3] Despite such a similarity between the 'Great Doubt' and 'Darkness', we should not overlook the fact that Christian mysticism is centring around the notion of God whereas Zen focuses on the problem of True Self. So, the negation of mystical darkness leads to an affirmation of God in Christian contemplation. But the negation of the Great Doubt leads to an affirmation of True Self in Zen practice.

However, besides these important differences, there still seems to be the similarity between Zen and Christian practice mentioned above. In both cases we must move beyond willful effort in meditation practice in order to discover or awaken to what each considers ultimate reality: God or Buddha-nature. And in both cases, this realization is fully transformative to our human existence.

Notes

1. D. T. Suzuki, *Essays in Zen Buddhism, First Series* (London: Rider, 1970).
2. Alan Richardson and John Bowden (eds), *A New Dictionary of Christian Theology* (London: SCM, 1983).
3. Gordon Wakefield (ed.), *A Dictionary of Christian Spirituality* (London: SCM, 1988).

15

Interfaith Relations and World Peace: A Buddhist Perspective

I understand that the theme of the dialogue 'Interfaith Relations and World Peace' implies a question: How can interfaith relations contribute to world peace? And in this regard the following two issues must be considered. First, what is true world peace? And second, in light of Marjorie Suchocki's paper, '*Sūnyatā*, Trinity and Community', what kind of interfaith relations can contribute to true world peace? I will discuss these issues from a Buddhist point of view.

Let me consider, first, what is true world peace? What kind of peace can be said to be the most authentic form of peace? In our daily life the term 'peace' is used as the opposite of 'war'. So peace is often understood only in terms of 'war and peace'. Thus peace is regarded as the absence of war or the cessation of war. However, people are not necessarily peaceful in their mind even when they are free from war. True peace can be attained by going beyond peace as the opposite of war, that is peace in a political and sociological sense, and by realizing peace of mind, that is peace at the innermost depth of human existence. To be sure peace without war is desirable but essentially speaking is it not an unreal and fictitious peace? The real peace must be a peace actualized from the basis of the peace realized at the innermost depth of human existence. This must be true not only for the peace of the individual, but also for the peace of society and the peace of the world.

In Judeo-Christian tradition *eirene* and *salom* denote peace. *Eirene* is general well-being, the source and giver of which is God – Yahweh alone. *Salom* embraces the idea of absence of war, but basically it indicates well-being or all that makes for wholeness and prosperity. In Christianity peace in the sense of inward spiritual calm is more distinctive. It indicates the serenity of a secure relationship with God which is sustained by grace through all kinds of tribulation and pressure.

Soteriologically, peace is grounded in God's work of redemption. Eschatologically it is a sign of God's new creation which has already begun. Teleologically it will be fully realized when the work of new creation is complete. Only in a secondary sense does peace describe human and divine–human relationships, in which case it refers to a psychological state consequent upon sharing in the all-embracing peace of God. (Luke 2: 14)[1]

Now, how is peace understood in Buddhism? The original Sanskrit term for peace is *śanti* which means calm, quiet or tranquillity. This peace of mind is called *nirvāṇa* in which all evil passions are extinguished. Gautama Buddha did not work miracles nor was he successful in reforming the broader Hindu society but rather calmly pointed out the most basic suffering of human life and waited for the people to become aware of it. To him the suffering innate in human existence is rooted in our fundamental ignorance and evil passion. *Śanti* is nothing but the state in which such ignorance and passion are overcome. In the *Dhammapāda*, one of the earliest Buddhist literatures, it is said:

If a man should conquer in battle a thousand and a thousand more, and another man should conquer himself, his would be the greater victory, because the greatest of victories is the victory over oneself; and neither the gods in heaven above nor the demons down below can turn into defeat the victory of such a man. (103–105)[2]

Buddha never fought against hostile powers with power. He always tried to persuade opponents to awaken to a deeper human reality prior to opposition and conflict. This basic attitude is well expressed in his following words:

Not by hatred is hatred appeased. Hatred is appeased by renouncing of hatred. It is so conquered only by compassion. This is a law eternal.[3]

Compassion, that is 'suffering together', accompanied with wisdom is the basic principle of Buddhist life. In Christianity, love and justice are always linked together. Love without justice is not true love; justice without love is not true justice. Likewise, in Buddhism compassion and wisdom always go together. Compassion without wisdom is not true compassion; wisdom without compassion is not true wisdom. This unity of wisdom and compassion is realized by awakening to the Buddhist truth, that is the truth of *anātman* (no-self) and the law of *pratītya-samutpāda* (dependent co-origination). The truth of no-self denotes that everything in the universe has no enduring, fixed, substantial selfhood. And the law of dependent co-origination indicates that all things in the universe are co-arising and co-ceasing: nothing exists independently. In Buddhism peace in the true sense can be established only on the basis of unity of wisdom and compassion.

Accordingly we see that to both Christians and Buddhists peace in the authentic sense is not the absence of war, nor the external well-being and security in the social and political dimension, but true peace is deeply rooted in the innermost depth of human existence. World peace in the authentic sense can be also established only on the basis of the internal security of humankind. The difference between Christianity and Buddhism in this regard is that in Christianity the internal security is grounded in God's work of salvation, whereas in Buddhism it is based on the awakening to no-self as true self.

So far we have discussed the problem 'what is true world peace'. Now we turn to the second problem: What sort of interfaith relations can contribute to true world peace? One of the serious problems all religions are now facing is the problem of religious pluralism. In the history of human religion almost no religions existed completely isolated from other religions. Generally speaking, religions have been living somewhat in a pluralistic situation on the local level. The problem of religious pluralism today, however, is qualitatively different. Due to the remarkable advancement of technology, the contemporary world is rapidly shrinking. Jet airplanes fly everywhere, and electronic communication happens almost instantly. East and West, North and South are encountering each other on a scale and depth never experienced before. This shrinking of the world, however, does not indicate that the world is now being united harmoniously. Rather, the difference and opposition among various value systems and ideologies become more and more conspicuous. How can we integrate this pluralistic world situation without marring the features of the cultures and religions of various nations? This is the urgent issue which humankind is facing today.

In this context, pluralism in religion presents us with a special difficulty in the attainment of an integrated unity. For all religions by their nature make claims to the ultimate truth which are often conflicting with each other. It is an ironical tragedy that religions which usually preach peace as an important tenet, fight each other, as we see in the case of the Middle East, Northern Ireland, Pakistan, Sri Lanka and so forth. In order to contribute to world peace all religions, especially the great world religions, must cooperate. What is, then, the basis for such interfaith cooperation while all faiths are making conflicting truth claims? What sort of unity is necessary to integrate the pluralistic situation of religion today? To answer this question I shall distinguish, as in 'Buddhist–Christian Dialogue' (Chapter 1), two kinds of unity or oneness: first monistic unity or oneness; secondly, non-dualistic unity or oneness. It is my contention that the latter kind of unity or oneness may provide a real common basis for the contemporary pluralistic situation of world religion. How, then, are monistic and non-dualistic oneness different from one another?

First, monistic oneness is realized by distinguishing itself and setting itself apart from dualistic twoness and pluralistic manyness, but non-dualistic oneness is completely free from any form of duality, including the duality between monism and dualism or pluralism. Secondly, the monotheistic God is somewhat 'over there', not completely right here and right now, whereas non-dualistic oneness is a kind of oneness which is based on the realization of 'great zero', or non-substantial emptiness realized right now. Thirdly, the true oneness which can be attained through the realization of 'great zero' should not be objectively conceived. Monotheistic oneness is oneness before the realization of 'great zero', whereas non-dualistic oneness is oneness through and beyond the realization of 'great zero' – it is not bound even by this concept. Fourthly, monotheistic oneness, being somewhat 'over there', does not immediately include two, many and the whole, but non-dualistic oneness, however, which is based on the realization of 'great zero' includes all individual things just as they are, without any modification.

The view of monotheistic unity does not *fully* admit the distinctiveness or uniqueness of each religion united therein, due to the lack of the realization of 'great zero' or non-substantial emptiness. By contrast, the view of non-dualistic unity thoroughly allows the distinctiveness or uniqueness of each religion without any limitation – through the realization of 'great zero' or emptiness. If monotheistic religions such as Judaism, Christianity and Islam place more emphasis on the self-negating, non-substantial aspect of God rather than the self-affirmative authoritative aspect of God, that is, if these religions understand the oneness of absolute God in terms of non-dualistic oneness rather than in terms of monotheistic oneness, then they may overcome serious conflicts with other faiths and may establish a stronger interfaith cooperation to contribute to world peace. On the other hand, if Buddhism learns from the monotheistic religions the importance of justice, and develops its notion of compassion to be linked not only with wisdom but also with justice, it will come closer to Judaism, Christianity and Islam in its interfaith relationship and may become more active in establishing world peace.

Let me conclude my presentation by saying that world peace in the authentic sense can be established only on the basis of the innermost religious security, and true and dynamic interfaith cooperation as the necessary condition for world peace can be realized only through the realization of the non-dualistic unity of all religions.

Notes

1. Colin Brown (ed.), *The New International Dictionary of New Testament Theology* (Exeter: Paternoster Press, 1985), Vol. 2, p. 780.
2. *The Dhammapāda*, trans. by Juan Mascaro (Harmondsworth: Penguin, 1973), p. 50.
3. Ibid., p. 5.

16

Faith and Self-Awakening: A Search for the Fundamental Category Covering All Religious Life

I

'What has faith to do with believing this or that? What has faith to do with being human?' Raising these questions in the opening pages of his book *Faith and Belief*,[1] Wilfred Cantwell Smith tries to clarify the nature of faith as distinguished from that of belief. He understands faith as 'a characteristic quality or potentiality of human life'.[2] This is an attempt to determine the essential human quality at the basis of man's religious life which is realized beyond the surface of all religions. It is important to do this in our time, since ours is one in which religious pluralism has become so prominent. An integral view of human life, though urgently necessary, is more and more difficult to achieve.

It is worth noting that Smith's approach has the following three characteristics: it is personalistic, historical-comparative, and global-and-integral. Let me briefly explain these three characteristics of his approach as I understand them.

First, the personalistic approach: Smith takes religion as a dynamic movement rather than as a static system with a fixed doctrine and practice. He emphasizes the personal involvement of religious individuals in religious truth as essential to man's religious life. He does not want to use the term 'religion' for a pattern of observable forms. He offers two concepts, 'faith' and 'tradition', as substitutes. 'Faith' means 'an inner religious experience of involvement of a particular person: the impingement on him of the transcendent putative or real'.[3] 'Tradition' he takes to mean the cumulative 'mass of overt objective data that constitute the historical deposit . . . of the past religious life of the community in question'.[4] Tradition is nothing but a potential pattern for personal involvement, which thus becomes religious as it expresses or elicits faith. 'Faith is nourished and patterned by the tradition, is formed and in some sense sustained by it – yet faith precedes and transcends the tradition, and in turn sustains it.'[5]

Secondly, Smith's person-centered approach does not entail a subjective, non-historical understanding of the matter. His personalistic approach is combined with the historical-comparative method. As a historian of religion, Smith makes a historical and comparative study of human religious ways of life across the centuries and around the world. His emphasis on the necessity of a distinction between faith and belief is based on his comprehensive survey of mankind's religious history.

As a result of the survey Smith states that 'religious beliefs have of course differed radically, whereas religious faith would appear to have been, not constant certainly, yet more approximative to constancy.'[6] He also reports two things: 'One is that the variety of faith seems on the whole less than the variety of forms through which faith has been expressed. The second is that such variety of faith as is found cuts across formal religious boundaries.'[7]

Smith criticizes the recent Western confusion between faith and belief as an aberration. He interprets 'belief' as the holding of certain ideas which constitutes an intellectual position, historically varied in differing forms among the traditions, even within each tradition. On the other hand, 'faith' is, in his view, a spiritual orientation of the personality, a capacity to live at a more than mundane level, and man's relation to transcendence that appears constant throughout human history.

The third characteristic of Smith's approach lies in the global and integral vision of 'a unity of humankind's religious history'.[8] In his recent book, *Towards A World Theology*, this global vision is evident. It is presented historically and also theologically. Smith insists: 'To suggest a unity of humankind's religious history . . . is not to propose that all men and women have been religious in the same way . . . It is, rather, to discern that the evident variety of their religious life is real, yet is contained within an historical continuum.'[9] For the historian 'unity is not sameness, but is interrelatedness. It is not system but development: not uniformity but continuity.'[10] Accordingly, Smith takes each one's religious life, Christian, Buddhist or Muslim, as a personal participation in the ongoing process of religious history in terms of Christian, Buddhist or Muslim.

Further, on the basis of this integral, global vision of the human history of religion Smith offers a 'Theology of Comparative Religion',[11] which is an appealing and significant proposal in our time. It is a 'theology for which "the religions" are the subject, not the object',[12] 'a theology of the religious history of humankind',[13] 'a theology of the faith history of us human beings'.[14] Emphasizing that truth is apprehended historically, Smith talks about the importance of the awareness of our human involvement simultaneously in the historical and the transcendent. His personalistic approach combined with the historical-comparative method, and his new vision of a 'theology of comparative religion', or a 'World theology', are realized in a context which has simultaneously historical and transcendent dimensions.

II

I hope this clarification of the three characteristics of Smith's approach is not off the mark. However, with all appreciation for his approach, I must raise a question about his standpoint. This question concerns his point of view which takes 'faith' as a 'foundational category for all religious life, and indeed for all human life'.[15] My question is inevitable, particularly from the point of view of Buddhism, which Smith regards as an important movement within the religious history of humankind.

Dealing mainly with the early Buddhist movement Smith says that Buddhism is atheist in the sense that it dispenses with the idea of divinity. However, Smith continues, the concept 'Nirvana' developed and emphasized by the Buddhists is 'some sort of counterpart to the Western concept "God"; or at the least, it played a role significantly comparable to that played by the concept "God".'[16] According to Smith, although the Buddha affirmed that within the ocean nothing persists, he affirmed a 'further shore' or 'other shore' as transcendence. He also preached the moral law as the enduring *Dharma*, the truth about right living. 'All else is evanescent. But the Saddharma, the True Law is eternal.'[17]

Smith insists that:

'The [early Buddhist] movement is religious because through it men and women's lives were lived in what the Western world has traditionally called the presence of God. Through their systems of beliefs, they were able to live lives of faith. They tasted transcendence; and accordingly their lives were touched by compassion and courage and serenity and ultimate significance.[18]

Concerning Smith's interpretation of the early Buddhist movement I have two interrelated questions. One is whether the early Buddhist movement is exhausted by using the term 'faith' as Smith understands it. Does his interpretation in terms of faith really touch the core of the early Buddhist movement, let alone Mahayana Buddhism? If the answer to these questions is negative, which I am afraid is the case, then the second question is whether it is legitimate to comprehend all human religions, Buddhism included, under the single term of 'faith'. Smith understands it to be 'a foundational category for all religious life, and indeed for all human life'. This interpretation not only confuses the distinctiveness of various forms of religion but also obscures what 'a foundational category for all religious life, and for all human life' is. Smith's generalization of the term 'faith' is expressed by the idea that faith is the relation to the transcendent. It is only possible to comprehend all human religious movements by eliminating the characteristics of faith in the Semitic religions such as faith is Yahweh, the Father of Jesus Christ, and Allah. On the other hand, his generalization of the term 'faith' is only possible by making ambiguous the authentic meaning of Buddhist notions such as *nirvāṇa*, *Dharma* and Emptiness. Although it is urgently necessary, as Smith insists, to find a global and dynamic category to comprehend the whole process of human history of religion, it is questionable whether we should take 'faith' as the foundational category.

III

To make my point clear, let me ask whether the core of meaning of the early Buddhist movement is exhausted by the term 'faith' as Smith understands it. What is the heart of the early Buddhist movement and the Mahayana Buddhist movement? The early Buddhist movement has an aspect of faith in *Dharma* or faith in *nirvāṇa*, as Smith argues. However, this alone does not give a central place to faith. What is central and essential to the early Buddhist and the Buddhist movement in general is not faith in *Dharma* or faith in *nirvāṇa*, but awakening to *Dharma* or self-realization of *nirvāṇa*.[19] Gautama Buddha is none other than one who awakened to *Dharma* or one who attained and realized *nirvāṇa* with his whole existence.

The Buddhist movement launched by the Buddha is a movement in which, just as Gautama Buddha did, each and every one may awaken to *Dharma* or attain *nirvāṇa* with his whole existence, that is become *a* Buddha. The Christian movement gives a central place to faith in Jesus Christ as the Messiah. This may be called a movement in which each and every one pertains to the Christ but not a movement in which each and every one becomes a Christ. Because of its emphasis on faith in Jesus as the Christ, Christianity, while it may be called the 'Teaching of the Christ', can never rightly be said to be the 'Teaching of becoming a Christ' except for a few views which have not been regarded as orthodox. By contrast, due to its emphasis on awakening to *Dharma*, Buddhism can be said to be the 'Teaching of becoming a Buddha' as well as the 'Teaching of the Buddha'. Smith insists that faith 'does not vary so much as, nor quite in accordance with, the variations of overt religious pattern.'[20] However, in the above sense it is hardly said that Buddhists live their lives only in a different pattern or form from that of Christians while their faiths do not vary so much.

Let me try to elucidate the basic standpoint of the Buddha. Shortly before his death, Gautama Buddha addressed Ananda, one of his ten great disciples, and others who were anxious over the prospect of losing the Master:

O Ananda, be ye lamps unto yourselves. Rely on yourselves and do not rely on external help. Hold fast to the Dharma as a lamp. Seek salvation alone in the Dharma. Look not for assistance to anyone besides yourselves.[21]

Obviously when he said to his disciples, 'Do not rely on external help' and 'Look not for assistance to anyone besides yourselves,' he included himself in terms of 'external help' and he excluded himself in terms of 'assistance'. He said this despite the fact that he, Gautama Buddha, had been a teacher of Ananda and the others for many years. It may not, however, at first be clear how the following two passages in his statement are related to each other: 'Rely on yourselves' and 'Seek salvation alone in the *Dharma*', or 'Be ye lamps unto yourselves' and 'Hold fast to the *Dharma* as a lamp.' In this address, the Buddha did not identify the *Dharma* with himself. He identified the *Dharma* with the individual disciple and, further, he emphasized this identity at the very time of his death.

In Buddhism, the *Dharma* is beyond everyone – beyond even Gautama Buddha, the initiator of the Buddhist movement. This is the reason why it is often said, 'Regardless of the appearance or non-appearance of *Tathāgata* [Gautama Buddha] in this world, the *Dharma* is always present.'[22] *Dharma* has a universality and transcendent character which is beyond time and space. However, who is qualified to talk about the *Dharma* in its absolute universality? Is one who does not realize the *Dharma* qualified to talk about it? Certainly not. In the case of such a person, through his conceptual understanding and his objectivization of it the total universality of the *Dharma* becomes an empty or dead universality. Hence, only one who has realized the *Dharma* with his or her whole existence can legitimately talk about it in its universality.

Although Dharma transcends everyone including Gautama Buddha and is present universally, there is no *Dharma* without someone to realize it. Apart from 'the realizer' there is no *Dharma*. The *Dharma* is realized as the *Dharma* with its universality only through a particular realizer. Gautama Buddha is none other that the *first* 'realizer' of *Dharma*. He is not, however, the one and only realizer of *Dharma*. In the sense that Gautama is a realizer of *Dharma* with its total universality he may be said to be *a* centre of the Buddhist faith. Yet he is certainly not *the* centre of the Buddhist faith, since everyone can become a centre as a realizer of *Dharma*, a buddha. The significance of Gautama's historical existence is equal to that of every other 'realizer' of *Dharma*, except that Gautama was the first.

How can we hold these two apparently contradictory aspects of *Dharma*: its total universality and its dependency upon a particular man for realization? The answer lies in the fact that one's realization of the *Dharma* is nothing but *the Self-Awakening of Dharma itself.* Your awakening is, of course, your own existential awakening. It is *your* awakening to the *Dharma* in its complete universality, and this awakening is possible only by overcoming your self-centeredness, i.e. only through the total negation of your ego-self. This self-centeredness, or the self-centered ego, is the fundamental hindrance to the manifestation of *Dharma*. Therefore when the self-centeredness is overcome and selflessness is attained, i.e. *anatta* or *anātman* is realized, *Dharma* naturally awakens to itself.

When *Dharma* awakens to itself *in you, you* attain *your true Self*; the selfless self is the true Self. Accordingly the Self-Awakening of *Dharma* has a double sense. First, it is *your* self-awakening of *Dharma* in your egoless true Self. In this case one may say that you are the subject of awakening of *Dharma* and *Dharma* is the object of your awakening. Secondly, it is the self-awakening *of Dharma itself* in and through your whole existence. In this case *Dharma* is the subject of its own self-awakening and you are a channel of its self-awakening.

$$\begin{array}{l} \longrightarrow \text{(You are the subject)} \\ \text{Your Self-Awakening of } Dharma \\ \longleftarrow \qquad\qquad (Dharma \text{ is the subject}) \end{array}$$

This double sense only indicates the two aspects of one and the same fundamental Reality, i.e. 'Awakening of *Dharma*' in which subject–object duality is originally overcome, or better, which is prior to the dichotomy between subject and object.

It was precisely on the basis of this 'Self-Awakening of *Dharma*' that Gautama Buddha said without any sense of contradiction, 'Rely on yourselves' and 'Seek salvation alone in the *Dharma*.' The statements 'Be ye lamps unto yourselves' and 'Hold fast to the *Dharma* as a lamp' are complementary and not contradictions. One's self as ultimate reliance is not the ego-self but the 'true Self' as the 'Realizer of *Dharma*'. Just as Gautama's awakening is the self-awakening of *Dharma* in the double sense mentioned above, so anyone's awakening to *Dharma* can and should be the self-awakening of *Dharma* in the same sense.

IV

This is the basic standpoint of Buddhism. It was clarified by Gautama himself through his life after his awakening and particularly, as mentioned above, as he approached death. This basic standpoint of Buddhism, that is 'Self-Awakening' of *Dharma* can hardly be grasped by the term 'faith' even if it is understood as 'the relation to the transcendent'. Smith's characterization of faith as the relation to the transcendent, I am afraid, confuses rather than clarifies the nature of human religion. *What kind of* relation a particular religion in question has with the transcendent is crucial for understanding the distinctive nature of that religion. Both faith and self-awakening may be said to indicate equally 'the relation to the transcendent'. Their relations to the transcendent, however, must be said to be radically different from one another. Though not necessarily theocentric, faith is usually theistic. As we see in Smith's own definition of the term, 'faith is man's participation' in God's dealing with humankind'[23] or 'faith is man's responsive involvement in the activity of God's dealing with humankind'.[24] On the contrary, self-awakening is clearly not theistic because in self-awakening there is no room for God to whom man must respond, although, roughly speaking, it may be said to be a kind of relation to the transcendent named *Dharma*.

Given this fundamental difference, further differences between faith and self-awakening may be expressed in three points.

First, in faith as man's participation or responsive involvement in the activity of God, *will* is included on the side of both man and God as the essential factor of their relationship. Even in its generalized form, faith is a matter of man's free will in relation to the positive or negative response to a transcendent will, although some intellectual component is also involved. On the other hand, the Self-Awakening of *Dharma* in Buddhism is completely free from will and intellectualization, whether human or divine. It is no less than self-awakening to *tathatā*, i.e. suchness or as-it-is-ness. The problem of free will is accounted for in Buddhism by *karma*, which is to be overcome through the self-awakening of *Dharma*.

Secondly, in faith as man's responsive involvement in the activity of God, the self is indispensable as the agent of free will, although ego-self, or self-centered self must overcome. One result is that man and nature are grasped differently in their relationship to

God, the transcendent. Self-awakening of *Dharma* is possible only through the realization of *anātman*, no-self. Once a man realizes his no-self, the absence of eternal self, he simultaneously realizes no-self-being or the non-substantiality of everything in the universe. Accordingly, in the realization of *anātman* implied in self-awakening of *Dharma*, the solidarity, not difference, between man and nature is realized in terms of non-substantiality. The teaching of dependent co-origination, instead of the doctrine of creation, comes on the scene in this connection.

Thirdly, faith as man's responsive involvement in the activity of God is teleological by nature. It is oriented by time and purpose. It is future-oriented and aim-seeking. Contrary to this, self-awakening is essentially free from teleological orientation. As the realization of suchness or as-it-is-ness of everything, including oneself, self-awakening of *Dharma* is not future-oriented but absolute-present-oriented. It is transtemporal, being beyond temporality in terms of 'God's time' as well as in terms of the past-present-future of secular time.

This, however, does not mean that self-awakening of *Dharma* or the realization of suchness is simply timeless. Instead, therein every moment of time is realized as beginning and end simultaneously. This is the meaning of its being absolute-present-oriented and of its being free from teleological orientation. *Telos*, that is end or purpose, is not given by the transcendent but is projected under the given situation along the flow of time through the self-determination of *Dharma*, i.e. through the self-development of 'suchness'. The principle of dependent co-origination is effective not only in terms of space but also in terms of time.

As stated in the three points above, 'Self-Awakening of *Dharma*' which was realized by Gautama Buddha and motivated the early Buddhist movement is categorically different from 'faith' as characterized by Smith as man's participation in God's dealing with humankind. I would like to suggest that, throughout the religious history of humankind, there are two not easily reconcilable types of religion, the religion of faith and the religion of self-awakening. The religion of faith, which may also be termed religion of grace, is exemplified by Christianity, Islam, some forms of Hinduism and Pure Land Buddhism. The religion of self-awakening, which may also be called religion of self-realization, is illustrated by early Buddhism, most forms of Mahayana Buddhism, and some forms of Christian mysticism.

In order to grasp the unity or coherence of humankind's religious history as Smith rightfully intends, one should not overlook the difference between these two types of religious movement. Instead of comprehending the whole of religious history of humankind by the category of faith, one must seek a more generic and more fundamental category through which both the religion of faith and the religion of self-awakening can be understood in their distinctiveness.

V

Before going on to ask what the most generic category to comprehend the unity of humankind's religious history could be, let me briefly discuss Mahayana Buddhism and its understanding of faith and self-awakening.

Like the early Buddhists, Nagarjuna emphasizes the importance of faith as the entrace to *nirvāṇa* and the indispensability of wisdom for attaining it. The following well-known quotation from *Mahā-prajñāpāramita-śāstra* shows his understanding of this point: 'The great ocean of the Buddha-dharma can be entered by faith whereas its other shore can be attained by wisdom.'[25] To reach the other shore of the ocean of Buddha-dharma, you must attain *nirvāṇa* by going across the flux of *saṃsāra*, which is the end of the Buddhist life. However, if one remains in *nirvāṇa* simply apart from *saṃsāra*, one cannot be said to attain the real end of Buddhist life. For one is still not completely free from selfishness and attachment in that, while enjoying the bliss of attaining *nirvāṇa*, one forgets the suffering of one's fellow beings still involved in *saṃsāra*.

Prajñāpāramitā-sūtra, one of the earliest and most important Mahayana sutras, emphasizes that the real end of the Buddhist life does not lie in attaining *nirvāṇa* by overcoming *saṃsāra*, but rather in returning to the realm of *saṃsāra* by overcoming *nirvāṇa* through compassion with one's fellow beings who are still in suffering. Although it is necessary to reach the other shore (*nirvāṇa*) by giving up this shore (*saṃsāra*), *prajñāpāramitā*, meaning the 'perfection of wisdom,' is not realized only by that attainment. To reach the other shore is not really 'to reach the other shore'. By giving up the other shore and returning to this shore one can attain *prajñāpāramitā*, i.e. the perfection of wisdom. This is the reason Mahayana Buddhists emphasize: 'For the sake of wisdom one should not abide in *saṃsāra*: for the sake of compassion one should not abide in *nirvāṇa*.' Indeed, the real *nirvāṇa* and the perfection of wisdom lie in the unhindered and free movement of going back and forth between this shore (*saṃsāra*) and the other shore (*nirvāṇa*).

It is precisely at this point that Mahayanists talk about the identity of *saṃsāra* and *nirvāṇa*. It is not a static but dynamic identity which can be realilzed only through the negation of *saṃsāra* and the negation of *nirvāṇa*. The realization of this dynamic identity of *saṃsāra* (immanence) and *nirvāṇa* (transcendence) is not faith in the transcendent. It is the self-awakening of *Dharma* (suchness) which is neither immanent nor transcendent and yet both immanent and transcendent. Just like the early Buddhist movement, the quintessence of the Mahayana Buddhist movement is not faith in the Buddha but to become a Buddha through self-awakening of *Dharma*. The difference between the early Buddhist (and Theravada Buddhist) and the Mahayana Buddhist movements is found in the static *versus* the dynamic understanding of *nirvāṇa*. The Mahayana Buddhist movement has given rise to various forms across the centuries in China and Japan. Rich diversity among the various forms of Mahayana Buddhism stems from the different paths recommended for how to become a Buddha. For instance, Zen Buddhism emphasizes 'becoming a Buddha through seeing into Original Nature' by seated meditation and *kōan* practice. However, the esoteric Shingon Buddhism stresses 'becoming a Buddha immediately with this body' through the attainment of the *sammitsu*, the three secrets of the Buddha. Pure Land Buddhism, which unlike most other forms of Mahayana, strongly emphasizes pure faith in Amida Buddha as the pivotal point for salvation, talks about 'becoming a Buddha through *nembutsu*'. Just like the Christian, for the Pure Land Buddhist 'faith' in Amida Buddha is absolutely essential for his salvation. But unlike the Christian and the followers of other theistic religions, his final end is to become a Buddha. Here again one can see the inadequacy of trying to comprehend the whole of humankind's religious history under the term 'faith'.

VI

We cannot comprehend the whole process of man's history of religion under the term 'faith', because one must recognize the existence of the religion of self-awakening which is not easily commensurable with the religion of faith. What, then, is the most fundamental category by which we can comprehend it? In a paper entitled 'A Dynamic Unity in Religious Pluralism' which I contributed to the book, *The Experience of Religious Diversity*, edited by Professor John Hick and Hasan Askari [see Chapter 2 above – Ed.], I made a proposal in this regard. My proposal suggests that, given the threefold notion of 'Lord', 'God' and 'Boundless Openness', the third is the ground of the former two. It is the most fundamental category by which we can comprehend the various religions of humankind in a dynamic unity. This threefold notion is an application of the Buddhist *trikāya* doctrine to the pluralistic situation of world religions in our time.

For a detailed discussion of the *trikāya* doctrine, the threefold Buddha-body doctrine, and its application to the contemporary pluralistic situation of world religions, see my paper mentioned above. I propose 'Boundless Openness' as a reinterpretation and generalization of the Buddhist notion of 'emptiness'. I suggest the possibility that it can serve as the fundamental category to comprehend the whole of the history of religion. It may be the principle of dynamic unity for world religions today.

Notes

1. Wilfred Cantwell Smith, *Faith and Belief* (Princeton: Princeton Univ. Press, 1979), Preface p. vii.
2. Ibid., p. 3.
3. Wilfred Cantwell Smith, *The Meaning and End of Religion* (New York: Macmillan, 1962), p. 156.
4. Ibid.
5. Smith, *Faith and Belief*, op. cit., p. 5.
6. Ibid., pp. 10, 11.
7. Ibid., p. 11.
8. Wilfred Cantwell Smith, *Towards A World Theology*. Typed manuscript, Part I: 1.
9. Ibid., Part I: 4.

10. Ibid.
11. Ibid.
12. Ibid., Part V: 22–3.
13. Ibid., Part V: 23.
14. Ibid., Part V: 24.
15. Ibid., Part V: 11.
16. Smith, *Faith and Belief*, op. cit., p. 23.
17. Ibid., p. 27.
18. Ibid., p. 32.
19. Both the doctrines of *pañca-indriya* (five faculties) and *pañca-balāni* (five powers), which were expounded in early Buddhism and which provide the ground for the practice of the subsequent Buddhist movement as the necessary faculties to attain *nirvāṇa*, emphasize *śraddhā* (faith), *virya* (assiduous striving), *smṛti* (mindfulness), *samādhi* (concentration) and *prajñā* (wisdom) in this order. This indicates that in order to attain *nirvāṇa*, *śraddhā* (faith) is essential as the entrance and foundation for the Buddhist practice, but that it is *prajñā* (wisdom) that all Buddhist practice aims at and ends with as ultimate. The Buddhist practice has a structure which starts from faith, goes through practice, and ends with wisdom.
20. Smith, *Faith and Belief*, op. cit., p. 11.
21. *Mahāparinibbāna Suttanta* – see F.A. Burtt (ed.), *The Teachings of The Compassionate Buddha* (New York: New American Library, 1955), p. 49.
22. *Samyutta Nikāya*, Vol. 12, Taishō Vol. II, p. 84b.
23. Smith, *Faith and Belief*, op. cit., p. 140.
24. Ibid.
25. *Mahā-prajñāpāramitā-śāstra*, Vol. I, Taishō Vol. XXV, p. 63.

17

God, Emptiness and Ethics

I have been asked to present an evaluation, from a Buddhist perspective, of the role of ethics in relation to ultimate reality as understood in Buddhism and Christianity. This is a question of the role of ethics in relation to the realization of Emptiness as ultimate reality in Buddhism and, in comparison with this, the role of ethics in relation to God as ultimate reality in Christianity. To clarify the Buddhist standpoint I will discuss (a) the relation between Emptiness and dependent co-origination, and (b) the two truths theory in Mādhyamika Buddhism.

Now, to encapsulate John Cobb's and George Rupp's interpretations of the Buddhist perspective, let me quote David Eckel's summary, which I think is quite accurate. In his paper Eckel says:

Cobb and Rupp approach the Mahayana material in different ways, but they end with remarkably similar judgments. They both emphasize the non-dualistic aspects of the Mahayana, found not only in the literary expressions of the Zen tradition, but also in such classic Indian statements as Nāgārjuna's 'There is no difference between saṃsāra and nirvāṇa, and there is no difference between nirvāṇa and saṃsāra' (*Mādhyamakakārikā*, 24.19). Cobb and Rupp then use this material to picture the Mahayana tradition as one that is so radical in its dissolution of conceptual distinctions' that the historical process, as a reality, simply slips away. The gradual transformation of what is into what ought to be is dissolved in the contemplation of the eternal truth reflected equally in every moment.

Against this understanding of the Mahayana position by Cobb and Rupp, Eckel, relying mainly on Svātantrika-Mādhyamika materials, emphasizes that 'the negative expressions of Mādhyamika thought are always balanced by statements that stress the purposeful practice of religious life.' He also emphasizes that 'the understanding of Emptiness is not an event outside time, but a continuous empty*ing* in which moral action plays a significant, indeed a crucial, part.' In this regard, Eckel further talks about the two-truths theory in the Mādhyamika school to which I will return later.

Robert Thurman also emphasizes the inseparability of the insight of Emptiness from ethical action and the interdependency of metaphysics and ethics in Buddhism. On this basis he criticizes both Cobb and Rupp, saying that they are not free from the typical Western understanding of Buddhism as ethically insufficient. In particular, Thurman strongly criticizes Cobb as if Cobb were attacking Buddhism. In my view, however, Cobb is actually emphasizing the different roles of ethics in Buddhism and Christianity, which are based on two different Ultimate Realities. He is stressing the need for a mutual transformation of Buddhism and Christianity through their encounter. I agree with Thurman, however, when he says that both Christianity and Buddhism have a kataphatic way and an apophatic way of dealing with the question of ultimacy, 'simply, both the movement from the relative to the ultimate (loving God, cultivating Wisdom), and the movement from the ultimate to the relative (loving one's neighbor since God is love, practicing selfless great compassion).'

As for Rupp's typology of the 'Zen-type' and 'Existentialist-type' of modern religious commitment, Thurman makes the criticism that Rupp's 'Zen-type' 'arises from his drastic oversimplification of Zen Buddhism'. I find Rupp's typology of 'Transactional vs. Processive' and 'Realist vs. Nominalist', quite interesting and provocative. Also his 'third type', Christian definition of God, is suggestive. We must give careful thought to the merit of Rupp's typological formulation. Nevertheless, I almost totally agree with Thurman's critique of the 'Zen-type' outlined by Rupp. To characterize Zen as a 'holistic acceptance' type of religion, Rupp quotes D.T. Suzuki and T.R.V. Murti. For instance, Murti's interpretation of *nirvāṇa* is quoted as support for this contention:

There is only change in our outlook, not in reality ... The function of *prajñā* [wisdom] is not to transform the real, but only to create a change in our attitude towards it. The change is epistemic (subjective), not ontological (objective). The real is as it has ever been.[1]

I completely disagree with this interpretation of *nirvāṇa*, for in his interpretation, Murti overlooks the discontinuity between *saṃsāra* and *nirvāṇa*. In Buddhism, *saṃsāra* is realized as the beginningless and endless process of living-dying. There is no continuous path from *saṃsāra* to *nirvāṇa*; in other words, what lies between *saṃsāra* and *nirvāṇa* is not a mere continuous epistemic change, but a discontinuous ontological change. Only when the beginningless and endless process of living-dying itself is realized as 'death' in the true sense is *saṃsāra*, just as it is, realized as *nirvāṇa* – *nirvāṇa* as the liberation from living-dying. Without the realization of *saṃsāra* as 'death' in the true sense, there can be no realization of *nirvāṇa* as 'new life' liberated from transmigration. 'Change in our outlook' or 'epistemic change' is only something which happens in the process of *saṃsāra*, and never leads us to *nirvāṇa*.

The same is true with Zen. The crucial point of Zen practice is *daishi ichiban zetsugo ni yomigaeru*, 'Upon the Great Death we are reborn through complete extinction' or *shinjin datsuraku; datsuraku shinjin*, 'Body and mind dropping off – dropped off body and mind.' This is far more than 'a transformation in the disciples' point of view'[2] as Rupp understands Zen practice to be. However, Rupp is perceptive enough to recognize that Murti's sharp distinction 'between epistemological and ontological change is problematic on the idealistic premises which inform this whole tradition.'[3] Thus, he says, 'For on those premises, a change in consciousness is also a change in the real.'[4] However, the interconnectedness of consciousness (subject) and the real (object) is legitimately realized not before, but only after the realization of Great Death. Accordingly, I cannot accept Rupp's characterization of Zen as manifesting a type of merely 'epistemological' transcendence.

On the basis of the above rough summary, we may formulate the points of discussion as follows: Does the non-dualistic nature of Buddhist 'Emptiness' eventually dissolve ethics and history? If not, how can Emptiness or *nirvāṇa* ground the Buddhist view of ethics and history? To promote interfaith dialogue, these questions must be clarified in comparison with Christianity. Both Eckel and Thurman have already presented their illuminating answers to these questions. In the following, I would like to offer my own understanding.

In the *Mādhyamika-kārikā*, dependent co-origination and Emptiness (and the Middle Way) are expressly declared to be synonyms.[5]

> It is dependent co-originating that we term Emptiness (*Śūnyatā*); this is a designation (*prajñapti*) based on some material. It alone is the Middle Way.

When dependent co-origination and Emptiness are grasped as synonyms two things are indicated: (a) dependent co-origination is Emptiness, and (b) Emptiness is dependent co-origination. The meanings of 'dependent co-origination' in (a) and (b) are not altogether the same. When Gautama Buddha preached dependent co-origination, he emphasized that everything in the universe without exception is co-arising and co-ceasing; nothing is self-existing or unchangeable; this mundane world is in *saṃsāra*, in the endless process of transmigration: to take this conditioned as unconditioned is the basic perversion which is the root of clinging and originates in *avidyā*, i.e., ignorance. The Buddha thus showed the way to attain *nirvāṇa* by realizing the dependent co-origination of everything in the process of *saṃsāra*. However, in the Buddha's teaching, although the transmigrational aspect of 'dependent co-origination' was clearly emphasized, emptiness or the lack of self-existent reality of phenomenal things was just implied. It was Nagarjuna who made explicit the notion of emptiness implied in 'dependent co-origination' and preached the way to enlightenment by awakening to the emptiness of things in this world. Hence, his emphasis on eightfold negation and the negation of all possible dualistic distinctions. Nagarjuna, however, equally stressed that *śūnyatā* is *upādāya-prajñapti* (designation or convention based on some material) which is a synonym of *pratītya-samutpāda*. Here dependent co-origination is regrasped in the light of Emptiness.

Accordingly, in his identification of *pratītya-samutpāda* Nagarjuna, by indicating that dependent co-origination is Emptiness, refers to 'dependent co-origination in *saṃsāra*' in which all dualism or conceptual distinction must be dissolved into Emptiness. On the other hand, by indicating that Emptiness is dependent co-origination he signifies 'dependent co-origination in *nirvāṇa'* in which all dualism or conceptual distinction is reconstructed in the realization of Emptiness without any possibility of clinging to distinction. These negative and positive meanings of Emptiness are implied when Nagarjuna discusses *pratītya-samutpāda* as a synonym of *śūnyatā*.

In order to make this point clearer, let me quote a well-known discourse of a Chinese Zen master, Ch'ing-yüan Wei-hsin of the T'ang dynasty. It runs as follows:

> Thirty years ago, before I began the study of Zen I said, 'Mountains are mountains; waters are waters.' After I got an insight into the truth of Zen through the instruction of a good master, I said, 'Mountains are not mountains; waters are not waters.' But now, having attained the abode of final rest (that is enlightenment), I say, 'Mountains are *really* mountains; waters are *really* waters.'

His understanding of mountains and waters in the first state before Zen practice indicates relativity or distinction realized in the mundane world or conventional realm. In the second stage in which he understands that mountains are not mountains and waters are not waters, he realizes Emptiness and the lack of self-existent reality in which relativity or distinction between things is resolved. All distinction is emptied and the non-duality of reality is realized. At this stage, however, Ch'ing-yüan Wei-hsin realizes only the negative aspect of Emptiness. But by emptying Emptiness, he finally realizes its positive or affirmative aspect at which point he says, 'Mountains are *really* mountains; waters are *really* waters.' In this awakening to true Emptiness, the relativity or distinction of everything is most clearly and definitely realized without attachment to it. The dependent co-arising and co-ceasing of everything in the universe is fully realized just as it is, without attainment and suffering. Along the lines of Wei-hsin, we can state with full justification:

> Before Buddhist practice, I thought 'good is good, evil is evil.' When I had an insight into Buddhist truth, I realized 'good is not good, evil is not evil.' But now, awakening to true Emptiness I say, 'good is *really* good; evil is *really* evil.'

Conventional ethics based on the dualistic view of good and evil must be dissolved in the realization of Emptiness for such ethics entail an endless conflict between good and evil. But this dissolution is just a negative aspect of Emptiness. In the positive aspect of the emptying of Emptiness, the distinction between good and evil is most clearly realized without any clinging to their duality. Hence, Buddhist ethics is established in the realization of true Emptiness.

As both Eckel and Thurman emphasize, Buddhist Emptiness is not merely an ontological ultimate reality devoid of practical commitment. The insight into Emptiness is always inseparably connected with ethical action. However, this unity of the ontological realization of Emptiness and ethical action must include the dissolution of conventional ethics and the construction of ethics in light of true Emptiness. This last point inevitably leads us to consideration of the two-truths theory in Mādhyamika Buddhism.

The two truths are *saṃvṛti-satya* and *paramārtha-satya*. *Saṃvṛti-satya* is the conventional or mundane truth which is valid for practical living. It includes common sense, ethical judgment, and scientific knowledge, all of which are based on conceptual distinction, and are constructed verbally. In contrast, *paramārtha-satya* is ultimate truth, which is *śūnyatā*, Emptiness completely free from conceptual distinction and beyond verbal expression. From the point of view of ultimate truth, conventional or mundane truth, however true it may be in its own right, is nothing but ignorance or falsehood. Thus, the two truths are essentially different from one another. The conventional and the ultimate do not constitute a twofold division of the world, however. It is not that one half is conventional and the other ultimate. Rather, the conventional and the ultimate are co-extensive; both pervade the entire world. This means that there is no continuous path from the conventional to the ultimate. However much conventional truth is accumulated, it can never reach ultimate truth. Only when conventional truth is realized as ignorance and thereby completely turned over does ultimate truth emerge. Being empty and non-dualistic, however, Emptiness not only negates conventional truth but also brings it to fruition.

Once ultimate truth is awakened to, it constructs conventional truth on the basis of Emptiness. Svātantrika terms this *vyavasthapana*, establishment of the conventional. In one sense, ultimate truth cannot express itself apart from the conventional realm. Only in the conventional world can ultimate truth be expressed. In short, only by the negation of mundane truth is ultimate truth realized: only through the self negation of ultimate truth does it express itself in the mundane world. This is the relationship between conventional truth and ultimate truth, in which they are dynamically identical while essentially different.

As I suggested before, ethics belongs to conventional truth. However true and genuine ethics may be in the mundane world, it cannot arrive at ultimate truth as Emptiness. There is no continuous path from ethics to Emptiness. In order to reach Emptiness ethics must be realized as 'ignorance' and be turned over completely. However, this is only the negative aspect of Emptiness. In its positive and affirmative aspect, in which Emptiness empties itself, ultimate truth expresses itself in the form of ethics and ethics is thereby re-established in light of Emptiness.

Accordingly, although ethics belongs to the conventional realm, it is not subordinate to the realization of Emptiness, for ultimate truth can express itself only in the mundane world. In this sense Emptiness may even be said to be subordinate to ethics. In *Mādhyamika-kārikā*, Nagarjuna says, 'The ultimate truth is not taught apart from practical behavior.'⁶ In Nagarjuna the ontological realization of Emptiness is always connected with practical and soteriological concerns.

In this connection it may be in order to examine the relation between *saṃsāra* and *nirvāṇa*. Originally, Buddhism rejects attachment to *saṃsāra* as something real and preaches the necessity of reaching *nirvāṇa*, in which one is emancipated from such attachment and the resultant suffering. *Nirvāṇa* is thus regarded as the goal of the Buddhist life. However, in the *Prajñāparamita-sūtras*, which constitute one of the most important groups of Mahayana sutras and form the background of Mādhyamika Buddhism, not only attachment to *saṃsāra* but also attachment to *nirvāṇa* is rejected. 'Do not abide in *saṃsāra* nor abide in *nirvāṇa*' is a main emphasis of the sutra.

When one overcomes attachment to *saṃsāra* through practice, one awakens to *śūnyatā* and attains *nirvāṇa*. At this point *avidyā* or ignorance ceases and *prajñā* or wisdom is realized. When the eye of wisdom is opened, one comes to realize that not only oneself but also everything in the universe is in *nirvāṇa*. This is why Mahāyāna Buddhism declares that *sōmoku kokudo shikkai jōbutsu*, 'All the trees and herbs and lands attain Buddhahood.' If one says, 'I have attained *nirvāṇa* but trees and herbs, he and she do not attain *nirvāṇa* as yet,' one's attainment is not an authentic one. The attainment of trees and herbs and other persons is *not* an objective event. Together with one's attainment the whole universe attains *nirvāṇa*. This is clearly termed by Dōgen *dōjijōdō*, simultaneous attainment of the way. Since the whole universe has now attained *nirvāṇa* with oneself, the flux of time is completely overcome and history ends in this *nirvāṇa*. This is the wisdom aspect of *nirvāṇa*.

Nirvāṇa as understood in this way, however, is still involved in at least the following two problems: (1) People who are understood by an enlightened one to have already attained *nirvāṇa* do not necessarily realize that they themselves are in *nirvāṇa*. Many of them view themselves as still involved in *saṃsāra*. 'Simultaneous attainment' is not yet *objectively actualized*. (2) Accordingly, if one abides in *nirvāṇa* and simply enjoys his or her own emancipation and is merely satisfied with 'simultaneous attainment', that person is not completely free from selfishness. Enjoying one's own *nirvāṇa* aloof from *saṃsāra*, one forgets the suffering in which fellow beings are still involved.

Due to these two problems, one should not abide in *nirvāṇa*, but return to *saṃsāra* to save others from suffering. Here, history begins in *nirvāṇa*, and it is endless, for those who take themselves to be unenlightened are innumerable in the world at present and will continue to appear forever in the future. Thus, history is the endless process of actualizing 'simultaneous attainment' in time and precisely this is the compassionate aspect of *nirvāṇa*.

Accordingly, true *nirvāṇa* in Mahayana Buddhism is not a quiet and static state of mind beyond the flux of *saṃsāra* as seen in the case of that Arhat, but rather a dynamic function of moving freely back and forth between so-called *saṃsāra* and so-called *nirvāṇa* as seen in the case of the Bodhisattva. The *perfection* of wisdom, i.e. *prajñāparamita*, is not realized in *nirvāṇa* beyond *saṃsāra*, but in the midst of *saṃsāra*, in which compassionate activities are going on through the abandoning of *nirvāṇa*. True compassion is not realized in the supramundane realm of *nirvāṇa*. Nor is it the humanistic love in the realm of the mundane world. Rather, it is compassion which is based on the wisdom realized in *nirvāṇa*, and yet is deeply working in the mundane world. In *nirvāṇa, mahaprajñā* and *mahakaruṇā*, i.e. true wisdom and true compassion, are not two but one. Buddhist ethics and history are established in this dynamic movement of true *nirvāṇa*. *Nirvāṇa* in Mahayana Buddhism is therefore not merely the goal of the Buddhist life but also the point of departure from which the Buddhist life properly begins. When *nirvāṇa* is simply taken as the goal, ethics may be dissolved in Emptiness and history may not be clearly realized. This is why throughout its long history Mahayana Buddhism has emphasized 'Do not abide in *nirvāṇa*' and severely rejected an attachment to Emptiness as a 'rigid view of nothingness' or a 'literal understanding of negativity'.

In conclusion, we can say it is of course not the case that Buddhism is less ethical than Christianity. Ethical action is equally essential to both Christianity and Buddhism. However, the *nature* or *character* of ethics as understood in the two religions is not the same. This difference in the understanding of the nature of ethics, as Cobb suggests, is related to the different realization of the 'ultimate' in the two traditions, that is, *the principle of rightness* in Christianity and Emptiness in Buddhism. Cobb says, 'In the Bible, Yahweh is portrayed as righteous, and the appropriate response to Yahweh's righteousness is human righteousness.' Due to the transcendent character of this divine righteousness, if I am not wrong, Christian ethics becomes an eschatological ethics which is somewhat future-oriented. According to so-called realized eschatology, the justice of God is *already* consummated, but in another sense, it is *not yet*. Christian ethics and its dynamism are based on this tension between *already* and *not yet*. In Christianity, however, 'already' and 'not yet' are not co-extensive: 'not yet' has priority over 'already'. This is why even the realized eschatology is future-oriented.

On the other hand, in Buddhism 'already' and 'not yet' are completely co-extensive and in a dialectical tension. This is because in light of the wisdom realized in *nirvāṇa*, the whole universe is *already* in *nirvāṇa* and time and history ceased there, but in light of compassion equally realized in *nirvāṇa*, innumerable fellow beings are *subjectively not yet* enlightened and time and history thus begin. This dialectical unity of 'already' and 'not yet' is possible because it takes place not in God whose essential nature is rightness, but in true *nirvāṇa* which is the realization of Emptiness. Buddhist ethics and its dynamism are based on this dialectical tension of 'already' and 'not yet', a tension which is not future-oriented but absolute-present-oriented. Thus, in Buddhism, at each and every moment of history, a development toward the endless future is *at once* the total return to the root and source of history, that is, unchanging eternity. Conversely, the total return to this root and source of history is *also* development toward the endless future. The process of history is a succession of such moments whose dynamic structure consists of an advance which is simultaneously a return, a return which is simultaneously an advance.

Christian ethics is an eschatological ethics, based on the principle of rightness as stressed in Protestantism, and it is future-oriented. Buddhist ethics is compassionate ethics, as stressed in Mahayana religiosity, based on the realization of Emptiness, and it is absolute-present-oriented. Since they are significantly different, they can learn greatly from each other. When they learn and deeply appropriate each other, Christianity will become Mahayana Christianity and Buddhism will become Protestant Buddhism.

Notes

1. George Rupp, *Beyond Existentialism and Zen* (New York: Oxford, 1979), p. 38. Originally from T.R.V. Murti, *The Central Philosophy of Buddhism* (London: Allen & Unwin, 1955), pp. 273–4.
2. Ibid., p. 38.
3. Ibid.
4. Ibid.
5. *Mādhyamika-kārikā*, XXIV: 18.
6. Ibid., XXIV: 10.

18

Responses to Langdon Gilkey

MASAO ABE: According to Langdon Gilkey, Christianity begins with a fundamental affirmation of the divine creation, of the essential goodness of the world. My question in this regard is: does this goodness of finite and creaturely beings in divine creation simply indicate goodness in the ethical sense or a goodness in the somewhat wider, transethical sense? According to Genesis, God saw everything that he had made and behold, it was very good. When God made birds and fish, they were very different from one another but equally good because birds were really birds just as they are and fishes were really fishes just as they are Everything created by God was created in its suchness, in its isness. Accordingly, the term God used in evaluating his creation is not good as distinguished from evil but the original goodness prior to the duality between good and evil – that is, goodness not in the ethical sense but in the ontological sense. This interpretation may sound too Buddhistic but when we move to the problem of suffering in connection with the doctrine of creation this interpretation may be helpful.

Referring to the problem of suffering, Gilkey notes that 'suffering, along with evil, enters as an alien or a spoiler – as, in fact, the enemy to what is. Either to what is already there or to what essentially is.' Let me briefly examine the Buddhist understanding of suffering. As Gilkey suggests, in Buddhism suffering and finitude arise and recede together, without contradiction. But I would express this in the following way: in Buddhism suffering, or *duḥkha*, comes from the attachment to things essentially impermanent as if they were permanent. Attachment is nothing but the human word for possessiveness, for human perception which blindly grasps everything as permanent. It is this *avidyā* – blind ignorance, unenlightenment – that engenders attachment. Thus *duḥkha* has its roots in attachment and ultimately in *avidyā* or ignorance. This attachment and blindness indicates a basic mode of human finitude. However, this does not indicate the necessity of evil and suffering in this life. That would be spiritually stifling and lead to an attitude of resignation. On the contrary, the Buddhist understanding of suffering is based on the human world of attachment and blindness. Such attachment and blindness is understood in Buddhism to be deeply rooted in human nature and is not understood as some kind of force operating outside or beyond human nature. Thus, there are credible and valid grounds for hope for emancipation from suffering, for enlightenment or awakening.

Let me now proceed to the Christian understanding of suffering, especially in relation to the Christian notion of the original goodness of finite beings. I would like to suggest that Gilkey's so-called contradiction peculiar to the Christian understanding of suffering may be significantly lessened, if not eliminated, if we understand the original goodness of creaturely beings as original suchness.

After the Enlightenment Schleiermacher distinguished natural evil from moral evil, and most theologians, following Schleiermacher, have explained natural evil in terms of the necessary conditions of a finite and good Creation and moral evil in terms of the symbol of the Fall. My question is, how can such a clear dichotomy between natural and moral evil be possible? In my view, both natural evil and moral evil should be understood both in terms of Creation and the

Fall. And the symbol of the Fall is more essential than that of Creation for understanding the problem of evil, both natural and moral.

Buddhism is not unaware of the distinction between natural and moral evil and its significance for understanding the peculiarity of human existence. In Buddhism, however, that distinction is less clear than in Christianity because Buddhism teaches that humans and nature are equally subject to change, equally transient, and equally involved in transmigration. This solidarity between humans and nature is clearly realized within Buddhism. But not at the expense of the peculiarity of human existence. Although transiency is common to humans and nature, only humans are self-conscious, realizing transiency as transiency and striving to overcome it. In other words, although man and nature are equally subject to transmigration and are involved in *saṃsāra*, only man, who has self-consciousness, can be emancipated from transmigration. This is the reason that Mahayana Buddhism has the following preamble to the verses which comprise the three-fold refuge in the Buddha, the Dharma, and the Sangha: 'Hard is it to be born into human life. We now live it. Difficult is it to hear the teaching of the Buddha. We now hear it. If we do not deliver ourselves in this present life, no hope is there ever to cross the sea of birth and death. Let us all together, with truest hearts, take refuge in the three treasures.' This verse expresses the joy of being born in human form and reveals gratitude for being blessed with the opportunity of encountering the teaching of Buddha. Finally, it confesses to a realization that so long as one exists as a human being, he or she can and must awaken to his or her own Buddha nature by practising the teaching of the Buddha. Otherwise, one may transmigrate on through *saṃsāra* endlessly. In this way the significance of individualized human existence is clearly realized in Buddhism.

There is, however, an existential difference between Christianity and Buddhism in understanding human existence and its relation to nature. In Christianity, man is always grasped in relationship to God. Nature is regarded as something peripheral around this central axis. Unlike nature, a human being who has free will must decide whether he or she will obey the will of God or not. In Buddhism, on the other hand, man is grasped not in relation to something supernatural, but in solidarity with nature, as a part of nature. Man's free will creates *karma* which works without beginning and without end and intimately affects the whole universe. Nothing in time and space is unrelated with our own *karma*. It is crucial for Buddhists to realize that even an event which is apparently unrelated to us is a result of our own being, our own *karma*. Accordingly, for a Buddhist, everything is taken as a matter of self-responsibility, as a result of his own work, not as the work of something else, nor even as the work of God. In this way not only moral evil but also natural evil is understood ultimately as a result of our own *karma* and is to be overcome as a matter of self-responsibility. This is called *jigō-jitoku*, self-*karma*, self-obtaining. This entails a clear realization of individualized human existence without losing its solidarity with nature.

Now I'll briefly discuss the problem of the Fall. As Gilkey clearly states, the ultimate cause of human suffering is the Fall, a person's rebellion against the will of God. According to Genesis, Adam and Eve partake of the fruit of knowledge, against the word of God, and that constitutes the Fall. I think this is a very, very significant understanding of the problem of evil or sin and human will. Again I would like to raise a question. When it is said that Adam and Eve partook of the fruit of knowledge of good and evil, is it good and evil merely in the ethical sense? There seems to be a broader meaning, perhaps the ability to make value judgments or the ability to make distinctions through one's own consciousness. The Genesis story is a mythological interpretation of how and why human beings came to be self-conscious.

Buddhism talks about human beings as having been originally pure and awake. Why then did evil or ignorance and suffering arise in human beings? In the classic philosophical treatise, *Awakening of Faith in Mahayana Buddhism*, it is said that 'suddenly a [deluded] thought arises.' This suddenness does not necessarily mean suddenness in the temporal sense, but rather in the ontological sense.

Redemption as divine participation in human suffering and resurrection, eternal life and the kingdom of God as eschatological transcendence of suffering are without a doubt the highlight of the Christian faith. I'd like to make a few critical comments on this. I'm somewhat uncomfortable with the phrase 'divine participation in our suffering'. Is the crucifixion or death of Jesus on the cross merely participation in our suffering? I believe that it is not participation in, but rather complete identification with our suffering.

LANGDON
GILKEY: I meant them both. You're the orthodox one here, I'm the heretic. You've got the whole church on your side, Masao.

ABE: I'm more Christian than you? [Laughter]

GILKEY: You're more orthodox! [Laughter]

ABE: Is that bad? [Laughter]

The term 'participation' implies a partial, not a total act. Here I'm not concerned with the verbal expression but with the reality understood as being behind the word. In my understanding of Christianity, that is, the orthodox understanding [laughter], the abnegation of the son of God, the Christ, actualized in the event of the crucifixion or death of Jesus, is not partial but total and thoroughgoing. If it is partial, the divine redemption of man's original sin may be only partial, and thus Christ's resurrection after death inconceivable. Only through the total abnegation of the son of God, the Christ, only through a total identity with human suffering could the new era of salvation history be opened. As Paul clearly says in the Epistle to the Philippians, 'Give us death on the cross with nothing but the expression of the kenosis of Christ,' that is, of Christ's self-emptying. The Son of God is Christ, the Messiah, simply because he completely, not partially, emptied himself, took the form of a servant and became obedient even unto death on the cross. If Jesus' crucifixion and death on the cross indicates the Son of God's total identity with human suffering, our resurrection together with the resurrection of Christ cannot be partial, but total and thoroughgoing. This means that our complete resurrection takes place in and through our faith in Jesus as the Christ at this present moment, and not at the end of history. All mankind is resurrected in principle at this present moment. This is a completely realized eschatology which is a necessary result of the total identification of the Son of God with human suffering. In this completely realized eschatology, divine salvation and the transcendence of suffering are already fulfilled, at least in principle. However, although all people may already be saved through Christ's complete identity with human suffering, they themselves may not realize that they are already saved. These unbelievers may be innumerable in the present world and may appear endlessly in the future. Accordingly, it is an essential task for believing Christians to help them realize that they are already saved. This process of helping others must be endless because the number of unbelievers in the present and the future world is endless. So we must say that the resurrection of mankind and the transcendence of human suffering is not yet realized. Thus, a Christian who believes in Jesus as the Christ, who died as the old man and was reborn as a new man through his complete identification with humanity, lives in a paradoxical position. To such a believer mankind is, on the one hand, already saved. On the other hand, the salvation of mankind is not yet fulfilled. Christian believers live a dialectic of 'already and not yet'.

GILKEY: I think I need not express my admiration for these remarks. I kept thinking all the while, he's the best Christian theologian in the room and we need him on our side. [Laughter] It is true that we start logically and ontologically with creation, but it seems to me that Christianity as a religion does not start here: it starts with the experience of rescue, of redemption, and so forth. I'm in thorough agreement that the word 'good' as it appears in Genesis and is interpreted in the tradition is not merely an ethical goodness. You're quite correct in saying that goodness does apply to nature. There's no question that in the early period it was taken in the Greek sense as the goodness of the structure, as the *arete* of finite being. That was what was meant by goodness. Later, as one moves into the modern period, that shifts a little from the structure to the possibility of fulfillment. I think that if one were to ask what contemporary theology means by that goodness, almost all the theologians that I know would probably describe it as a combination of structure and fulfillment. With humans, as far back as Augustine this issue of structure drives them to the problem of decision and the question of ethics arises. But it isn't as if there's a large discontinuity about the word 'good'. The word 'good' refers basically, as you have said, to structure, which I think you are right in identifying as suchness.

It seems to me that whether emancipation is in fact emancipation from finite being was really the subject of our discussion earlier, when we were talking about the issue of the self. When we speak of finite being I think most of us are thinking not only about the various creatures of nature but about human beings in particular. At that point the distinction between an authentic self and an inauthentic self is very important. I would say this is the point: is the goodness of finite being such that redemption is not the abdication of finite being? I don't mean to imply that in Buddhism it is the abdication of finite being: I must say I myself find this difficult to be clear about.

I think you're absolutely right about the distinction between natural and moral evil as raising some very interesting and difficult questions for Christianity. As I indicated, I think that distinction was not very important in the tradition because it was assumed, partly because earlier theologians didn't know anything about the early history of the earth and partly because they thought they had an authoritative account, that what we call natural evils were more or less the result of the Fall in Eden. We must reinterpret the Genesis story as did Schleiermacher and Hegel and others. With this reinterpretation one finds the distinction between natural and moral evil beginning to appear. I agree thoroughly that the distinction tends to enforce what is certainly one of the major problems of all three of the religions that stem from the Hebrew religion, namely the separation of humans from nature. I here have played with the idea, completely heretical to the tradition, that maybe we ought to talk about nature as being in the image of God as well.

I think you're also absolutely right that Buddhism has a much more positive view of nature, a much more creative view of nature than we do. In fact, when I was in Kyoto and Yoshinori Takeuchi and I used to talk about that, we parted on the agreement that what we Christians had to do was to start working on nature. And when I said that what he has got to do is start working on history he shook my hand on that point [laughter], and we rather agreed. The only point that I would make as a kind of friendly nudge like you've been giving me – is that the problem of nature is now a political problem. It was a theoretical problem until industrialism and technology but now it's a political problem. And a political problem is a problem of the meaning of history in the social ethic. So at this point we've got to go into this solution together rather than separately. I myself feel that much more could be said than Christians have said about nature and I would suggest the 'image of God' as an appropriate category for nature. I think the psalms are full of this feeling. Yet we also cannot ignore the modern scientific understanding of nature, and thus the problem has become an exquisite one in the West following the Renaissance.

Another problem, one which I have learned from you, is that of transmigration and its meaning with regard to nature, a problem which raises the question of the status of *karma*. In a very interesting way, I gather that this might be demythologized. If it's demythologized into existentialism then you land in our problem because the existentialist tradition has been perhaps the most elegant forgetting of nature of anything that the West has produced. There is a way in which the collapsing of religion into existentialism leaves out a lot of things, the political aspect among them, but it also leaves out any conception of nature. This is very clear in all the existentialist traditions. I think that the Buddhist view of nature depends on not demythologizing all the way and is very dependent upon *karma* for its force. That is, as you so powerfully put it, we have not been separated forever from the natural world – we have participated in it. You said this to me one time and I've never forgotten it.

I appreciated very much your remarks about the Fall and I know that you are very aware that the Fall as a symbol has been a prime subject for hermeneutic analysis by contemporary theologians. A great deal of really very creative theology has been done by Harvey Cox, John Cobb and others and there have been many very different interpretations of what that story meant and how it's to be interpreted. I think your interpretation is quite accurate, that it is not to be taken point by point too literally but is in some sense to be interpreted in terms of some contemporary view of human beings. Nevertheless, most modern theology doesn't regard it as the historical cause of our problem. Instead, the story is seen as the symbolic disclosure of our problem. That was what I tried to say and that's a very real difference in the function of this symbol. I hesitate to use the word demythologizing as if we put it aside and add something else. It is a disclosive symbol for us, not merely an exegetical problem of that story.

I suggested that with the Enlightenment the temporal distinction between the good Creation and then the Fall was lost. I think Tillich is perhaps the one who saw this most clearly and was somewhat unfairly accused of identifying the two. I suggested that in the discussion with Mahayana Buddhists the identity of *saṃsāra* and *nirvāṇa* was a helpful analogy in thinking about two things that are distinguishable from one another. We think it's important to talk about both of them, but in actuality they both characterize our experience. They're distinguishable in thought, but in any particular moment one is not free of the other. I'm suggesting that Christians adopt this way of perceiving Creation, the Fall and redemption: they are distinguishable yet do not exist independently at any given moment in time, and this is characteristic of our actuality. I think most of us are trying to think about them in this way.

Also, we're talking about the absoluteness of

God here, rather than the issue of the participation of Christ in suffering which, I agree with you, must be total. The issue I think being raised in contemporary theology is a much more fundamental point about God. It certainly involves the related God, in some sense a conditionness on the part of God, and implies a vulnerability on the part of God. Actually I found myself fascinated with the concept of nothingness, *mu*, in relation to this point. I think here the dialectic of being and non-being was closer to the authentic Christian message than the conception of pure being. I don't want us to resign entirely the concept of being because I think our first affirmation (of Creation) depends upon it in some sense. But it seems to me that as one moves through these moments of the Fall and redemption, not only suffering but the role of non-being begins to take a different form, although I'm not sure the church has been aware of that. On that point I think the Buddhists have a great deal to teach us. One might say that self-emptying may be the nature of God. As for the positive meaning of nothingness and of non-being, we've been inclined to reserve it for special occasions like the atonement, rather than thinking it out in terms of the whole structure of our theology. I think Karl Barth really saw this very clearly and that is one of the reasons he said we won't say anything about God. But I'm not sure he took it far enough. Anyway, I'm very grateful for what you said. I wish you were a Christian theologian. It would do us some good.

ABE: Thank you very much, Professor Gilkey. You said that Creation, the Fall and redemption should not be taken in a temporal sequence. I completely agree with you, and I think that Creation and the Fall should be understood in the light of redemption. Talk about these three stages is only for convenience of explanation.

GILKEY: With the only qualification that redemption in Christianity – and to some extent in Buddhism too – does come. That is a character of our faith that means it's asymmetrical at this point. I don't want to go all the way to say that all three are always there. I don't think that would be an accurate expression of the Christian consciousness, to use Schleiermacher's language.

ABE: I said that I am somewhat uncomfortable with your phrase 'divine participation in human suffering'. As I said, the crucifixion of Jesus on the cross must not have been partial, but a complete identity with human suffering. And this implies that the subnegation of the Son of God is not partial, but total and thoroughgoing. Therefore I said that the Son of God, precisely because he is not the Son of God, is really the Son of God. You mentioned that this self-sacrificialness of the Christ may be also related to God himself. Without the self-emptying of God the Father, the self-emptying of the Son of God is inconceivable. The kenotic God is the ground of the kenotic Christ. God the Father who does not cease to be God in the self-emptying of the Son of God is no true God. Accordingly, we may say that our faith in God, is faith in God who is not God, for he is completely self-emptying, but precisely because he is not, God is truly God, for through complete self-emptying God is totally identical with everything, including the sins of man. This means that kenosis, or emptying, is not an attribute, however important it may be, of God, but the fundamental nature of God himself. God is God, not because he had the Son of God take a human form and be sacrificed, but because he himself is suffering God, self-sacrificed God, through his total kenosis. The kenotic God, who totally empties himself and totally sacrifices himself is, in my view, true God.

GILKEY: That's much better said than I said it.

COBB: Better watch it, Langdon. It's going to get taken further than you may want. [Laughter]

GILKEY: Well, I always like to be seduced. [Laughter] What I meant is that the self-emptying is not the emptying of the Godness into something else, but is the character of the divine itself. Now, obviously this is a dialectical matter which frightened the church because who's minding the store when all this is taking place? They realized that if they were going to assert that God is the continuing reality behind the reality of the world, that there had to be some dialectic here, and they tended to make the) Father one and the Son the other. Many contemporary theologians are really wanting to change that.

HANS KÜNG: Well I only want to tell Langdon that I think he's a little confused here. I admire greatly the clarity of Professor Abe's original paper that I heard earlier. It referred to Philippians 2. I think the literary character of this passage is more or less a hymn. It is not to be taken as a dogmatic statement. There is a whole library written about these few verses of this hymn. It is not originally a Pauline hymn, and Paul added something to it, the death on the cross. But Professor Abe omitted that Christ has been exalted, and he stops with the death on the cross. The exaltation was omitted and not taken into account. So I ask first, how can you just identify Christ and God himself? I have nothing against Langdon Gilkey's views of the relatedness of God, God not just above but in this world, committed and involved. I think here we have to make our corrections regarding the immutability of God in the classical sense. But to identify Christ and God is really not the line of the New Testament. As a matter of fact, the Jewish background would not permit such a thing.

Secondly, I had the same troubles with Masao's interpretation of the self-emptying of God, because the self-emptiness of God means to empty God, in order to resolve God into emptiness. This is very good Buddhism, not equally good Christianity. John Cobb has a lot of hesitations in his new book about considering God as emptiness, and I think it's an open question how to handle this. Identification of Christ and God doesn't explain the resurrection. Masao never answered the question, who resuscitates God if he dies completely? A Buddhist doesn't need the second part of the hymn, but for us it is a real problem and maybe we cannot identify God with this kind of nothingness. That's the beginning of the conversation, not the end. Nevertheless I seriously hesitate to consider this real Christianity.

GILKEY: I wasn't raising that point, Hans. I think that there is a bit of a contradiction for a faith that asserts unequivocally the being of God and then has its centre in the death of the Son of God. I remember when Takeuchi was talking about human freedom and authenticity, and I said you need a little more being in that non-being. And then we agreed we need a little more non-being in our being. Buddhists might well think about what the source of that positive estimation of the self is. But we've been a little too strong on the being side, and I think that we can learn a good deal, though obviously we cannot have an identical theology at this point.

SEIICHI YAGI: With the kenotical God, do you mean the death of Christ on the cross of Creation as well? If you understand kenosis as death of Christ on the cross, then it's through kenosis, an event, a temporal event, an event in history. But if you understand Creation also as an act of kenosis, then I think it's more structural.

GILKEY: I noticed everybody nodded in agreement when you said Creation has got to be in some sense a kenosis if redemption is a kenosis. Probably most of us would make a distinction between the relationship of God to the finite world of Creation and the redemptive nature of God; nevertheless the two cannot be completely contradictory to one another. I suppose what we don't like about the tradition is that God was defined as unrelated to the world and this contradicted the message.

The spelling out of how creation is also the kenosis of God or the self-emptying of God, or the giving of the divine itself is pretty complicated. I'm very happy not to identify Creation and redemption but to put the two in the same set of categories.

It's only on the basis of the knowing of God and the power and love of God that one can have hope. We don't have a particularly higher consciousness as such in which the validity of our symbols comes clear, but I think that there is a kind of experiencing, liturgical and devotional, as well as in one's ordinary life, that is the basis of our hope. Certainly the hope is founded upon the relationship to God, and not the reverse, it seems to me.

GORDON
KAUFMAN:

My question I think is along the same line as Professor Yagi's. You presented really two different possible ways of reading the Christian three moment scheme. The traditional is a historical way which no longer seems credible to many. In place of that you proposed a dialectical-structural kind of account in which these three moments form a kind of structure. Now Professor Abe tried to push you all the way on that one and said, in effect, if you're going to go the structural way, then you should make the whole thing structural. But you resist that and want to have a kind of mix in which there is a structure of the first two moments, Creation and Fall, and then a sort of historical kind of redemption of some sort. It really isn't clear to me what that could mean. If the redemption is a kind of super-added historical event, that means redemption must be from finitude, because finitude is really defined by the first two events. That's the structure of things out of which redemption lifts us in some way. But you don't want that either, you don't want redemption to be from finitude. If redemption isn't from finitude then we're going to have to say that the problem as well as the redemption is historical, so the Fall (the second moment) is going to have to be in some way historical and progressive as well as redemption (the third moment), or else the third moment is just completely out of line with the argument. Now I think, Langdon, you just felt it all pretty fuzzy as to whether this is a structural understanding or a historical understanding or some combination that isn't yet clear.

GILKEY: I hate to agree with everybody [laughter] but I find it very fuzzy too. You said so in your systematic theology, and it was one of the things I felt was really true in that book...

KAUFMAN: I don't like that book very much any more, Langdon. [Laughter]

GILKEY: I know you don't. But I think you are going to like this part [laughter], namely that the Fall must've begun even if we didn't take it as an event. I agree thoroughly with that in so far as we're analysing the human. In so far as our present experience is concerned this is where we are.

Now with regard to the asymmetry, I agree with you, but I will stick with that whatever the problem is. I have a big brother on my side in Tillich who said that the paradox – and this is the fundamental paradox – is that against all expectation something has come into the human situation. Now I think that is our experience. I can't understand either one of our Jewish or Christian faiths without that experience of coming in. Now the minute one has said that one has to say that this is a coming in of what God apparently about all the time, and that there is a redemptive activity of God that is universal, as is the creative and the judging activity of God.

KAUFMAN: Then, of course it is structural rather than historical.

GILKEY: I do not agree that salvation appeared for the first time here. I think the loss, the decline of hell is the most important thing that's happened in our tradition. I think the universality of grace and the universality of truth, which is why we're here

JOHN HICK:

SCHUBERT
OGDEN:

ABE:

really, is the other important thing. However, we are historical beings and apparently God in some sense relates to that. Now at that point I'll stick with the contradiction. I'd be afraid of losing the historical entirely if we made all three structural. I wanted to insert a note of warning. The idea of divine self-emptying is, I think, a poetic or a metaphorical idea. It's extremely vague. One can make large, quick moves with it but sooner or later it's going to be very important to give them precise meaning. If we say that God empties himself are we saying that God ceases to exist? That he commits suicide? Are we saying that he throws aside and ceases to have certain attributes of his? If he throws them aside can he take them back again? If he can't take them back again has he really thrown them aside? Does he cease to be good, to be loving, to have knowledge, to have the capacity to bring things about, etc. I just find the phrase 'divine self-emptying' dangerously vague.

On the one hand Jesus Christ is the manifestation of God's participation in or identification with the non-being and suffering of finitude and estrangement, and on the other hand, he is the meritorious cause of this atonement. To say that the atonement of Jesus Christ is the meritorious cause of our redemption does indeed put things in a radically historical way, but for many of us it also puts it in a mythological way that we can no longer find credible. The alternative to that isn't simply structural, because one can still distinguish between God's history, which is the history of atoning life relative to the creatures, and the manifestation of that divine history of atonement in the history of Jesus Christ. That distinction should be made, and I don't think that involves a contradiction, Gordon, I think the distinction is clear.

The kenosis of Christ should not be understood to mean that Christ was originally the Son of God and then emptied himself and became identical with man. Such a view in the temporal order or sequential order is nothing but the conceptual and objectified understanding of the issue. So we should understand the kenosis of God to mean that Christ as the Son of God is essentially and fundamentally self-emptying. It is not that the Son of God became man through the process of self-emptying, but he is essentially true man and true God at one and the same time in the dynamic manner. It is based on the will of God, the love of God.

19

Spirituality and Liberation: A Buddhist-Christian Conversation (with Paul F. Knitter)

I   A CHRISTIAN INTRODUCTION
Paul F. Knitter

In introducing the topics for our Buddhist-Christian conversation, I would like to follow the advice of my feminist theologian friends and take a personal approach. I think I can make clear why I am eager to talk with Professor Abe by first speaking about what I did in the summer of 1987 and what happened to me.

First of all, I went to Japan. It was my first visit to the Orient, and I had all of six weeks. The official reason for my trip was research: I was working on a history of Zen Buddhism at Nanzan University. But the real, the impelling, reason I went to Japan was to immerse myself in the history, the spirit, the experience of Buddhism, especially of Zen. As much as possible, I wanted to *practice*, to sit, to follow the guide of a master, and to do all this in the land where, after its birth in China, Zen had taken on a new identity that has endured through the centuries. Especially during the days I spent in the old monastery of Hosshinji, in Obama, in the southwestern mountains of the main island, my wish was granted. I sat, and chanted, and worked, with the thirty monks and nuns who carry on the Sōtō Zen tradition of Hosshinji.

Why did I want to do this? Why this pressing need to 'pass over', as John Dunne puts it,[1] to Buddhism? It certainly was not because of any fundamental or serious dissatisfaction with Christianity. I was not running away. On the contrary, I would say that the need to taste of Buddhism came out of my own Christian faith and experience. Here Thomas Merton helps me understand what I felt. His own life and experience illustrates that the more one enters into the fullness of the mystery of Christ, the more one is open to others and the more one can appreciate the beauty and richness of other religious ways. In his *Seven Storey Mountain*, Merton had little good to say about Eastern religions; in fact he gave up his explorations into Hinduism as a waste of energy; it was only after his entrance into Gethsemane, only after the years of deepening his own Christian mysticism, that he was, as it were, able to return to the East and read the Zen and Taoist classics, as well as the works of D.T. Suzuki, with new eyes and a new heart. He saw and felt what he had earlier missed. And as his *Asian Journal* attests, his study and experience of Zen had a penetrating influence on his own spirituality. (I would argue that it helped make Merton's spirituality more 'this-worldly'.[2]) In any case, I experienced just a little of what Merton discovered – that to know Christ is to be open to the presence of truth or ultimacy wherever it may play. This is part of what drew me to Japan.

But there was more. It was not just a question of being open to or *appreciating* other religions, but of *needing* them, of *having to* dialogue with followers of other paths. This is difficult to explain. There is a paradox here, something that more and more Christians, especially in Asia, are sensing. What called me to Japan was a sense that something was missing in the fullness of Christian faith if I did not open myself to the riches of other ways. Or, the more I know of Christ, the more I realize that something is missing in Christ if I do not also know Buddha. Merton, I think, felt that.

And so I went to sit and study with the Buddhists of Japan. And what I realized convinced me that John Cobb was indeed right when he suggested a few years ago that Christians and Buddhists, through dialogue with each other, can be 'mutually transformed'.[3] It is a transformation not just in 'technique' or practice ('Now I use Zen for my prayer!') but in self-understanding (doctrine) and in experience itself (new ways of experiencing the Ultimate). My Japan experience confirmed for me what many Christians like Thomas Merton and Buddhists like Professor Abe have been discovering over the past decades – that interreligious dialogue is an ever-more pressing challenge and opportunity for all people of faith. In order really to be Christian, we must also, as it were, be Buddhist (or, Hindu, Muslim, Jewish).

But I did something else that summer. In August, I went to El Salvador. With thirteen other Cincinnatians, my wife and I (for the third summer in a row) travelled to Central America to learn more about what is happening there, to be with and learn from the people who are the victims of war and unjust social structures, and to protest here at home what we think is the unwise and immoral policy of our government in Central America. Much of the motivation for our trip came out of our work in the Sanctuary Movement in Cincinnati.

But we went not just as concerned citizens. We went primarily as Christians. As with the trip to Japan, it was my Christian faith that drew me to El Salvador – a faith that for me has best been articulated by Vatican II and liberation theologians. With so many other Christians in both South and North America, I have felt, more and more clearly/uncomfortably, that to be a Christian, one who follows the way of the Nazarene, we cannot remain in the warmth of our churches; we must enter the grime and mess of the world, especially the world of victims. In El Salvador, familiar post-Vatican II themes took on impelling reality: that God wills to save us not just for heaven but in the world; that the Kingdom is to come on earth, as it is in heaven, that sin is social, and to be saved is to be saved from sinful social structures; that Christians therefore must be part of the world, including the world of politics and economics – and most sharply and demandingly, that to know God is to do justice. But as Jon Sobrino told us in San Salvador, the reverse is perhaps even more accurate: to do justice, to be active with the struggling poor, is to know God – i.e. to experience God, perhaps, as one has never before experienced the Divine. In short, Christian life must be lived in and out of some form of *liberative praxis* – some concrete action that seeks to liberate people (ourselves included) from that which prevents them from living a full human life, whether it be in El Salvador, or in South Chicago, or in our own neighborhood.

All this was confirmed for me in El Salvador. From our visits to the many refugee camps, our reflection and prayer with the base Christian communities, our fear of the ever-lurking military and Cherokee vans of the death squads – from the oppressed of El Salvador we were enriched. We returned home with much more than we could ever give them.

Yet when I look back at that summer, I am, in a sense, perplexed. It is a familiar perplexity. It was out of my Christian faith that I went to both Japan and El Salvador. And that Faith was abundantly enriched by both experiences – by both sitting with the monks of the Hosshinji Temple and by talking and praying with the victims of bombing in the Bethania refugee camp. Both experiences were so good, so necessary. But how do they fit together? Do they fit together? Does one have a priority over the other? Must I continue doing both?

This is where I think Buddhism can help us Christians. Both on the basis of their practice and their teaching, Buddhists can aid us to respond, in our contemporary world, to the time-tried question of how to combine 'contemplation and action', 'prayer and work', 'Martha and Mary', spirituality and liberation – Japan and El Salvador. In the context of my summer's experience, here are some of the questions and issues I would like to discuss with Professor Abe.

– Are both sitting in meditation and acting for social-political liberation necessary in order to be a follower of Jesus – or of Buddha? Why? The same question from another angle: Christian theologians urge us all to make a preferential option for the poor, maintaining that today the primary concern of the churches must be for the oppressed and the marginalized of our society and world. How does this fit into what seems to be Buddhism's 'preferential option for meditation and enlightenment'? Would Buddhists agree with the claim of liberation theologians that unless we are involved in some form of praxis of liberation, our meditation-prayer will be empty and/or self-serving?

– The liberation claim is that we do not really know God or the Ultimate unless we are working for justice – that it is in the very experience of acting with and for the oppressed that God can be discovered in new and necessary ways today. I realized this in El Salvador. But I also sensed, as I sat for seven hours a day facing the wall of the Hosshinji Temple, that in *zazen* the Ultimate was present to me in ways I had not really known before. Again, is the Ultimate present differently in sitting with an empty mind than in acting for justice?

– A question that pursued me especially in El Salvador: do people who sit, who meditate, act differently as they go about their liberative praxis, than people who do not sit? What happens to us in sitting?

– Also, what does sitting tell us about what we can hope for, what we should strive for, in our acting and involvement in the world? From his own experience of *zazen*, his own spirituality, what does Professor Abe hope we can do with this world of suffering and injustice? Can we really change this world?

What I want to talk about with Professor Abe is summed up for me in a feeling I had while I sat in one of the beautiful gardens of the Zen Temple of Ryōanji in Kyoto and watched the tall pine trees swaying Zen-like in the wind. I realized that in two months I would be in the squalor and pain of the refugee camps outside of San Salvador. And I knew I wanted to be in both places; I was certain of that. But I don't know why.

II   A BUDDHIST PERSPECTIVE
Masao Abe

In his introduction, Professor Paul Knitter vividly talked about his experiences in Japan and El Salvador two summers ago, the experiences in which his Christian faith prompted his involvement. He told us that his faith was abundantly enriched by both experiences – by both sitting in meditation with the monks of Hosshinji Zen Temple in Japan and by talking and praying with victims of bombing in the Bethania refugee camp in El Salvador. Then Professor Knitter raised the question: 'How do they [these two experiences] fit together? Do they fit together? Does one have a priority over the other? Must I continue doing both?' This question, that is how to combine 'contemplation and action', 'prayer and work', 'spirituality and liberation', is one of the most fundamental and crucial questions that any religionist must confront – especially in our contemporary world.

I myself have been struggling with the same kind of question since my student days. I was a university student in Japan during the Second World War. As the war developed, students were enlisted and ordered to the battlefield by the government. Around that time my Buddhist professor, Shin'ichi Hisamatsu[4] and his disciples including myself had organized an association named *Gakudō-dōjō*[5] which emphasized Zen meditation as the basic forum of practice. By joining the army, we students were to give up academic studies and Zen meditation, and were to be confronted by death on the battlefront. What is the meaning of Zen meditation in relation to national and world peace? This was a serious question for all students of our association.

After the War which ended in 1945 with Japan's unconditional surrender, we continually grappled with the same problem. In 1951, shortly after the Korean War, addressing the question of how we were to reform the world and create true history, we formulated 'The Vow of Humanity'. It runs as follows:

> Keeping calm and composed, let us awaken to our true Self, become fully compassionate humans, make full use of our gifts according to our respective vocations in life; discern the agony both individual and social and its source, recognize the right direction in which history should proceed, and join hands without distinction of race, nation, or class. Let us, with compassion, vow to bring to realization humanity's deep desire for self-emancipation and construct a world in which everyone can truly and fully live.

Hisamatsu was highly critical of the concept of the nation-state, in particular its self-interested sovereignty, which he saw as being at the source of international conflict. He insisted that true sovereignty rests with humanity as a whole[6] and emphasized the necessity of establishing a political system 'of all humanity, by all humanity and for all humanity'.

In 1958, we reorganized our association, *Gakudō-dōjō* into the FAS Society[7] in order to make clear our threefold understanding of human existence which, we believe, is essential to religious awakening and social change. (We used this English acronym, FAS, because there is no adequate Japanese abbreviation to express this threefold notion.)

What, then, is FAS? 'F' stands for 'Awakening to the *F*ormless Self' referring to the dimension of depth of human existence, i.e. the True Self as the ground of human existence. 'A' stands for 'Standing on the Standpoint of *A*ll Humanity', referring to the breadth of human existence, i.e. human beings in their entirety. And 'S' stands for 'creating history *S*uprahistorically' referring to the dimension of the chronological length of human existence, i.e. awakened human history. Accordingly, the three aspects of FAS indicate a threefold structure of human existence, that is depth, breadth and length of human existence – more concretely speaking: self, world and history. (This threefold notion may correspond to the traditional Western threefold notion of the soul, the world and God. In our threefold notion, however, God is absent.) In the notion of FAS, these three dimensions of human existence are grasped dynamically, and though different from each other they are inseparably united with each other.

The first dimension, that is 'F', which stands for 'Awakening to the Formless Self', signifies nothing other than *satori* in the Zen sense. Traditionally, it has been said that the primal concern of Zen is *Koji-kyūmei*, 'investigation of self', that is, enquiring and awakening to one's True Self, or original face. Hisamatsu calls True Self the 'Formless Self'[8] because, being entirely unobjectifiable, True Self is without any form that can be objectified. True Self is realized to be really formless by going beyond both form (being) and formlessness (non-being). Traditional Zen greatly emphasized the importance of investigating and seeing into the Self, but it also admonished not to remain in silent illumination or fall into a nihilistic demon cave by becoming attached to the formlessness of the self. Zen thus stresses the necessity of great dynamism or the wondrous function of helping others. Hisamatsu, however, criticizes this formulation of traditional Zen by saying that if the so-called 'wondrous function' signifies only the process leading other individuals to awaken to their True Self, its function remains limited to the problem of self without penetrating more widely beyond it even by one step. He says:

> If, as in traditional Zen, wondrous function remains a compas-
> sionate act of enlightening others from beginning to end, then
> it has nothing to do with the formation of the world and the
> creation of history. Being apart from the world and history Zen
> eventually becomes a mountain Buddhism or a temple Buddhism,
> or at best becomes a meditation hall Buddhism. After all it
> cannot escape from the demon cave Zen.[9]

> A complete compassionate act in Zen must be to form a true
> world and to create true history freely without any bondage,
> through having people awaken to their authentic, True Self, i.e.,
> the Formless Self which is solitarily emancipated and
> nondependent.[10]

According to Hisamatsu, a formation of the true world necessi-
tates the second dimension of human existence, that is 'A' which signifies 'Standing on the Standpoint of *All* humanity', because unless we grasp racial, national and class problems from the perspective of all humankind, we cannot solve any of them adequately. Thus, in addition to the 'investigation of Self', what I call *sekai-kyūmei*, an 'investigation of the world' is needed to discover the nature and structure of the world.

Furthermore, a creation of true history requires the third dimension of human existence, that is 'S', standing for 'Creating history *S*uprahistorically', because true history cannot be created by an approach immanent in history, such as class struggle in Marxism or social reform in humanism. Unless we take a suprahistorical religious standpoint, that is, in Hisamatsu's case, the awakening to the Formless Self as our basis, we cannot create true history. Therefore, what I call *rekishi-kyūmei*, 'investigation of history', is necessary to understand the real meaning of history and its origin and purpose.

Currently, we have various forms of peace movements, human rights movements, and various other social reform movements. If these movements, however, are pursued only from a political and social standpoint *without a basis* in our deep realization of True Self, such approaches may not yield adequate solutions. Even if those who participate in such movements are full of much good will and possess a strong sense of justice, if they lack an awakening to the original nature of self and others, their actions are without real power, or worse, they create more confusion. On the other hand, if only the internal religious aspect of the human being is emphasized and priority is given to one's own salvation, thereby neglecting affairs of the world, however serious individuals may be in their religious quest they cannot attain a profound religious solution. Mere concern with self-salvation is contrary to even the Bodhisattva's 'Four Great Vows'.[11] Today's Buddhism is apt to be removed from social realities and confined to temples, and engrossed only in the inner problems of the self.

Koji-kyūmei, the 'investigation of self', will necessarily become superficial and without reality if it is sought only for its own sake. Therefore, we should work upon *sekai-kyūmei*, the 'investigation of the world', that is, the problem of what is the true world, what is the root and source of the world in which we live. Accordingly, the 'investigation of the world' is not separate from the 'investigation of self'. But to study and clarify the world is also inseparably linked with *rekishi-kyūmei*, the 'investigation of history', that is, studying and clarifying the origin and true meaning of history.

In short, the questions of what the self is, what the world is and what history is, are all related to one another. The problem of what the self is cannot be resolved in its true sense if it is investigated independently of those problems of the nature of the world and the meaning of history. On the other hand, world peace, for example, cannot be established in the true sense, nor can history be truly created, unless one clarifies what the self is. These three problems are inseparably related and united at the root of our existence.

In order to respond to the questions raised by Professor Knitter concerning how to combine spirituality and liberation, I would like to answer that we should clearly realize that we are always standing and working at the intersection of three dimensions: 'investigation of self', 'investigation of the world' and 'investigation of history'. Each approach must include the other two, otherwise each may fail even for its own sake.

III A CHRISTIAN RESPONSE
Paul F. Knitter

Professor Abe, as in past conversations with you (and with other Zen Buddhists), I have found your remarks as inspiring and challenging as they are intriguing and elusive. Your threefold distinction of the dimensions of reality – the investigation of the self, the world and history – was extremely helpful not only in clarifying the relation between spirituality and liberation but in clearing away certain Christian misunderstandings of Buddhism. Yet your distinctions – what you mean by the terms and how you interrelate them – left me with as many questions as answers. I would like to formulate my part of our conversation at this point in two general questions, each of which goes in a different direction. The first expresses what I think is a central Buddhist challenge for Christians; the second formulates what might be a Christian challenge for Buddhists.

'You cannot change the world unless you sit'

If I can summarize what for me was your main message, it would be something like: 'You cannot change the world unless you sit.' That is, we will not be able to liberate the world and transform it unless we sit in meditation and are internally transformed ourselves, unless we are enlightened or experience *satori*, unless we investigate the self and realize (or start to realize) the Formless Self. As you put it, 'if they lack an awakening to the original nature of the self and others, their actions are without power, or worse, create more confusion.' '[W]orld peace . . . cannot be established in the true sense, nor can history be truly created, unless one clarifies what the self is.'

There is a danger that in listening to you we Christians will sit back and say, 'Oh yes, I know what he means. All actions must flow out of contemplation. That is what our Christian mystics have said all along, what every true spiritual adviser will insist on. It is even what Cardinal Ratzinger has stressed in the Vatican's recent statement on liberation theology: social transformation must be preceded by personal conversion and devotion.' The danger is that what you have told us may sound too familiar – or that we too quickly translate what you said into our familiar Christian categories. I suspect that when you and other Buddhists insist that one must realize the Formless Self before being able to be truly involved in the world and history, you are saying something more than what is already familiar to us Christians. This is your challenge to us. To sharpen its message, I would ask you, Professor Abe, to challenge us more by telling us more.

I think it would be helpful, perhaps even unsettling, if you can state more clearly what you mean by the Formless Self, the True Self. Here is where I suspect there might be significant differences in what Buddhists and Christians take to be a necessary condition for social transformation.

What happens to a person when she or he begins to experience the Formless Self? What does such a person see or feel? Is it appropriate to ask whether there is an *object* to this experience? *What* is the person experiencing?

What I am trying to get at with these questions can be approached from a different direction: Why is it necessary for us to experience the Formless Self before trying to change the world? You said that without this experience our actions in the world are without energy, or they create confusion. Is the experience of our True Self an experience of a kind of cosmic energy – the 'Force' of *Star Wars*? And just how does the experience keep us from causing further confusion? What does it reveal that prevents this confusion?

I come closer to the intent of my questions when I raise an even more difficult issue: why are you apparently reluctant to associate this experience of the Formless Self with God? You mentioned that in your distinction of self/world/history, you leave God out.

Why? Do you feel that the traditional Christian notion of God gets in the way of an authentic experience of the Formless Self or that it prevents the full integration of the self with the world and history?

All these questions are trying to nudge you to formulate more expressly and uncomfortably what I think is the Buddhist challenge to Christian spirituality and liberation. I suspect that Buddhists refuse to speak of God because they want to make sure that the experience of the Formless Self or of the Ultimate is genuinely an experience in and of oneself – an experience of the Ultimate *as* oneself, *as* the world, i.e. not separate from oneself. I sense that the Buddhist fear of the Christian insistence on the otherness and transcendence and personality of God is that such a God, in *God's own* otherness, does not allow for the kind of religious experience that calls forth the full promise and potential of the human self and of the world and of history. Buddhists are challenging Christians, I think, to explore a much more *immanent* concept and experience of the Ultimate, an experience in which one senses the inadequacy of speaking of God as other or as a person. For the Zen Buddhist, only such a non-dual, immanent experience of God as the Formless Self will truly enable an affirmation of this world and of the need for human action and responsibility in it.

'You cannot sit unless you change the world'

The second issue I would like to discuss with you might be summarized in the overly simplified statement: 'You cannot sit unless you change the world.' By that I mean the Christian insight – as formulated by liberation theologians – that we cannot taste the fruits of meditation or prayer, we cannot experience the Ultimate or the Formless Self, unless we are first, or at the same time, acting to transform the world. Meditation will not work unless it is preceded/accompanied by action for social transformation. We cannot realize our Formless Self in the meditation hall unless we are also realizing it in actions for justice. Perhaps here too there is a certain danger that Buddhists might too quickly agree with what liberation theology is saying, claiming this to be something they already hold. Perhaps Christianity, in its modern dress of liberation theology, is saying something quite different from traditional Buddhism (and traditional Christianity!).

To try to clarify this Christian challenge to Buddhism, let me ask you some questions about what you mean by 'investigating the world and history'. While I clearly understood your insistence on the interrelatedness of investigating the self-world-history, I did not grasp *how* you go about your investigation of world and history. To be more precise, I am not sure just what the investigation of the world and history really adds to what you already have discovered from the investigation of the self. In your remarks, you insisted that the investigation of self, world and history are 'inseparably related'. But it seems to me that there is a certain priority in this relationship, with 'investigation of the self' holding the priority.

Even for Hisamatsu, enlightenment takes place essentially *within*, in meditation, in discovering the Formless Self; when one investigates the world and history, one applies or lives out what one has discovered in *satori*. The essential discovery takes place in the enlightenment experience, not in and through investigating and acting within the world. In other words, it seems to me that the enlightenment one gains through sitting or practice has a certain *epistemological priority*. As you said, when we investigate the world we find that we are one family, all interrelated; and we discover that history must have a transhistorical source of meaning and energy. But these are discoveries that we already knew in realizing our Formless Self through enlightenment.

Liberation theologians, if I understand them correctly, would hold that by itself faith or prayer or meditation or personal enlightenment is *not* enough for investigating and understanding the world and history. By acting in the world, i.e. by getting involved in some form of action for justice and social transformation, especially by a preferential option for the poor in which we act with and share the experience of the poor – by such forms of 'praxis' we discover and see things not only about the world and history but also about God and the Ultimate that we could never see in our prayers or meditation or traditional understanding of religious experience. Also, the liberation theologians suggest that to investigate the world and history we need, besides our spiritual perspectives born of faith, some form of concrete social-economic analysis. Without some hard-nosed social analysis, our faith-or-*satori* perspective on the world may easily turn out to be an ideology that deludes ourselves and exploits others.

In other words, liberation theologians, drawing on what they think are biblical insights, suggest that *action* has a certain *epis-*

temological priority over prayer or meditation or the explicitly religious. Yes, if we can never really transform the world unless we are enlightened, liberation theologians would respond that we can never attain enlightenment unless we have made a prior option to act for justice and love for and with others. Only out of the soil of such action or liberating praxis will true enlightenment, true experience and knowledge of God, grow. In fact, they would argue – and they feel that history makes this clear – to engage in sitting or prayer or intense religious practice without some concrete involvement in trying to transform the world easily leads to a false image of God, to inauthentic religious experience, to a Self that is not truly Formless. Praxis or working for justice, therefore, holds a certain priority (which does not mean that praxis can ever stand by itself, i.e. without contemplation and sitting).

These claims for a certain priority of praxis are based on what some have seen as a fundamental difference between Christianity and Buddhism.[12] Christianity emphasizes *agape* or love, which then leads to and needs gnosis or knowledge, whereas for Buddhism (both Theravada and Mahayana?) the emphasis falls on gnosis or contemplative knowledge which then includes *karuṇā* or love. Christian life and identity are first of all a matter of *agape* – of living God's life, of loving, or doing what God does, of working for the Kingdom, before it is a matter of praising God or clearly knowing God; not those who proclaim 'Lord, Lord' but those who *do* the will of the Father are called blessed. The living of God's life, the praxis of love and justice, leads one to know God, to celebrate God, to express this life in liturgy and sacrament and religious doctrine. We do before we know. The spirit lives within us before we confess the Lord Jesus. In Buddhism, I think, the emphasis is on first knowing, on enlightenment, on sitting, which then, by its very nature, will embrace acting. Gnosis before *agape*; *prajñā* before *karuṇā*. The differences between the two spiritualities are clear and significant, though not at all contradictory or exclusive.

Again, Professor Abe, can you tell me whether these observations on the relation between *agape* and gnosis, and on the priority of acting over knowing, make any sense from your Buddhist perspective? If Buddhists insist that we cannot change the world without sitting and enlightenment, would they also agree that we cannot sit and experience enlightenment unless we are trying to transform the world?

IV A BUDDHIST RESPONSE
Masao Abe

Professor Knitter has made a very insightful and penetrating response to my Buddhist perspective on the problem 'Spirituality and Liberation'. It is indeed an important challenge for Buddhists, one which no Buddhist can avoid in the contemporary social situation.

A

Professor Knitter summarized the Buddhist standpoint in the statement, 'You cannot change the world unless you sit,' whereas he summarized the Christian message in the statement, 'You cannot sit unless you change the world.' And, in his conclusion, he states that in Christianity, 'We do before we know. The Spirit lives within us before we confess the Lord Jesus.' In Buddhism, the emphasis is on first knowing, on enlightenment, on sitting, which, then, will embrace acting. Gnosis before *agape*; *prajñā* before *karuṇā* (that is, wisdom before compassion). This is a clear analysis of the difference between Christian and Buddhist spiritualities. On the basis of this understanding, Professor Knitter raises a very challenging question to Buddhists: 'Why is it necessary for us to experience in Formless Self *before* trying to change the world?'

In this connection, I would like to raise a counter-question to Professor Knitter. When in referring to Christianity, you say, 'We do before we know' and in referring to Buddhism, 'wisdom before compassion', what do you mean by the word 'before'? Does this 'before' indicate 'before' in the temporal sense? Do you understand Buddhists to believe that the attainment of enlightenment must precede working for others and transforming the world? If this is your implication, there remains a misunderstanding of Buddhism. Buddhism, particularly Mahayana Buddhism, strongly emphasizes the way of *bodhisattva* which tries to help others awaken while attaining enlightenment. This is because Mahayana Buddhism insists that one can attain true enlightenment only through helping others become enlightened. Buddhism teaches us to overcome *saṃsāra*, i.e., living-dying transmigration, and attain *nirvāṇa* by awakening to wisdom. But if one stays in *nirvāṇa*, being apart from *saṃsāra*, one is still selfish because abiding in *nirvāṇa*, one may enjoy one's own salvation while forgetting the suffering of one's fellow beings who are still involved in *saṃsāra*.

To be completely unselfish one should not stay in *nirvāṇa* but return to the realm of *saṃsāra* – that is, this actual world – to respond compassionately to suffering fellow beings. This is the reason Mahayana Buddhism emphasizes that 'In order to attain wisdom, one should not abide in *saṃsāra*; in order to fulfil compassion, one should not abide in *nirvāṇa*.' Not abiding either in *saṃsāra* or *nirvāṇa*, and freely moving from *saṃsāra* to *nirvāṇa*, from *nirvāṇa* to *saṃsāra*, without becoming attached to either – this dynamic movement is true *nirvāṇa* in Mahayana Buddhism. In this dynamic movement of true *nirvāṇa* there is no before-and-after duality.

Sitting in Zen meditation does not necessarily indicate a quiet sitting by physically taking the full lotus posture. Tradition emphasizes: 'Walking is Zen, sitting is Zen, whether talking or remaining silent, whether moving or standing quiet, the Essence itself is ever at ease: Even when greeted with swords and spears, it never loses its quiet way.' Even in walking, moving and talking, Zen meditation must be realized. What is essential for Zen meditation is not physical sitting but the well-composed, quiet mind under any circumstances. This is the reason Zen emphasizes 'stillness in movement, movement in stillness', and that, 'meditation practice in movement is far more important than meditation practice in stillness.' Accordingly, Zen sitting in meditation does not exclude activities but provides the basis for our vital activities. In the case of the FAS Society, this activity includes the investigation and formation of the world and history.

When I said, 'World peace . . . cannot be established in the true sense, nor can history be truly created, unless one clarifies what the self is,' I did not mean that the clarification of one's self must come temporally before a world peace movement and historical change. Rather, I mean that the clarification of the self, that is, the awakening to the True Self, is necessary as the existential or ontological *ground* for our social movement. Without the awakening to the True Self as the existential ground, we cannot establish world peace in the true sense.

For this reason, I emphasized the inseparability of investigating the self-world-history. In other words, the true investigation of the self must include the investigation of the world and history, and the true investigation of world and history must include the investigation of the self. In their inseparability, there is no before-after relation in the temporal sense. They take place simultaneously.

B

In this regard, however, I must listen more carefully to Professor Knitter's testimony concerning liberation theology. In his response, he states: 'We cannot know God or experience God *unless* we are working for justice.' I would like to know the implication of this statement clearly. Does Professor Knitter mean by this statement that working for justice is a necessary worldly and practical condition for experiencing God or is an essential *ground* for experiencing God? It seems to me that by that statement, based on liberation theology, he indicates that working for justice is not merely a practical condition for experiencing God but rather an essential ground or source for experiencing God. I have such an impression especially when he states:

> By such forms of 'praxis' (i.e. by getting involved in some form of action for justice and social transformation], we discover and see things not only about the world and history but about God and the Ultimate that we could never see in our prayers or meditation or traditional understanding of religious experience.

If Professor Knitter means by these statements that our religious experience of God is deepened and expanded by our action for justice, I can well understand and agree to it. However, if he and liberation theologians mean that our action for justice is the *ground* which yields a new religious experience of God himself, I cannot agree. For the authentic religious experience of God must come from God himself because God is the ground and source of revelation. It is the character of religious experience of God that may be conditioned by our actions in time and space. Our action in time and space, however serious and important it may be, cannot become a *ground* or *source* of our God-experience while it can certainly deepen and expand our God-experience.

The same is true with the Buddhist notion of awakening to True Self. Awakening to True Self is self-awakening, not awakening caused by something else. This is the reason why the True Self to which one must awaken is called 'Formless Self' because True Self can never be objectified in any sense. But, just as God's revelation is not separated from human activities in time and space, awakening to Formless Self is not apart from human activities in the world and history. Human actions in the world and history are indispensable for our God-experience or for our self-awakening. However, they are indispensable not as the ground or source of our religious experience, but as the practical condition or worldly occasion for our religious experience. We should not confuse what should be *ground* with what should be *occasion*, what should be *source* with what should be *situation*. If we take our praxis of transforming the world not as an occasion but as a source of religious experience, it is mistaken.

Professor Knitter asked: 'Why are you apparently reluctant to associate this experience of the Formless Self with God?' This question touches upon one of the most crucial problems of Buddhist–Christian dialogue. Fundamentally speaking, Buddhism considers the notion of one absolute God who is other than ourselves to be inadequate. Gautama Buddha did not accept the age-old Vedantic notion of *Brahman* as the sole foundation underlying the universe, although it is believed to be identified with *Ātman*, the eternal self at the core of each individual. Instead, the Buddha emphasizes as the ultimate principle *pratītya-samutpāda*, that is dependent co-origination or relational origination. Even the divine and the human co-arise and co-cease. The otherness of a personal God that necessarily implies the objectification of the Ultimate is not acceptable to Buddhism to which the awakening to one's True Self is crucial.

In Christianity, however, the otherness of God is inseparably connected with the clear realization of human finitude, that is the realization of sinfulness and death. Human sinfulness can be redeemed not by our works but only by pure faith in the love of God. (Even such faith is believed to be the gift of God.) From this Christian point of view, the Buddhist emphasis on the awakening to one's True Self may sound unreal, even self-deceptive, at least lacking serious realization of human finitude. In this regard, however, Buddhists are led to raise the following questions: Can human finitude in terms of sinfulness be fully overcome by faith? What is the ground of this faith and hope in which our death and sin can be completely redeemed? Is humanity's finitude one which can be overcome by such faith? To Buddhists, human finitude is so deep and so radical that it cannot be overcome either through pure faith or through the work of God as the divine other power. Hence the need for the realization of absolute nothingness. Awakening to Formless Self is just another term for the realization of absolute nothingness.

C

Professor Knitter also asks: 'How [do] you go about your investigation of world and history? . . . What [do] the investigation of the world and history really add to what you already have discovered from the investigation of the self?' Again, in this respect, we should not confuse what should be ground or source with what should be situation or occasion. Although the awakening to True Self is the ground or source of our activities, it cannot be historically actualized in the world without certain conditions. The necessary conditions for the historical actualization of this awakening are natural and socio-scientific knowledge and political and economic policy and strategy. If one thinks that this knowledge and strategy can be spontaneously derived from the awakening to True Self, one is mistaken. True investigation of the self, however, includes the investigation of the fundamental meaning of the world and history just as the awakening to True Self includes the realization of this fundamental meaning. From there one can properly use the knowledge, policy and technology necessary to transform the world.

In sum, however essential religious experience may be as the ground of activities, the ground without particular situations is abstract. For this reason, I said earlier 'If only the internal religious aspect of the human being is emphasized and priority is given to one's own salvation, thereby neglecting affairs of the world, however serious individuals may be in their religious quest, they cannot attain a profound religious solution.' On the other hand, however important the action to transform the world may be, if it is not based on God-experience or awakening to True Self, it is also inauthentic. And for this reason, I said earlier, 'If these movements (peace movements, human rights movements, and various social reform movements) are pursued only from a political and social standpoint *without bases* in our deep realization of True Self, such approaches may not yield adequate solutions.' To be precise, ground and condition, source and occasion must always be combined. And in my understanding, at the depth of human existence, the problem of self, the problem of the world and the problem of history are inseparably connected with one another. Thus, we must realize that we are always standing and working at the intersection of three dimensions of self, world and history.

From this integrated and dynamic point of view, I would like to examine further Professor Knitter's standpoint. He states that in Buddhism the enlightenment has a certain *epistemological priority* over practice, whereas in Christianity action has a certain *epistemological priority* over prayer. To this understanding, I would like to raise the following two questions: first, when Professor Knitter speaks of an *epistemological* priority, does he imply that there is no *ontological* priority between enlightenment and practice, prayer and action, but only an *epistemological* one? – or, does he also admit the issue of an *ontological* priority among these realities?

Second, when Professor Knitter speaks of priority within Buddhism or within Christianity, where does he take his stand? As a Christian who is sympathetic with liberation theology, Professor Knitter must have taken his stand on action rather than prayer as an epistemological priority. However, in order to discuss a priority between two items, he must have initially distinguished those two items from one another. Accordingly, my question may be restated as follows: When he makes a distinction between prayer and action, enlightenment and practice, where does he take his stand? Does he stand within prayer (enlightenment) or action (practice) in making such a distinction? Since it is impossible to make a distinction between two items by taking one of them as one's standpoint, Professor Knitter must have, consciously or unconsciously, taken a *third* position *outside* of the two items in question. But such a third position outside of prayer and action, enlightenment and practice is nothing but a conceptual construction. It is a projected position established through speculation. In our non-conceptualized living reality, prayer and action, enlightenment and practice are indistinguishable. Speaking from the non-conceptualizable and unobjectifiable depth of our existence, questioning the priority of enlightenment or practice, prayer or action, is already inauthentic. In the *ontological* dimension, that is, the most profound existential dimension, both in Buddhism and Christianity, meditation and practice, prayer and action are not two, but one.

Phenomenologically speaking, however, I agree with Professor Knitter when he states that in Buddhism enlightenment has a certain epistemological priority over practice whereas in Christianity action has a certain epistemological priority over prayer. By saying this, I mean that Buddhism tends to put priority on enlightenment over practice and thereby threatens to become a quietism. Conversely, Christianity tends to put priority on action over prayer and thereby threatens to develop a crusade. To avoid such a tendency and overcome quietism, Buddhists must learn from Christianity, and especially from liberation theology. However, if liberation theology insists that 'Only out of the soil of such action or liberating praxis will true enlightenment, true experience and knowledge, grow,' the Buddhist must disagree. For as I said before (Part I), this understanding takes action and praxis in time and space – which cannot be more than practical occasion or worldly condition – as if it were a ground or source for our religious experience which originates in God or true self-awakening. If liberation theology takes liberating praxis as the *only* source for genuine God-experience by putting priority on action over prayer, I am afraid it deviates from Christianity. For as I said earlier, in Christianity as in Buddhism, if I am not mistaken, in its ontological dimension, that is, its most profound existential dimension, prayer and action, faith in God and working for justice are not two but one.

D

Each human being is a single dynamic existence who encompasses both horizontal and vertical dimensions. The horizontal dimension indicates the dimension of space and time, world and history, whereas the vertical dimension signifies the trans-spatial and trans-temporal dimension, namely the dimension of Self or God, that is religion. What I call practical condition, occasion or situation indicates the horizontal dimension, whereas what I call ground or source refers to the vertical dimension. At this point, we must clearly realize that although the horizontal dimension and the vertical dimension are qualitatively different, in living reality they are undifferentiated. They are one not two, and yet not a fixed one, but are distinguishable into two. In sum, the horizontal dimension (spatio-temporal condition) and the vertical dimension (trans-spatio-temporal ground) are neither one nor two, and yet both one and two. We are always standing and working *in* this dynamism. More precisely speaking, we *are* this dynamism and this dynamism *is* us. Unless we start from this dynamism, we cannot solve the problem of how to combine 'meditation and action', 'spirituality and liberation', and the problem of which has a priority, enlightenment or practice, action or prayer.

Notes

1. John S. Dunne, *The Way of All the Earth* (New York: Macmillan, 1972).
2. See Paul F. Knitter, 'Merton's Eastern Remedy for Christianity's Anonymous Dualism', *Cross Currents*, Vol. 31 (1981), pp. 285–95.
3. John B. Cobb, Jr., *Beyond Dialogue: Toward a Mutual Transformation of Christianity and Buddhism* (Philadelphia: Fortress, 1982).
4. Shin'ichi Hisamatsu (1889–1980), Professor of Buddhism at Kyoto University in Japan. See Masao Abe, 'Hisamatsu's Philosophy of Awakening', *The Eastern Buddhist*, Vol. 14 (1981), pp. 26–42 and 'Hisamatsu Shin'ichi, 1889–1980', *The Eastern Buddhist*, Vol. 14 (1981), pp. 142–9.
5. A Zen association established in 1944, *Gakudō dōjō* literally means 'the place for learning and practising the way'.
6. Masao Abe, 'Sovereignty Rests with Mankind', in *Zen and Western Thought* (New York: Macmillan; Honolulu: Univ. of Hawaii Press, 1985), pp. 249–60. This essay was inspired by Hisamatsu's idea of true sovereignty.
7. Masao Abe, 'A History of the FAS Zen Society', *FAS Newsletter*, Autumn 1984, pp. 1–12.
8. Shin'ichi Hisamatsu, *Zen and the Fine Arts* (Kodansha International, 1975), pp. 18–19, 45–52.
9. Shin'ichi Hisamatsu, 'Ultimate Crisis and Resurrection', *The Eastern Buddhist*, Vol. 8 (1975), p. 64.
10. Ibid.
11. Bodhisattva's 'Four Great Vows' read as follows: However innumerable beings are, I vow to save them; however inexhaustible the passions are, I vow to extinguish them; however immeasurable the Dharma are, I vow to master them; however incomparable the Buddha-truth is, I vow to attain it.
12. I draw this understanding of complementary differences between Buddhism and Christianity especially from the writings of Aloysius Pieris. See his 'A Theology of Liberation in Asian Churches?' in *Asian Theology of Liberation* (Maryknoll, NY: Orbis, 1988), pp. 111–26, and especially his soon to be published *Love Meets Wisdom: A Christian Experience of Buddhism* (Orbis), as well as his essay in this volume of *Horizons* [Vol. 15, No. 2, 1988].

Index